P9-DVD-848

Management Research Methods

Management Research Methods is a comprehensive guide to the design and conduct of research in management-related disciplines such as organisational behaviour, human resource management, industrial relations, and the general field of management. The book provides an overview of the research process and explains the main types of design used in management research – experimental and quasi-experimental designs, correlational field studies (surveys), case studies, historical analysis, and action research. It also describes the methods of data collection – interviews, questionnaires, documentation, and obsevation – commonly employed by management researchers. In addition, the book examines the issues of reliability and validity, the construction of multi-item scales, and the methods of quantitative and qualitative analysis. It concludes with a practical guide explaining how to report research findings and a discussion of ethical issues in the conduct and practice of research.

Management Research Methods is an essential guide for students, managers and researchers.

Phyllis Tharenou is Dean of Research in the Division of Business, University of South Australia.

Ross Donohue is a lecturer in the Department of Management, Monash University.

Brian Cooper is a lecturer in the Department of Management, Monash University.

Management Research Methods

PHYLLIS THARENOU, ROSS DONOHUE,
AND BRIAN COOPER

CAMBRIDGE
UNIVERSITY PRESS

CAMBRIDGE UNIVERSITY PRESS
Cambridge, New York, Melbourne, Madrid, Cape Town, Singapore, São Paulo

Cambridge University Press
477 Williamstown Road, Port Melbourne, VIC 3207, Australia

Published in the United States of America by Cambridge University Press, New York

www.cambridge.org
Information on this title: www.cambridge.org/9780521694285

© Phyllis Tharenou, Ross Donohue, Brian Cooper 2007

First published 2007

Printed in Australia by Ligare

A catalogue record for this publication is available from the British Library

National Library of Australia Cataloguing in Publication data

Tharenou, Phyllis.
Management Research Methods.
Bibliography.
Includes index.
ISBN-13   978-0-52169-428-5 paperback
ISBN-10   0-52169-428-0 paperback

1. Management – Research.   2. Management – Research – Methodology.   I. Donohue, Ross.
II. Cooper, Brian.   III. Title.
658.0072

ISBN-13   978-0-52169-428-5 paperback
ISBN-10   0-52169-428-0 paperback

Reproduction and Communication for educational purposes
The Australian *Copyright Act 1968* (the Act) allows a maximum of one chapter or 10% of
the pages of this work, whichever is the greater, to be reproduced and/or
communicated by any educational institution for its educational purposes provided
that the educational institution (or the body that administers it) has given a
remuneration notice to Copyright Agency Limited (CAL) under the Act.

For details of the CAL licence for educational institutions contact:

Copyright Agency Limited
Level 15, 233 Castlereagh Street
Sydney NSW 2000
Telephone: (02) 9394 7600
Facsimile: (02) 9394 7601
E-mail: info@copyright.com.au

Reproduction and Communication for other purposes
Except as permitted under the Act (for example a fair dealing for the purposes of study,
research, criticism or review) no part of this publication may be reproduced, stored in a retrieval
system, communicated or transmitted in any form or by any means without prior written
permission. All inquiries should be made to the publisher at the address above.

Cambridge University Press has no responsibility for the persistence or accuracy of URLs for
external or third-party internet websites referred to in this publication, and does not guarantee
that any content on such websites is, or will remain, accurate or appropriate.

Contents

Preface   *page* vii

Part 1 Introduction   **1**
1   The research process   3

Part 2 Research designs   **31**
2   Experimental and quasi-experimental designs   33
3   Correlational field study (survey) designs   45
4   Case study research designs   72
5   Action research designs   88

Part 3 Methods of data collection   **99**
6   Asking questions: Questionnaires and interviews   101
7   Documentation and observation   123

Part 4 Measurement   **147**
8   Reliability and validity   149
9   Scale development   160

Part 5 Methods of data analysis   **187**
10 Quantitative data: Data set-up and initial analysis   189
11 Quantitative data: Multivariate data analysis for answering
    research questions and hypothesis testing   220
12 Content analysis   250

Part 6 Reporting research findings and ethical
         considerations   **273**
13 Writing up a quantitative or qualitative project   275
14 Ethical issues and conduct in the practice of research   316

Index   329

Preface

In order to conduct sound research in the discipline of management, it is critical that you develop an awareness of research approaches and techniques. The purpose of this text is to foster your capacity to understand the appropriate method of research to undertake and what outcomes you could reasonably expect from that research. By using this text, you will be encouraged to become critical of the use of different techniques and methods applied in this research field.

Aims and objectives

The aim of this text is to develop your understanding of the research process suitable for the management discipline. Having completed this text, it is expected that you will be able to:

- critically analyse, interpret, and understand basic research designs in the management discipline;
- identify management-related issues for research;
- build the capacity to develop research questions grounded in a theoretical and conceptual framework;
- compare the appropriateness and use of qualitative and quantitative data collection and analysis techniques as a means of investigating and answering research questions in the management discipline;
- outline the process of collecting primary data, and identify, search for, and locate secondary data and knowledge relevant to management research;
- summarise the role and introductory use of computer software packages and facilities in the collection, analysis, and presentation of research findings;
- demonstrate a general understanding of the role of management research in academic, industry, government, and professional and community organisations; and

- develop academic writing skills appropriate to the discipline for reporting on business management research projects.

Text content

Every day, managers are involved in designing projects, jobs, organisational or departmental structures, and ways of matching individual and group needs in organisations. They base their decisions on existing knowledge resulting from what they or others have learnt from applied or pure academic research. In fact, designing questions to solve management problems is such a fundamental skill that we overlook its significance as a major factor contributing to quality management.

Management Research Methods aims to foster in readers an understanding of the basic research processes and a capacity to identify management-related research questions. Readers will learn the manner in which others have designed and conducted research studies to answer management-related questions, the sources of the main existing literature in management-related studies, the procedures involved in collecting primary data, the purposes of techniques for analysing and presenting data, and the necessary structuring and writing skills to generate a research report.

This text therefore provides a basic introduction to research design in management, types of research designs, data collection and measurement techniques, coding data, reliability and validity, qualitative and quantitative methods of analysis, interpreting and discussing results, structuring and writing the research report, and integrating individual research into the overall management literature.

Organisation

This text is organised into six parts. Part 1, *Introduction*, contains Chapter 1, which outlines the research process, discusses foundational issues, defines key terms, and provides readers with an overview of topics discussed more comprehensively in subsequent chapters. Part 2, *Research Designs*, is comprised of chapters examining experimental and quasi-experimental designs (Chapter 2), correlational field study (survey) designs (Chapter 3), case study research designs (Chapter 4), and action research designs (Chapter 5). Part 3 of the book is focused on *Methods of Data Collection* and includes chapters on asking questions using questionnaires and interviews (Chapter 6) and documentation and observation (Chapter 7). Part 4, *Measurement,* consists of chapters discussing reliability and validity (Chapter 8) and scale development (Chapter 9). Part 5 of the text groups the *Methods of Data Analysis* and contains chapters on quantitative data set-up and initial analysis (Chapter 10), quantitative multivariate analysis (Chapter 11), and content analysis (Chapter 12). *Reporting Research Findings and Ethical Considerations* is the final part and comprises chapters on writing up a qualitative or quantitative project (Chapter 13) and ethical issues and conduct in the practice of research (Chapter 14).

Learning outcomes

The main components involve:

- developing a critical understanding of basic research designs (for example, experimental and quasi-experimental designs, correlational field study designs, case study designs, and action research designs) in order to conduct applied management research;
- developing skills in designing research studies in relation to contemporary management issues, including ethical considerations in design;
- devising or locating techniques to generate or collect primary data, and identifying and locating sources of secondary data;
- developing basic, introductory skills in data collection – for example, interviewing, using questionnaires, observation techniques, and documentation;
- developing skills in the construction of multi-item scales;
- developing an understanding of basic data analysis concepts in relation to answering research questions and testing hypotheses;
- developing skills in writing up an academic research study in formal research report format; and
- having an appreciation of the overall steps in research design and of integration of the individual research skills that comprise effective research designs in management.

Having completed the text, readers will be able to:

- prepare research questions both from applied and theoretical perspectives for management research;
- conduct computerised literature searches for management research;
- prepare research designs for a range of management research questions;
- design and conduct research in keeping with ethical considerations;
- identify and locate sources for data collection and design questionnaires, interviews, and multi-item scales;
- appreciate the broad purpose and applicability of data analytic techniques for quantitative and qualitative data analysis; and
- develop skills in writing an academic research report.

Acknowledgements

The authors gratefully acknowledge Cathy Miles for her meticulous assistance during the editing process of this book and for her assistance during the production stages. The authors are also appreciative of the excellent support and guidance provided by Cambridge University Press, specifically the managing editor, Kate Indigo, as well as the freelance editor, Robyn Fleming.

Part 1

Introduction

1 The research process

At the end of this chapter you will be able to:

- *describe the overall research process;*
- *describe each step in the research process and explain why it is conducted;*
- *develop a research question and hypotheses;*
- *differentiate between research questions and hypotheses;*
- *discriminate between independent and dependent variables and give examples of each;*
- *explain what control, mediator, and moderator variables are;*
- *define 'theory';*
- *explain why you need theory to generate research questions and hypotheses;*
- *describe what an empirical study is;*
- *explain how an empirical study can test the relationship between independent and dependent variables;*
- *summarise the use of empirical studies to write a literature review;*
- *define 'causality';*
- *explain why causality is difficult to establish; and*
- *outline the broad types of research designs used and methods of data collection.*

CONTENTS

Overview of the research process   4
Developing the research question   5

Finding the theory or underlying frameworks	6
Finalising the specific research questions or hypotheses	11
Choosing the research design	16
Choosing the method(s) of data collection	21
Choosing the method(s) of data analysis	25
Interpreting the results against the research questions or hypotheses	26
Reporting the findings	26
Conclusion	27
References	28
Chapter review questions	28

Overview of the research process

This chapter presents an overview of the research process, from generating the idea to writing up the research report. The first section covers in detail:

- developing the research question;
- finding the theory;
- how to critique past studies; and
- how to develop hypotheses and consider issues in relation to causality.

The second section of this chapter examines how to design the study, the different kinds of research methods available, the use, type, and design of measures, how to initially manage the data, the broad categories of approaches for analysing the results, and how to write up the results and the overall project. These issues are explained only briefly in this chapter, as they are covered in depth in other chapters to which the reader is directed.

The research process may be thought of according to the following stages:

- Developing the research question.
- Finding the theory or underlying frameworks.
- Finalising the specific research questions or hypotheses.
- Choosing the research design.
- Choosing the method(s) of data collection.

- Choosing the method(s) of data analysis.
- Interpreting the results against the research questions or hypotheses.
- Reporting the findings.

Developing the research question

The first step in beginning a research project is to decide: *What is the research question?* A research question is a question about the problem to be addressed; it is therefore focused on the content of the topic of interest (i.e., substantive). According to Graziano and Raulin (1993), the research question:

- is a statement about the expected relationship between variables;
- is a question; and
- implies the possibility of an empirical test.

An empirical test is where data are gathered specifically to test the research question. Empirical tests may be conducted on primary data (e.g., data directly gathered by the researcher), or on data obtained from secondary sources (e.g., archival data, company documentation, or company or public records). Whatever the type, the data are analysed expressly for the purpose of answering the question. The research question might begin as: *'What causes people to advance into management?'* This question, however, is too broad, so the researcher might change it to: *'What are the organisational and individual factors that cause people to advance into management?'* This question may still be too broad, and so the researcher may choose to focus on organisational factors and then on one specific organisational factor (e.g., mentors). The refined research question might now be: *'Does mentoring influence managerial career advancement?'* Researchers should aim to end up eventually with as precise and specific a question as possible for their topic. Often the development of a research question requires considerable thought and rumination and while researchers may not end up with the final question at this point, they still need a direction and focus to set them on the right path.

Depending on the focus of the research question, the researcher needs to decide whether the study will be exploratory, descriptive, or hypothesis testing. Sekaran (1992) explained *exploratory studies* as those where the researcher knows little about the situation, or has no information on how similar research problems have been solved. Therefore, preliminary work needs to be done to comprehend the nature of the problem (e.g., the initial studies on the nature of managerial work where it was not known what managers did each day). *Descriptive studies* are those undertaken to describe the characteristics of variables in a situation. Descriptive studies may be conducted in organisations to learn about and describe the characteristics of particular employees (e.g., those with high levels of absenteeism) or organisations that follow common practices (e.g., those following best practice or implementing total quality management, or TQM). *Hypothesis testing studies* try to explain the nature of certain relationships, or to establish the differences among groups. Hypothesis testing goes beyond describing the relationships in a situation to understanding the relationships among factors (variables) in a situation.

Finding the theory or underlying frameworks

Having developed the initial research question, the researcher's task is then to find out what the literature indicates on the first formulation of the question. The most efficient way to do this is to find three or four major papers on the topic that are recent. (More comprehensive reading and the literature review will follow.) Papers published in the last five years are considered recent. The papers should be written by major scholars in the area and may be reviews of the specific topic or of the broader area, major theoretical pieces, and so on. They are usually journal articles.

Major papers provide researchers with an overview of the broad topic, allow them to see what has previously been done, and present them with reference lists to track down more specific papers of interest. Major papers also indicate what needs to be done next on this topic, provide criticisms of the approaches, and detail the extant studies in the area. Again, researchers should focus particularly on the most recent major papers, as they will provide discussion of the most up-to-date findings and approaches. What researchers should be looking for in these major papers includes terms, conceptual frameworks, criticisms, empirical studies, and ideas for future research.

Terms

The *terms* that are used in the literature on this topic need to be identified (e.g., for the above research question, the relevant terms may be *managerial advancement, career advancement, managerial level, career outcomes,* and *careers*). This knowledge is vital to researchers, as productive computerised searches of electronic databases require the use of the correct search terms. (There are usually several.) Getting the terms right is very important in starting the search, and researchers should ensure that the correct terms are used consistently in their manuscripts so as to reduce confusion and increase precision.

Theories

Researchers also need to ensure that they develop a clear understanding of the *theories/explanations* or *conceptual frameworks* underlying their research area. There are usually theories/models/frameworks that have been used in the literature on this topic, and it is the researcher's task to locate these explanations of the phenomenon which the researcher is interested in investigating. There are often broad approaches and specific theories/explanations. For example, in terms of explanations of managerial career advancement, the broad approaches have been that the phenomenon is explained by a combination of organisational (opportunity structures, selection, and promotion processes), interpersonal (social structures and interpersonal support), and individual factors (personality, human capital, skills, and competencies). However, there are several specific theories linked to each of these approaches. If the emphasis of the study was organisational opportunity structures through promotion ladders, then the researcher would look at the theory of internal labour markets. If the researcher were to look at interpersonal factors, he or she would look at theories of social capital. If the emphasis were on individual accomplishments through education, work experience, and training, the researcher would look at human capital theory. If the emphasis was placed on personality, he or she might use gender-role theory and examine the impact of masculinity/instrumentality on advancement.

A theory offers a satisfactory rationale of the 'why' question and testable explanations for relationships. A testable theoretical explanation of a phenomenon is one that can be disproved (falsified). According to Jackson (1988), a theory has three key elements:

- a set of concepts, or a conceptual scheme;
- a set of propositions, each stating a relationship between some of the concepts; and
- some of the propositions must be contingent; that is, they must be amenable to some form of empirical test.

Sekaran (1992) has also provided a very useful account of the properties of a theory for management research. These properties are:

- The variables in a theory considered relevant to the study are clearly identified and labelled for discussion; that is, dependent, independent, moderator, and mediator variables.
- The way in which the two or more variables are related to each other is stated. This is done for the important relationships hypothesised between the variables.
- If the nature and direction of the relationships can be theorised, an indication is still given (e.g., positive or negative).
- A clear explanation is given of why we would expect these relationships to exist.

A schematic diagram of the theoretical framework can be given so that the theoretical relationships can be visualised.

Theories consist of relationships between constructs. Following Edwards and Bagozzi (2000), a construct is a conceptual term for a phenomenon of theoretical interest. Put simply, constructs are theoretical concepts. Most constructs of interest to researchers are conceptualised as variables; that is, they can take on different values or states. Identifying relevant variables is a major task early in any research project. For research purposes, variables may be treated as independent or dependent.

Independent variables are those that are hypothesised to influence others, as they are the presumed cause or determinant or antecedent. In the hypothesis above (page 5), the independent or causal variable is mentor support.

Dependent variables are those that are presumed to be affected by another variable; that is, the effect or outcome. In the above hypothesis, the dependent variable is the number of managerial promotions.

A *moderator variable* is that which influences the strength and/or direction of relationship between the independent and dependent variables. It influences the relationship between the two variables, so that the nature of the relationship between the two variables is different when it varies (see also Sekaran, 1992). Moderator variables are said to have a conditional influence (see Jackson, 1988).

A *mediator variable* is one that transmits the effect of the independent variable to the dependent variable. Mediator variables have an intervening influence, hence they are also called *intervening variables*.

Some variables may cause the relationship between the independent and dependent variables and need to be controlled for that relationship not to be spurious (see Jackson, 1988). These are called *control variables*. 'Spuriousness' means that the relationship between the two variables is really caused by another variable. That variable confounds the relationship and needs to be controlled.

Literature evaluation

The next phase in the research process involves the critique of the previous literature on this topic, as criticisms of earlier studies point the way to new research. The major papers will usually have a section called 'Limitations' (usually outlined at the end of the discussion section of the paper) that leads to future research. Limitations of past research on a topic or of specific studies are usually substantive and methodological.

The *substantive/content-based criticisms* of past research concern the nature of the topic, problem, or theory/explanation. Substantive/content-based criticisms relate to issues such as:

- what has not been done yet and what we still do not know about;
- what we still do not understand, or a further explanation that has not been covered;
- inconsistencies in the prior results;

- failure to consider the context (e.g., situational factors when assessing the impact of individual factors on managerial career advancement);
- the relative importance of several factors; or
- the lack of a theoretical basis for the question/problem, including explaining the process (mediators) or the conditions affecting the relationship (moderators).

The criticisms of how previous studies have been conducted can also be *methodological*. (They usually concern research design, samples, measures, and methods of analysis.) Methodological criticisms may relate to issues such as:

- inadequacy of research designs and approaches used to test the questions, such as the nature of the design (quantitative versus qualitative designs), the types of measures (subjective versus objective measures), or the level at which the test has been done (individual-level versus organisational-level tests);
- the limited types of samples that have been used and lack of generalisability;
- the quality of the measures (unvalidated or unreliable); or
- the types of analyses (descriptive rather than multivariate techniques).

Empirical studies

Empirical studies are those in which data were gathered to assess if the variables were related. Often empirical studies are looking for an explanation of a variable, and therefore there are analyses of data that examine the relationship between an independent variable or several independent variables and one or more dependent variables. It tries to ascertain *if* – or *how* – one variable affects another.

Any empirical studies that have been conducted are valuable. If few studies have been carried out on the topic it may not be worth trying to do a literature review, as researchers need to summarise the results of extant studies to carry out a review. If a large number of studies have been conducted, the literature may have been reviewed quite recently and therefore reviewing it again may not be useful.

Why is it important that a researcher should know how to interpret or how to conduct these empirical research studies? The reason is because they examine the causes of outcomes. For example, knowing what an empirical study is, knowing how to interpret it, and knowing how to conduct it, can help researchers to:

- understand research studies conducted on a problematic question – for example, *'Does enterprise bargaining increase wages?'*
- judge research; that is, whether the results of studies conducted on a vexing topic are valid (true) or could be interpreted another way – for example, *'Does protection of employment and employment rights affect people's decisions to join unions?'*
- conduct a research investigation themselves and come to valid answers about a research question.

Future research

Future research may need to be conducted on the topic. The authors of major papers will normally tell you what they think should be done now in terms of future research, usually following on from the substantive and methodological criticisms in the last sections of their papers. All researchers also need to ensure they outline in their papers the future research directions by identifying the limitations in their own study and delineating what is not known about the topic.

In summary, researchers need to understand from these major papers:

- what are the major constructs in this research;
- how these constructs are defined;
- what is (are) the major theory(ies)/explanations of your topic;
- the criticisms of the work already done;
- the recent empirical studies conducted on the question you are interested in answering; and
- the directions needed for future research.

Finalising the specific research questions or hypotheses

Often the aim in research is to test a theory. In theory testing studies, hypotheses are formulated. A research hypothesis is a statement about the relationship between two (or more) variables that allows measurement or manipulation of the variables (Graziano & Raulin,

1993). Consequently, a hypothesis is operational – it is a specific prediction about the effects of the specific, operationally defined independent variables on the specific, operationally defined dependent variables (Graziano & Raulin, 1993). By having a hypothesis, a researcher can compare the data he or she gathered against it, to determine if there is a level of support.

Formulating a hypothesis for the study

A hypothesis can be constructed in various ways. For example, a researcher's hypothesis might be that (this is stated as a relationship type of hypothesis): *'Mentor support is positively related to the number of managerial promotions received.'* Another version of this hypothesis (still a relationship type) is: *'Mentor support will be greater for those who have had more managerial promotions than fewer managerial promotions.'* Alternatively, the hypothesis might be couched in terms of group differences (this is a difference between group type) and therefore may state: *'Those who have been promoted into management are more likely to report mentor support than those who have not been promoted into management.'* Other examples of hypotheses are:

- *'Enterprise bargaining is negatively related to increasing gender equity at work (i.e., wage parity between the sexes).'*
- *'Wage increases are likely to be lower under enterprise bargaining than under a centralised system.'*
- *'Wage increases under enterprise bargaining will be greater for more powerful groups of employees (e.g., full-timers, men, non-migrants) than for less powerful groups (part-timers, women, migrants).'*

Note that the first hypothesis in the examples above is a relationship-type hypothesis, while the second and third are group difference-type hypotheses. In summary, a hypothesis is a propositional statement about a relationship between two variables, or it is a statement that proposes the difference between groups (see Graziano & Raulin, 1993). Researchers may not need a hypothesis, but they always need to know what they are testing. Therefore, in order to address a question, researchers need to have a basis against which to assess it.

Qualities of a hypothesis

A hypothesis should be both *testable* and *directional.* As a consequence, it should:

- be phrased in the *positive/negative.* It should not be that there is no relationship, as in a null hypothesis. For example, you cannot say that mentor support will not be related to managerial advancement. The reason for this is that it is impossible to test.
- be *specific,* saying what is related to what. If, for example, a researcher believes that mentor support, as opposed to another type of individual relationship, is positively related to the number of managerial promotions received, then he or she is implying that the amount of 'support', as opposed to just having/not having a mentor, is important.
- automatically lead to *what the researcher will measure* (e.g., mentor support, or number of managerial promotions);
- include in the hypothesis the *type of relationship* to be tested (e.g., positive/negative, greater than, or differences between groups);
- include in the hypothesis the *variables* to be tested (e.g., mentor support, or number of managerial promotions); and
- be developed *ahead of data collection.* The researcher might change it later.

The variables in hypotheses need to be operational; that is, the researcher can measure them. A hypothesis should redefine the concepts in terms of clearly observable operations that anyone can see. However, as explained by Ray (1993), there are usually several ways to measure the same phenomenon or construct. For example, if the researcher was assessing motivation at work, should he or she measure:

- the individual's self-report of the experience of motivation?
- the individual's self-report using a psychometric measure of motivation (a standardised scale that has been examined for reliability and validity)?
- the individual's performance of the job?
- days off work not due to illness or other justifiable reasons?

- others'-report, such as their bosses' or co-workers' evaluations of the individual's motivation?

   What happens if a researcher does not have a hypothesis(es) to test? In management research, hypotheses are not always required. A researcher may be working in a relatively new area (exploratory research) where little is known about the problem; therefore, there may be insufficient knowledge to formulate a hypothesis. Alternatively, a researcher may have a preference for an inductive approach to research. *Inductive reasoning* is generalising from a specific instance, or several new facts, to a more general idea. In an inductive approach, the initial identification of research questions and the theoretical framework is usually tentative and then developed further as information is gathered and analysed. Inductive approaches are used to generate theory from data. Observations are made (through collecting and analysing qualitative or quantitative data), and the theory regarding how the relationships exist in the real world is then induced. This is very different from the deductive approach, where the researcher already has a well-developed theory that makes predictions; that is, deduces what will happen next by formulating a hypothesis and then testing it by observation for support (Ray, 1993). It is unlikely that many researchers use pure induction or deduction. In practice, most research is a combination of both inductive and deductive reasoning, with different degrees of emphasis on theory building or theory testing depending on the nature of the research question.

Alternatives to a hypothesis

If researchers do not have a hypothesis, they:

- still require specific research propositions (i.e., usually phrased as questions or sometimes objectives);
- need to have some theoretical/conceptual foundation (no matter how tentative);
- still need to check what the literature has found, and to know the results of past theories and empirical studies and what are likely kinds of hypotheses, even if they do not use them;

- may break up their broad research questions into subparts for direction to carry out the study; and
- need to know how to carry out an inductive approach; that is, how to make observations and induce theories of how relationships arise.

Causality

Researchers often desire to make causal inferences about the relationship between variables. Inferences of causality, according to Shadish, Cook, and Campbell (2002), have three necessary conditions:

- The cause precedes the effect in time.
- The cause and the effect co-vary.
- No plausible alternative explanation exists for the co-variation.

In most social science research the causal relationships are not clear, as researchers have to contend with:

- a context/environment that affects the relationships;
- a multi-determined event (there are many causes);
- relationships that are probabilistic; and
- effects that are indirect (they are caused through other variables) or through interaction with other variables.

In order to explain events, therefore, a researcher needs a theoretical basis that he or she can test and disprove. This requires converging evidence from:

- multiple research approaches (quantitative, qualitative);
- experimental and non-experimental designs;
- multiple measures (self-report, others'-report, hard data);
- methods of analyses that can include simultaneously a number of variables (e.g., multivariate analyses);
- usually a program of research, so that the researcher conducts a sequence of studies that get sequentially closer to solving the research problem; and
- a theory, so that if the variables are related to each other, the researcher can speculate on an explanation for the relationship.

Following the steps above does not enable the researcher to 'prove' causality; however, it does allow him or her to develop a likely, or most likely, or defensible explanation. The extent to which causal inferences can be made is often referred to as the *internal validity* of the research. For instance, just because two variables are correlated, a researcher cannot necessarily infer that one causes the other. The relationship may be spurious (caused by a third variable), or reciprocal (each variable influences the other), or reversed (the impact is counterintuitive, or the reverse of what is commonly thought; for example, that job dissatisfaction leads to absence). Each type of research design discussed in this book has difficulties associated with internal validity. The strongest causal inferences can be made with experimental designs (see below).

Choosing the research design

Types of research designs

Having settled on the nature of the study, the next step is for the researcher to decide on the type of design he or she will apply to answer the research question. The research design is the overall plan or structure used to answer the research question. The researcher needs to ensure that the design chosen suits the particular research question. Therefore, it is best to start with the question and then choose the design. The researcher may also be constrained, for example, by the resources available and by what participating organisations will allow him or her to do, in relation to the research. From the choice of research design, the researcher then needs to choose the specific techniques for data collection. The main types of research designs are experimental and quasi-experimental designs, correlational field study (survey) designs, case study designs, and action research designs.

Qualitative and quantitative designs
Most textbooks emphasise the distinction between qualitative and quantitative research (Creswell, 2003). We feel that this distinction is overdrawn. Most research designs and data collection techniques can generate both qualitative (words) and quantitative (numbers) data. A major theme of this book is that issues of design need to be carefully

matched to the underlying purpose of the study. A simple qualitative–quantitative divide does little to address the complexity of issues at work here. We believe the critical issue between qualitative and quantitative is not in the type of data gathered, but in the methods of analysis applied. Qualitative analyses provide detail, process, richness, and sensitivity to context. They are appropriate if the aim is to understand meaning and to build theoretical explanations from participant understandings. Quantitative analyses are more appropriate for questions involving 'how many' or 'how much'; that is, questions of incidence and measurement. Quantitative analyses are best used when the aim is to test theoretical predictions with precise measures of variables. Throughout this book, we highlight a variety of approaches that can be used for conducting qualitative and quantitative analyses.

Experimental and quasi-experimental designs

Studies following an experimental design are normally conducted away from where the phenomenon usually occurs (e.g., in a laboratory), and attempts are made to control as many extraneous influences as possible in that setting. True experimental designs enable strong causal inferences to be made about the effects of an independent variable. They are, therefore, the most powerful way to test theoretical hypotheses. The important characteristic of true experimental designs is that there is random assignment of participants to experimental and control groups. Quasi-experimental designs are similar to experimental designs but are carried out in real (naturalistic) settings (e.g., organisations). The term *quasi* means 'almost', 'semi', or 'more or less'. With a quasi-experimental design, the researcher is able to manipulate the independent variable; however, unlike true experimental designs, participants cannot be randomly assigned to experimental and control groups. Experimental and quasi-experimental designs are discussed in Chapter 2.

Correlational field study (survey) design

A correlational field study is a study based on survey data, conducted in the field (i.e., a non-contrived setting such as an organisation), in which the relationship(s) between one or more dependent variables and one or more independent variables is (are) examined. Many management studies are based on correlational field designs, of which the mail (postal) survey is the most common. Correlational field surveys usually (but not always) gather quantitative data analysed using statistical methods. Correlational field study (survey) designs are discussed in Chapter 3.

Case study design

A case study is a comprehensive inquiry, conducted in the field, into a single instance, event, or setting. The purpose of the case study is to explain the processes of a phenomenon in context. The unit of analysis (i.e., the case) in these designs may be as circumscribed as an individual or as large as a country. One of the benefits of using a case study design is that it affords highly in-depth analyses of specific empirical issues. Case studies can use both qualitative and quantitative data to answer the research question. The main drawback of this design is that it is difficult to generalise to other cases; however, generalisability can be improved by using more than one case. Chapter 4 provides a detailed discussion of case study research designs.

Action research designs

Studies applying an action research design iteratively cycle through the processes of diagnosis (research) and intervention (action) until there is understanding of, and change in, the social system (e.g., an organisation) under investigation. With each iteration, interpretations are developed which, in turn, inform the next stage of the process. In action research the researcher and members of the social system under investigation work collaboratively to understand and improve the social system. Action research designs are discussed in Chapter 5.

The unit of analysis

Another consideration related to the type of research design selected is the unit of analysis (Sekaran, 1992). The unit of analysis may be:

- *Individuals*: each employee's response is an individual data source, such as individual measures of job satisfaction and absence.
- *Dyads*: two-person interactions, such as several supervisor–subordinate pairs.

- *Groups*: unit of analysis at the group level, such as teams, group effectiveness (dependent variable), and group size or structure or cohesiveness (independent variable).
- *Organisations*: the company/institution is the unit of analysis. Usually questions are asked about the independent variables of the organisation as a whole (across the organisation), such as business strategy or company training. The dependent variable is usually measured at the organisational level, such as return on investment, profit per employee, market share, etc. In some circumstances, companies as a whole are not used but rather business units within companies or plants.
- *Industries*: the variables are measured across industries, not companies.

In recent years, there has been increasing interest in research using multi-level models. A multi-level model is indicated where there is a hierarchical (or nested) structure to the data. Hierarchical data structures, consisting of two or more levels, are very common in organisational research. For example, a higher level might refer to organisational teams and a lower level might refer to the team members. In this example, individual team members are nested within teams. Multi-level designs enable one to conduct cross-level analyses. Cross-level analyses examine the relationships among variables at different levels of analysis (Klein & Kozlowski, 2000). For example, team characteristics could be used to predict individual team member performance outcomes. Conventional quantitative methods are designed for single levels of analysis and are not appropriate for hierarchical data structures. Specialised statistical techniques are now available to examine multi-level models (e.g., hierarchical linear modelling). An excellent user-friendly discussion of multi-level modelling in organisational research can be found in Klein and Kozlowski (2000).

Length of studies

Cross-sectional
In studies using a cross-sectional design, all data for all variables are gathered at the same time. The data are often called contemporaneous

data. Consequently, if a researcher measures participation in training and development on a survey and at the same time measures the independent variables of training attendance motivation, organisational training policies, supervisor and peer support, motivation to learn, and the control variables, then this is a contemporaneous or cross-sectional design.

It is important to keep in mind that cross-sectional designs are weak on internal validity. As noted above, internal validity relates primarily to whether 'the cause' results in 'the effect'. If a researcher found that training attendance motivation and participation in training and development were related in a cross-sectional design, one might not lead to the other. In fact, they may both be caused by a third variable. Alternatively, the direction of the effect might be the opposite of what the researcher first hypothesised. It might also be the case that participation in training and development leads to the higher motivation to attend training. As the researcher measured both at the same time, he or she cannot know which occurred temporally prior to the other. Hence, cross-sectional designs are by their nature inherently limited. This would be the same whether the researcher were to obtain these measures by questionnaire or any other method of data collection.

Longitudinal
In studies applying a longitudinal design, data are gathered with an intervening time period, usually between the predictor and predicted variables. The independent variable therefore predicts the dependent variable. Consequently, if a researcher measured training attendance motivation at one time (Time 1) and then measured training attendance at a later time (Time 2), he or she would be able to predict training attendance in that time from training motivation attendance. A longitudinal design can be called predictive, as the researcher is predicting something that has not yet happened.

Choice of comparison

In order to test a research question, a researcher often requires a comparison group. By comparing the groups on the relationships of interest, he or she is able to obtain a better way of explaining the results. The researcher may also need comparison norms (for surveys or for interviews). Without these comparison norms, he or she has an absolute measure and no idea of what is high, medium, or low for this variable in the population of interest. The norms therefore indicate to the researcher whether his or her group is high, low, the norm, and so on.

Sampling

Most research has a specific population to which the findings should apply. That may be a broad population (university students) or a narrow one (management students). The sample from which the researcher gathers the data needs to be representative of the population to whom the researcher would like to generalise the results. The ability to generalise the findings of a study to the population from which the sample came is an important aspect of external validity. 'External validity' refers to the extent to which the findings of a study can be generalised to people and settings beyond the immediate study. If a sample is not representative, the researcher needs to be able to say how it differs from that population, or justify why the approach (e.g., opinion leaders) was used. The sample also needs to be of sufficient size to have adequate power to detect relationships in quantitative analyses. The different sampling approaches are discussed in Chapter 3.

General

There are problems and pitfalls with each type of design, as well as advantages. The main caution is to design the study so that it answers the research questions and so the researcher knows *before he or she gathers the information/data* exactly how it will be analysed.

Choosing the method(s) of data collection

Questionnaires and interviews

Questionnaires and interviews are usually conducted for the purpose of determining the respondents' thoughts about, and feelings towards, issues, events, behaviours, and so on. They may be used as a research technique singly, or they may form part of a larger mixed-method research design, such as in case studies, to achieve triangulation.

Self-administered questionnaires are commonly used in correlational field (survey) designs, of which the mail questionnaire is the most common. Questionnaires are a cost-effective and efficient way to gather verbal data from a large sample. Due to their structured format, questionnaires are used where the aim is to generate quantitative data to test research questions and/or hypotheses.

Interviews are typically conducted face-to-face, but telephone interviews are also common. Interviews vary from structured through to unstructured. In the case of the former, the researcher may wish to measure specific variables and interviews may provide the technique to measure those variables. Unstructured interviews are typically naturalistic, interpretive, and inductive. Like questionnaires, structured (also called standardised) interviews tend to be used where the aim is to conduct statistical analyses with quantitative data to test research questions and/or hypotheses. Semi-structured interviews fall in-between the two. Interview structure is therefore linked to the nature of the research question being asked. Who is interviewed depends on whom the researcher wishes to make inferences about (i.e., individuals or groups). Interviews may also be conducted of groups, such as in focus groups.

The design of questions for interviews and questionnaires needs to be based on the theoretical framework underlying the research question, and the purpose of each question needs to be clear. The questions for structured interviews will often look much like questionnaires, with an emphasis on closed-ended response categories. However, unlike questionnaires, structured interviews may also include probing questions to arrive at respondents' answers on rating scales, as well as clarifying and confirmation questions. Semi-structured interviews will use both open- and closed-ended questions, with probing questions, as well as clarifying and confirmation questions. Unstructured interviews will primarily use open-ended questions, probing (including complex probes, reflective probes, and cross-checks), story-telling, and verbal cues. As a consequence, designing questions for structured interviews requires skills akin to those used with questionnaires. Alternatively, in order to conduct effective unstructured and semi-structured interviews, the skills associated with establishing and maintaining complex interpersonal dialogues are required.

Analysis of interview data parallels the underlying philosophy of the approach and the types of research questions being asked, ranging in a continuum from statistical analysis to qualitative analyses. Reliability, to obtain consistent data, and validity, to measure the actual construct that is thought to be measured, require substantial effort in research interviews and questionnaires to achieve rigour. The use of interviews and questionnaires as methods of data collection is discussed in more detail in Chapter 6.

Documentation and observation

Document analysis involves the study of documents such as the minutes of meetings, official and unofficial company documents, newspapers, personal journals, diaries, letters, and documents developed from narratives and life histories. Also included as documentation are archival or public records, including government statistics. Documents are the permanent product of exchanges and communications of individuals and groups across the various levels of the organisation. Therefore, document analysis affords the researcher the opportunity to understand how different employees and groups interpret organisational life. Documentation may be used as data in their own right or as preliminary data to inform a primary data collection method such as interviews, or for the purpose of triangulation to offset the biases of other methods. Documentation may be qualitative or quantitative in nature. The use of documents can engender problems such as gaining access to them if they are protected, difficult to locate, incomplete, or inaccurate. However, the advantages of documents are that they enable the researcher to obtain data based on the words, language, and vernacular of informants; they record the exchanges between different subgroups and organisational politics; their collection is unobtrusive and non-reactive; and their need for transcription is often minimal.

Studies using an historical document analysis attempt to uncover the ways in which individuals in the past constructed their unique reality. The purpose of historical analysis is to examine how the meaning and value of past human intentions, decisions, and actions were related to phenomena and events. The analysis of documents, like interviews, may be qualitative or quantitative, depending on the underlying philosophy of the approach and the types of research questions being asked.

Observation is the process of systematically recording observed behaviours and occurrences. Observation may vary according to the extent of researcher participation in what is being observed, from non-participant observation through to participant observation. In participant observation, the researcher attempts to immerse him- or herself in the phenomenon being observed. This occurs through an extended period of interaction between the researcher and the subjects, in the subjects' environmental setting. Throughout this period, detailed field notes are obtrusively and methodically gathered. The advantages of participant observation are that it provides direct and synchronous (real-time) information about organisational phenomena, as they transpire in a non-contrived environment, without distortion from post hoc verbal descriptions. The disadvantages of participant observation are the potential for reactivity (i.e., the subject being self-conscious or acquiescent because he or she is being observed), the possibility that illegal or unethical behaviour may be observed, and the potential that the researcher may over-identify with those he or she is studying.

Observation also varies in terms of the extent to which the observations themselves are structured. With unstructured observation the researcher maintains a 'running record' by recording everything that occurs during the observation period. With structured observation the researcher develops prearranged categories of expected behaviours, and during the observation period behaviours are checked against the categories. The sources of error from structured observation are reactive effects, observer error, and sampling error. Structured observation is typically used in quantitative analyses of behaviour. Reliability for structured observation can be estimated by having multiple observers and then calculating their level of agreement. In-depth descriptions of document analysis and observation are provided in Chapter 7.

Reliability and validity

Irrespective of the type of design or type of data gathered, the measures applied in a study need to be reliable and valid. Reliability is concerned with how much random error there is in the measurement of a variable. Validity is whether the researcher is measuring the construct he or she purports to be measuring; that is, the extent to which the measure measures what it is supposed to measure. The main types of validity are construct validity, criterion validity, and content validity. The issues relating to reliability and validity are discussed in detail in Chapter 8.

Developing a new scale

Researchers often use multi-item scales to measure complex constructs. The construction of a new scale is a highly complex process. Generally, it is unwise for researchers to develop their own measures, unless there are no established measures of the construct or their own measure is used merely to supplement validated scales. The steps required to develop a multi-item scale to measure a variable are covered in Chapter 9.

Choosing the method(s) of data analysis

Techniques of quantitative analysis

Initial analyses
Initial analyses are preliminary tests undertaken on quantitative data to examine the properties of the data, the assumptions underlying the technique of analysis, and the reliability of the measures, and to obtain sample description data. The issues associated with initial analysis of quantitative data are covered in Chapter 10.

Multivariate analyses
Multivariate techniques are useful because they allow variables to be simultaneously analysed, controlling for each other's effects. In analysing data, initially researchers are advised to examine similar studies on their topic, or a closely related one, to see how those data were analysed. These techniques can then be modelled or extended.
     Examples of multivariate techniques are:

- multiple regression;
- multiple regression for moderated and mediation analysis;
- logistic regression; and
- structural equation modelling.

The techniques of multivariate data analysis are described in more detail in Chapter 11.

Techniques of qualitative analysis

There are various established techniques for analysing qualitative data. We highlight a generic approach called content analysis, including template and editing analyses. Specialised techniques for analysing qualitative data include grounded theory and pattern patching. There are also computer-based approaches for analysing qualitative data. These approaches are discussed in more detail in Chapter 12.

Interpreting the results against the research questions or hypotheses

It is important that the researcher interprets the results against the research questions and hypotheses (if he or she has hypotheses). If the study does involve hypotheses, the researcher needs to examine the results and determine whether they support, or do not support, the hypotheses. The researcher also needs to compare the findings in relation to his or her research questions with the relevant theory, and to consider other plausible explanations and unexpected findings. The procedures for interpreting specific quantitative data analytic techniques are discussed in Chapter 11, while the steps involved in interpreting qualitative data analytic approaches are discussed in Chapter 12.

Reporting the findings

The final step in the research process involves writing up the findings of the study so that they are communicated to a wider audience (e.g., through publication in an academic journal or through submission of a thesis). This is a critical phase in the research process, as even a well-designed and executed study is compromised by a poorly written research report. The report should follow a publication style guide such as the *Publication Manual of the American Psychological Association* (American Psychological Association, 2003) and typically it is structured according to the following sections: abstract, introduction, method, results, and discussion. Chapter 13 details the steps involved in writing up both quantitative and qualitative research reports.

Conclusion

Before beginning to undertake a study, a researcher needs an understanding of the entire process, including the final write-up and what the report will look like. Probably the most important aspect that a researcher needs to carry out is the development of an appropriate research question. This question may be adjusted as the research proceeds, but it should be formulated in order for the literature review to be written, for specific propositions to be derived, and for the research to be designed. The initial stages of understanding the theory and the past empirical studies, and the critique of both, should be well advanced before contemplating the design. It is advisable to keep the design stage separate from the conceptual phase.

Once the conceptual phase has become sufficiently determined, several options are available to test research propositions. Whichever method of research design is used, data need to be reliable and valid, whether quantitative or qualitative. Prior to gathering data, the methods of analysis also need to be fully understood. The overall aim in the design phase is to produce an interpretable result, in terms of the confidence that can be placed in the design for answering the initial research question. The results gained from analysis need to be examined in terms of support for the specific research propositions and then interpreted for meaning. That interpretation should focus back on the theory and past studies to decide what the results mean with respect to the initial research question and what they offer in terms of a contribution to answering the problem.

References

American Psychological Association (2003). *Publication manual of the American Psychological Association* (5th ed.). Washington: American Psychological Association.

Creswell, J.W. (2003). *Research design – qualitative, quantitative and mixed method approaches* (2nd ed.). Thousand Oaks, CA: Sage Publications.

Edwards, J.R. & Bagozzi, R.P. (2000). On the nature and direction of relationships between constructs and measures. *Psychological Methods*, 5, 155–174.

Graziano, A.M. & Raulin, M.L. (1993). *Research methods*. New York: HarperCollins.

Jackson, W. (1988). *Research methods – rules for survey design and analysis*. Ontario: Prentice-Hall.

Klein, K.J. & Kozlowski, S.W. (2000). From micro to meso: Critical steps in conceptualizing and conducting multilevel research. *Organizational Research Methods*, 3, 211–236.

Ray, W.J. (1993). *Methods toward a science of behavior and experience*. Monterey, CA: Brooks/Cole Publishing Company.

Sekaran, U. (1992). *Research methods for business: A skill-building approach* (2nd ed.) (pp. 114–147). New York: John Wiley & Sons, Chapter 5.

Shadish, W.R., Cook, T.D., & Campbell, D.T. (2002). *Experimental and quasi-experimental designs for generalized causal inference*. New York: Houghton Mifflin.

Chapter review questions

1 What is a research question?
2 What are the types of substantive and methodological criticisms that are made of past research?
3 What is a theory?
4 What is a hypothesis?
5 What is a variable?
6 What is an independent variable, dependent variable, mediator variable, moderator variable, and control variable?
7 What is an empirical study?
8 Why is causality hard to show in the social sciences? What should you do to help overcome this problem?
9 What is research design?
10 What are the different types of research designs?
11 What is the difference between qualitative and quantitative designs?

12   What do the individual, dyad, group, organisational, and industry level of analysis mean?
13   Why are longitudinal designs predictive?
14   Define the various types of data collection.
15   How do you interpret your results?

Part 2

Research designs

2 Experimental and quasi-experimental designs

Objectives

At the end of this chapter you will be able to:

- *compare and contrast experimental and quasi-experimental designs;*
- *explain the purpose of experimental and quasi-experimental designs;*
- *discuss the advantages and disadvantages of experimental and quasi-experimental designs; and*
- *identify when experimental and quasi-experimental designs might be suitable for use in management research.*

CONTENTS

Introduction	33
The main types of experiments	34
Commonly used experimental designs	37
Conclusion	42
References	42
Chapter review questions	43
Appendix: A checklist of questions for designing an experimental procedure	44

Introduction

In order to conduct an experiment to assess the effects of an independent variable on an outcome, the researcher needs to decide on an appropriate experimental design. Cook and Campbell (1983) and Shadish, Cook, and Campbell (2002) have provided very comprehensive overviews of the various types of experimental designs. The following is a discussion of the main types and applications of experimental designs.

The main types of experiments

Research designs typically vary in terms of the extent of researcher interference (Sekaran, 1992). In some research designs (e.g., correlational field studies – see Chapter 3), researchers may minimally interfere and study events as they normally arise. Researchers may also interfere and manipulate and/or control and/or simulate the situation. Experimental designs are characterised by manipulation or control over the independent variable (often called a treatment or intervention).

The study setting can also vary from contrived (i.e., artificial) to non-contrived (i.e., natural environments where events normally occur). Contrived settings are usually those of laboratory experimental studies or sometimes field studies, where conditions are imposed by conducting experiments. Laboratory experiments are conducted away from where the phenomenon is usually found and the researcher attempts to control as many extraneous influences as he or she can in that setting.

In other words, contrived settings offer the highest level of researcher interference. Non-contrived settings are typically field studies where variables are allowed to operate as they would normally, such as correlational field studies, and case studies conducted in organisations. In field experiments, there is researcher interference, but this occurs in less contrived settings than laboratory experiments. There are two main types of experiments: true experiments, which are often conducted in the laboratory; and quasi-experiments, which are often done in the field or naturally occurring settings.

A true experiment

A *true* experiment can be defined as having the following characteristics:

- an *experimental condition or group* derived by a manipulation or intervention to force it to occur (e.g., introducing a stimulus); this is the *independent variable*;
- a *control group* (or several groups) called controls that do not get the experimental treatment;
- a *controlled environment* where no other event can influence what is happening. The experimental manipulation is therefore the only thing that changes;
- *random allocation* of participants to experimental and control groups so that an individual could just as likely end up in the experimental group as the control group; and
- the dependent variable is measured after the introduction of the treatment, in both the experimental/treatment group and the control group, to see if there was a change in the experimental group but not in the control group.

The central features of a true experimental design therefore are *manipulation and control* (Sekaran, 1992). An essential element of true experiments is randomisation of cases to experimental and control groups. A thoughtfully designed experiment provides the required controls that enable the researcher to reject alternative explanations, thereby allowing him or her to draw strong causal inferences (Raulin & Graziano, 1995). True experiments are strong on internal validity; that is, the ability to make causal inferences. They do so by controlling all the variables, other than the cause, then manipulating the cause to introduce it as a treatment, and then comparing the effect on the dependent variable (the effect). Creswell (2003) has provided a useful checklist of questions for designing an experimental procedure. This checklist is presented in the appendix at the end of this chapter.

Quasi-experimental designs

Quasi-experimental designs also provide the researcher with the opportunity to assess the effects of interventions or manipulations. However, it is important to keep in mind that they are not true experiments. The reason quasi-experimental designs are not true experiments relates to the fact that they do not occur in completely controlled environments. Although the researcher may manipulate the independent variable (the experimental treatment), there are likely to be other changes occurring that are not being manipulated specifically for the experiment, which may be causing the effect. Therefore, manipulation may occur in quasi-experiments (e.g., experiments in organisations); however, the level of control is weaker than in a true experiment.

Unlike a true experiment, there is no random allocation of participants to groups (experimental vs. control) in quasi-experimental studies; however, people fall into those groups for other reasons. For example, training may be staggered over time and some groups are trained first, providing the later groups as natural control groups whose pre- and post-test measures can be taken at the same time as the experimental groups.

Quasi-experiments have the essential form of experiments, including a causal hypothesis and some type of manipulation to compare two (or more) conditions (Graziano & Raulin, 1993). When conducting experiments in organisations, participants often cannot be randomly assigned to experimental and control conditions. Studies following this design do control for some confounding variables, but do not have as high a level of control as true experiments. As a result, causal inferences can be drawn from quasi-experiments, but not with the same degree of confidence as with true experimental designs. Quasi-experiments are, however, useful when true experiments cannot be carried out, on practical or ethical grounds. There are many variants of quasi-experimental designs (e.g., non-equivalent control group designs, interrupted time-series designs, reversal designs, multiple baseline designs, single-subject designs).

For example, a researcher may wish to know if democratic leadership is more effective than autocratic leadership. In this study, one group might use autocratic decision-making (all decisions made by the leader), another might use democratic decision-making (decisions made by the group), another laissez-faire (the leader deliberately keeps out of the decision-making), and another group just be told to do the task (a true control group). The last two groups might be considered controls or comparisons. If democratic decision-making works, productivity should be highest in that group compared to the three others.

Table 2.1 The pre-test–post-test experimental design

Group	Pre-test score	Treatment	Post-test score
Experimental	O_1	X	O_2

Treatment effect $= (O_2 - O_1)$

Commonly used experimental designs

One-group pre-test–post-test design

Some authors do not classify the one-group pre-test–post-test design as a quasi-experiment, because it does not involve an experimental group and a control group. Creswell (2003) referred to this design as 'pre-experimental', as it has no control or comparison group to compare with the experimental group on the dependent variable. In this design a group is given a pre-test (e.g., supervisory behaviour), is exposed to a treatment (e.g., training), and is then administered a post-test (supervisory behaviour) to measure the effects of the treatment (Sekaran, 1992). The effects of the treatment are measured by the difference between the pre-test and the post-test. Table 2.1 provides an overview of the design. In Table 2.1, X represents the exposure of a group to an experimental variable, the effects of which are to be measured; O represents a measurement; Xs and Os in the same row are applied to the same persons and in different rows are applied to different persons, but simultaneously.

The design, although commonly used, has weak interpretability because anything could have caused a change in the dependent variable. It may just as easily have happened to a control group if one had been included.

Randomised pre-test–post-test experimental and control groups design

This classical experimental design has an experimental/treatment group and a control group both measured at pre-test and post-test on the dependent variable. It is a true experiment, because there is

Table 2.2 The pre-test–post-test experimental and control groups design

Group	Pre-test score	Treatment	Post-test score
Experimental	O_1	X	O_2
Control	O_3		O_4

Treatment effect $= (O_2 - O_1) - (O_4 - O_3)$

random allocation of cases to experimental and control groups. Randomisation ensures that the experimental and control groups are equivalent prior to the treatment, at least within the limits of random error. With randomisation, observed effects can be attributed to the manipulation of the independent variable (e.g., the effect of the intervention) and not to other factors that may influence the outcome, such as pre-existing group differences. The only difference between the two groups is that one received the treatment and the other did not. Measuring the difference between the pre-test and post-test for the two groups and comparing them should test if the treatment had an effect. For example, there should be a greater increase in the dependent variable for the experimental/treatment group than the control group. The randomised pre-test–post-test experimental and control groups design, which is presented in Table 2.2, is interpretable and allows strong causal inferences to be made about the effects of the independent variable.

Non-equivalent pre-test–post-test control group design

If there had been no random allocation to groups, the design in Table 2.2 becomes a non-equivalent control group design. As a quasi-experimental design, the non-equivalent pre-test–post-test control group design is not as interpretable as a study where random allocation had occurred. Unlike a 'true' experimental design where random assignment is used, the non-equivalent control group design uses naturally occurring or intact groups. Interpretability is strengthened if the groups have been matched (e.g., by stratified sampling or some other method) on characteristics and then divided into the treatment groups and control groups. The key issue in a non-equivalent control group design is that the experimental and control groups cannot be assumed to be equal prior to the treatment/intervention.

For example, a researcher might want to know if the introduction of a performance feedback program influences employee perceptions of feedback and if their performance improves. This is an example of a quasi-experiment, conducted in a large Australian government department by the lead author (Tharenou, 1995). In this quasi-experiment, the researcher randomly sampled persons who will have had a performance feedback program (the treatment) introduced (they were appraised) and other persons who did not have the program yet (the controls) and who did not get the performance feedback (they were not appraised). Measures were taken of the dependent variables (e.g., usefulness of feedback, satisfaction with feedback, improved performance) before and after the introduction of the program for those in the treatment group. As the control group did not have a program introduced, they were merely assessed on the variables at two intervals (but they had received nothing). The researcher might do this by 'staggering' the introduction of the program, so that the treatment group is first to receive the treatment and then the control group subsequently receives the treatment.

The groups are not necessarily groups situated in one place. Individuals in a 'treatment group' can be spread over a country in a particular organisation, as can individuals in the 'control group'. The researcher would also usually measure the 'independent' variables here (amount of feedback given, supervisor behaviour, etc.) to determine whether the independent variable 'took' or actually occurred. People who are supposed to receive performance feedback often report that they do not receive it. Measures also need to be taken of the individuals' characteristics to make sure the control and treatment groups do not differ on something that affects the results (e.g., job type, managerial level, or education level).

Alternatively, a researcher might want to evaluate whether a first-line supervisory training and development program works, and so randomly place people in the training program and the control group and also measure leadership style both before and after the training (Tharenou & Lyndon, 1990). This would be an example of a true experiment. The supervisors are randomly allocated to the treatment and control groups. Measures are then taken of the dependent variable (supervisory behaviour) for both the treatment and control groups before the treatment group is trained (the pre-test). Then measures are taken of supervisory behaviour again (the post-test) for both the treatment and control groups. If supervisory behaviour changes in the expected direction (in this case, more consideration and more structure), the training program can be said to have been effective.

There are a number of variations that can be made to improve the non-equivalent pre-test and post-test experimental and control groups design. One way that researchers can improve this design is by using a double pre-test, where participants are measured on the same pre-test twice. (It is best when the intervals between all observations are equivalent.) The additional pre-test enables researchers to test for biases such as maturation. If the experimental and control groups are maturing at differing rates, this can be identified if there is a change from pre-test 1 to pre-test 2. Another way that researchers can improve on the pre-test and post-test experimental and control groups design is by using switching replications. With this variation there are two phases. In phase 1 of the design, both groups are pre-tested; one is then given the intervention/treatment, and then both are post-tested. In phase 2 of the design, the group that was initially the control is given the intervention/treatment, while the initial experimental group serves as the control. One advantage associated with using switching replications is that the researcher can determine whether, after having received the intervention/treatment, the original control group 'catches up' to the original treatment group (Shadish, Cook, & Campbell, 2002). As both groups receive the treatment/intervention, the potential for social threats (e.g., compensatory behaviour) is reduced. It is also fair from an ethical perspective, because all participants receive the treatment/intervention. Also, as there are two independent administrations of the treatment/intervention, the external validity (generalisability) is increased.

Interrupted time-series design

The interrupted time-series design involves multiple pre-tests and multiple post-tests. The logic underlying this design is that if the treatment/intervention has had an effect, the slope or level of pre-test

Table 2.3 Interrupted time series with a non-equivalent no-treatment comparison group design

	Pre-test score	Pre-test score	Pre-test score	Treatment	Post-test score	Post-test score	Post-test score
Experimental	O_1	O_2	O_3	X	O_4	O_5	O_6
Control	O_7	O_8	O_9		O_{10}	O_{11}	O_{12}

observations will differ from that taken after the treatment/ intervention (Shadish, Cook, and Campbell, 2002). In other words, there is an 'interruption', at the point of the treatment/intervention, to an otherwise consistent series of observations (Fife-Schaw, 2000). One advantage of this design is that it controls for regression towards the mean (an extreme score on an initial test). As there are multiple comparison points, the researcher can check for any effects due to regression towards the mean (Raulin & Graziano, 1995).

The simple interrupted time-series design has a single group that is measured several times, prior to and after the treatment intervention. However, there are a number of different types of interrupted time-series designs; indeed, Cook and Campbell (1979) have listed six variants. One type, the interrupted time series with a non-equivalent no-treatment comparison group design, is presented in Table 2.3.

The improvement of this design, over the simple interrupted time-series design, is that the inclusion of a control or comparison group allows the researcher to control for history effects. The reason for this is that any historical event that has an effect (increase or decrease) on the dependent variable in the experimental group would also have the same effect on the dependent variable in the control group. There is still the possibility of an historical event being a threat, but this bias would have to be unique to the experimental group. The researcher can also test for maturation effects using this design, by examining whether each group appeared to be changing at equivalent rates prior to the treatment/intervention (Shadish, Cook, and Campbell, 2002).

Conclusion

Experimental designs, whether conducted in the laboratory or the field, are designed to test cause–effect relationships. They are strong on internal validity – that is, the ability to make causal inferences. They do so by controlling all variables, other than the cause, then manipulating the cause to introduce it as a treatment, and then comparing the effect on the dependent variable (the effect). What the researcher is comparing is the change in the dependent variable in the treatment group with the change in the dependent variable in the control group, to whom nothing is done. The main characteristics of experiments are control and manipulation. True (randomised) experiments are difficult to conduct in organisational settings for both practical and ethical reasons. The non-equivalent pre-test–post-test control group design is an interpretable and commonly used quasi-experimental design. It allows the researcher to test if the treatment/intervention had an effect (e.g., a greater increase in the dependent variable for the experimental group than the control group). Modifications, such as utilising a double pre-test and/or switching replications, can improve this design. Studies using an interrupted time-series design involve several observations prior to, and after, the treatment/intervention. The simple interrupted time-series design involves only a single group, observed on multiple occasions before and after the intervention/treatment. However, by adding a non-equivalent no-treatment control group time series to this design, the researcher can attempt to control for historical and maturational threats.

References

Cook, T.D. & Campbell, D.T. (1979). *Quasi-experimentation: Design and analysis for field settings*. Chicago, ILL: Rand McNally.

Cook, T.D. & Campbell, D.T. (1983). The design and conduct of quasi-experiments and true experiments in field settings. In M.D. Dunnette (ed.), *Handbook of industrial and organizational psychology* (pp. 223–326). New York: John Wiley & Sons.

Creswell, J.W. (2003). *Research design – qualitative, quantitative and mixed method approaches* (2nd ed.). Thousand Oaks, CA: Sage Publications.

Fife-Schaw, C. (2000). Quasi-experimental designs. In G.M. Breakwell, S. Hammond, & C. Fife-Schaw (eds.), *Research methods in psychology* (2nd ed.) (pp. 75–87). London: Sage Publications.

Graziano, A.M. & Raulin, M.L. (1993). *Research methods*. New York: HarperCollins.

Raulin, M.L. & Graziano, A.M. (1995). Quasi-experiments and correlational studies. In A.M. Coman (ed.), *Psychological research methods and statistics* (pp. 58–77). London: Longman.

Sekaran, U. (1992). *Research methods for business: A skill-building approach*. New York: John Wiley & Sons.

Shadish, W.R., Cook, T.D., & Campbell, D.T. (2002). *Experimental and quasi-experimental designs for generalized causal inference*. New York: Houghton Mifflin.

Tharenou, P. (1995). The impact of a developmental performance appraisal program on employee perceptions in an Australian agency. *Group and Organization Management, 20*, 245–271.

Tharenou, P. & Lyndon, T. (1990). The effect of a supervisory development program on leadership style. *Journal of Business and Psychology, 4*, 365–373.

Chapter review questions

1   What is an experiment? What are the different types?
2   What is a true experiment? What are its main characteristics?
3   What is an experimental field study?
4   What is a quasi-experiment? How may it differ from a true experiment?
5   What are the types of experimental designs commonly used in the field?
6   What is a one-group pre-test–post-test design?
7   Explain why a one-group pre-test–post-test design is an uninterpretable design.
8   What is a randomised pre-test–post-test experimental/control groups design? What is the non-equivalent version and how does it differ from a true experiment?
9   Explain why a non-equivalent pre-test–post-test control group design is an interpretable (quasi-) experimental design.
10   What variations can be made to improve the non-equivalent pre-test–post-test control group design?
11   What is an interrupted time-series design? What are the advantages of the interrupted time series with a non-equivalent no-treatment comparison group design over the simple interrupted time-series design?
12   What would be real-life phenomena where conducting an experiment would be the best way to assess if the independent variable causes the dependent variable; that is, explains the phenomenon?

Appendix: A checklist of questions for designing an experimental procedure

1 Who are the subjects in the study? To what populations do these subjects belong?

2 How were the subjects selected? Was a *random selection method* used?

3 How will the subjects be randomly assigned? Will they be *matched* (e.g., measured on a particular variable at pre-test and then assigned to their conditions on the basis of their score on that variable)? How?

4 How many subjects will be in the *experimental and control groups*?

5 What is the *dependent variable* in the study? How will it be measured? How many times will it be measured?

6 What is the treatment condition(s) – that is, the independent variables or factors – in the study? How was it operationalised?

7 Will variables be co-varied in the experiment? How will they be measured?

8 What experimental research design will be used? What would a visual model of the design look like?

9 What instruments will be used to measure the outcome – that is, the dependent variable – in the study? Why was it chosen? Who developed it? Does it have established *validity and reliability*? Has permission been sought to use it?

10 What are the steps in the procedure; for example:
   • random assignment of subjects to groups;
   • collection of demographic information;
   • administration of pre-test;
   • administration of treatment(s); and
   • administration of post-test?

11 What are potential threats to internal and external validity for the experimental design and procedure? How will they be addressed?

12 Will a *pilot test* of the experiment be conducted?

13 What statistics will be used to analyse the data (e.g., descriptive and multivariate)?

(*Source:* J.W. Creswell, *Research design – qualitative, quantitative and mixed methods approaches* (2nd ed.), p. 163. Copyright 2003 by Sage Publications, Inc. Reprinted by permission of Sage Publications, Inc.)

3 Correlational field study (survey) designs

Objectives

At the end of this chapter you will be able to:

- *describe a correlational field study (survey) research design;*
- *list the essential characteristics of a correlational field study (survey);*
- *compare the advantages and disadvantages of a correlational field study (survey);*
- *describe how a correlational field study (survey) is conducted;*
- *outline how to overcome, in practice, the disadvantages of a correlational field study (survey) research design;*
- *explain the importance of a theoretical basis to a correlational field study (survey);*
- *explain why control, mediator, and moderator variables are used in a correlational field study (survey) and how they help overcome the limitations of the design; and*
- *list ways to overcome the main problems in correlational field research.*

CONTENTS

The correlational field study (survey)	46
Characteristics of an interpretable/rigorous correlational field study (survey)	48
Collecting better data and increasing return rates	64
Overcoming the problems in correlational field studies (surveys)	67
Conclusion	68
References	69
Chapter review questions	71

The correlational field study (survey)

One of the most ubiquitous research designs in management research is the correlational field study (survey). Correlational field studies are also called survey or non-experimental designs. We prefer the term 'correlational field study' to 'survey', as the latter is commonly associated with a questionnaire. Historically, correlational field studies typically involve the administration of mail (postal) questionnaires to gather data to test a research question(s) and/or specific hypotheses. However, correlational field studies can be used with any data collection technique, including interviews (face-to-face and telephone) and observation. They are a type of research design, rather than a specific technique of data collection.

Correlational field studies (surveys) usually require the measurement of several independent variables and one or more dependent variables, as well as control and other variables (e.g., mediators, moderators). Unlike an experimental design, a correlational field study (survey) is less able to make strong causal inferences. The interpretation is usually correlational in nature. In other words, the aim of a correlational field study (survey) is to assess the extent of the relationships (correlations) between the independent variables and dependent variable(s). The variables are selected to help answer a research question, to test hypotheses, and are usually chosen based on a theory or theories that underlies the explanation proposed for the phenomenon being examined.

In a correlational field study (survey) the relationships (associations) between the independent and dependent variables are usually examined using multivariate analyses to provide statistical control in the absence of experimental control. The dependent and independent variables, in correlational field studies (surveys), exist in the field (usually the organisation) and they are measured in situ, as they exist, without interference. Hence, correlational field studies (surveys) use a non-contrived setting with minimal researcher contamination (Sekaran, 1992). For example, the researcher might want to know if organisational commitment is related to intentions to quit. In order to answer this research question, he or she would choose a relatively large sample and measure participants' organisational commitment (as well as other control variables and predictors that need to be taken into account) and their intentions to quit.

In summary, Mitchell (1985) argued that a correlational field study (survey) typically:

- aims to measure the relationship between a dependent variable(s) and several independent variables;
- uses a questionnaire (or other data collection device) to measure the variables;
- is conducted in the field (e.g., an organisation);
- is naturalistic and has limited interference by the researcher;
- invokes no manipulations; and
- makes associational (relationships) inferences.

When to utilise a correlational field study (survey) design

In general, correlational field studies (surveys) are most suitable for use under a combination of certain circumstances. For example, they are used to:

- test a theory that includes not just the independent variables (influences) and dependent variables (outcomes), but also perhaps mediator variables (transmitters) or moderator variables (conditions under which the relationship exists); that is, differential predictions and alternative explanations are tested, not just the direct relationship between the independent and dependent variable;
- test the hypotheses/research questions on a large sample of people;
- examine real-life settings and use people (e.g., employees) facing those situations every day;
- examine the extent to which the dependent variable and each independent variable are related;
- generalise the findings – therefore, a large sample is chosen to be representative of a particular and predefined population;
- test questions when there is a solid literature base (i.e., theory, empirical studies) from which to choose the variables to measure in the survey; and
- assess the effects of several variables (e.g., independent variables) while taking into account other variables (e.g., controls such as individuals' demographics, or organisational characteristics).

Problems with correlational field study (survey) designs

Mitchell (1985) outlined some of the problems associated with correlational field study (survey) research designs:

* the use of unreliable measures;
* the use of statistical tests that have low power (e.g., small sample, poor measures, too many variables for the sample size);
* inadequate and poorly planned sampling designs (e.g., convenience sampling);
* use of non-pre-tested instruments; and
* results inappropriately generalised beyond the sample.

Other problems include:

* cross-sectional data (all data collected at one point in time); and
* potential method problems such as socially desirable responding, common method variance (variables related because they are measured by common methods at the same time; explained later in this chapter), and acquiescent responding.

Characteristics of an interpretable/rigorous correlational field study (survey)

Correlational field studies (surveys) can be interpretable and valid if they are conducted rigorously. In order to conduct a robust and interpretable correlational field study (survey), the following processes are required.

Variables to be measured are chosen based on a strong theoretical basis

Like all good research, a correlational field study (survey) should be based on a theory or theories. A theory is a set of interrelated constructs/variables that present a systematic view of a phenomenon by specifying relationships among the variables, with the purpose of explaining the phenomenon (see Creswell, 2003). The systematic view might be an argument or a rationale that helps to explain phenomena that occur in the real world. Theories explain why and how the variables provide an explanation of a phenomenon. Independent, mediating or moderating, and dependent variables are combined to form research questions and hypotheses about the type of relationships (i.e., positive, negative, or none) and their magnitude (i.e., weak, medium, or strong). Theories are often a series of logic statements ('... if ... then ... '). The presentation of the theory shows a causal ordering of the variables.

In correlational field studies (surveys), theory is applied deductively in order to test or verify it. (The results may show the theory is wrong or needs modifying.) Data are collected on independent, dependent, and other variables to test a theory, and the theory is either confirmed or disconfirmed by the results of the study. The theory is the framework for the study, an organising model for the research questions and hypotheses as well as the data collection and analytic procedures. Hence, the researcher tests a theory, tests hypotheses or research questions derived from the theory, operationalises concepts or variables derived from the theory, and uses instruments to measure the variables in the theory. The theory leads to research questions and hypotheses, which are also developed from empirical studies. Hypotheses are usually posed, which are declarative statements that represent the relationship between two or more variables (Creswell, 2003).

Measurement of dependent and independent variables

A correlational field study (survey) always includes measures of the independent and dependent variables and calculates the relationship between them. Hence, a researcher may wish to know if the motivation to attend training (called training attendance motivation) is related to participation in training activities. The researcher could measure training attendance motivation (the independent variable) using a multi-item scale. He or she would also measure how many times employees attended training activities within a predefined time period (the dependent variable). Typically, the dependent variable is also measured via a multi-item scale (e.g., averaging how many internal training courses, external training courses, and conferences each participant attended).

Measurement of control variables

A well-designed correlational field study (survey) should include the measurement of control variables, because the unique, uncontaminated relationship between the independent and dependent variables needs to be determined by the statistical analysis. Control variables that could have any impact on the dependent variable should be measured and their effects removed from the relationship, so that the unique impact added by the independent variable can be determined. Consequently, the researcher needs to decide what could affect the dependent variable, other than the independent variable, and then measure those controls. Their effect is then controlled statistically by a process called partialling (partial correlation if there is one independent variable, or multiple regression if there is more than one independent variable).

In the example study described above, several individual and organisational variables would need to be controlled in order to determine the unique effect of training attendance motivation on attendance at training sessions. Control variables often include personal demographic variables (e.g., age, education level, gender, marital status) and work demographic variables (employment gaps, company tenure, occupation type, full-time vs. part-time employment status, permanent vs. temporary employees, organisation size, and public sector vs. private sector employees). These variables need to be measured because the extent to which motivation to attend training affects actual participation in training may be influenced by these variables; therefore, their effects need to be removed. Additionally, research indicates that younger employees are usually provided with greater opportunities for training than middle-aged and older employees, because there is a greater return on investment to the employer from training younger employees. Full-time and permanent employees are usually trained more than either part-time or temporary employees, again because the employer can more easily recoup the cost of the training. Similarly, the skill level of the occupation needs to be measured. Those who are in higher skill-level occupations, such as managers and professionals, are likely to be trained more than those in lower skill-level occupations such as tradespersons, sales and service workers, clerks, semi-skilled or unskilled employees. Again, the reason for this discrepancy is that there is a greater return on training investment for the higher productivity of skilled workers when compared with their unskilled counterparts. Those in the public sector are often trained more than those in the private sector, because the public sector often has greater financial resources than the private sector and it is less subject to economic downturns. Similarly, larger organisations often provide more training opportunities than smaller firms, because they can capitalise on economies of scale.

Measurement of multiple independent variables

Often in a correlational field study (survey) there will be more than one independent variable, which the researcher is interested in examining. The main interest lies in the link between the independent and dependent variable(s), but the interrelationship between the independent variables is also assessed. Returning to the example study, in addition to training attendance motivation, attendance at training sessions might be predicted by favourable organisational training policies, supervisor support for attendance at training, and employee motivation to learn. This is in addition to the control variables that the researcher needs to measure. Hence, it is a multivariate study, as it has multiple independent variables. The researcher would need to measure each of these and then examine the relationship between each of the independent variables and the dependent variable. Additionally, the researcher would want to know how unique the link was between each of these independent variables and the dependent variable. He or she could use multiple regression analysis in order to examine these unique associations.

Inclusion of mediator or moderator variables where theoretically needed

A correlational field study (survey) may also have different types of relationships being assessed. The theory may indicate that there is a mediator variable or a moderator variable, or the researcher may wish to test if the theory is improved by the calculation of these theoretically meaningful relationships. Consequently, the researcher may measure mediating or moderating variables, which are other types of variables that may affect the relationship between the two main variables of interest.

Mediator variables

Mediator variables are those that intervene between the independent and dependent variables so that the mediator transmits the effect of the independent variable to the dependent variable. There are special kinds of analyses that can be conducted to determine whether a variable has mediator effects; these are described in Chapter 11. Mediator variables explain *how* the process operates to transmit the independent variable to the dependent variable.

Moderator variables

A moderator is a variable that influences (moderates) the strength and/or direction of relationship between two variables. Thus, the relationship between the independent and dependent variables may vary according to another variable (moderator variable) in a systematic way. This is called an interaction effect. For example, job dissatisfaction has been found to be related to absenteeism more strongly for women than for men. Often, if men are dissatisfied this does not result in their absence; however, if women are dissatisfied it does impact on their absenteeism. Hence, gender is a moderator variable. The relationship between the independent and dependent variables varies according to different categories of the moderator variable. Therefore, moderator variables explain *when* a relationship exists (Lindley & Walker, 1993).

Longitudinal designs used rather than cross-sectional designs

With correlational field studies (surveys), it is preferable that researchers apply longitudinal rather than cross-sectional designs, as the former allow prediction. A way to strengthen a cross-sectional correlational field study (survey) is to have a very strong theoretical basis for the tests. (Theory explains 'why' and 'how' and 'what leads to what'.) Using mediator or moderator variables if it is theoretically logical to do so, as well as controls, also strengthens the researcher's explanation in a cross-sectional study, as he or she is proposing a very specific pattern of relationships that may be difficult to obtain unless the theory is correct.

A better correlational field study (survey) design is one that is longitudinal, where the researcher can see if the independent variable actually predicts the dependent variable. Longitudinal data have a time period in-between the measurement of the predictor (independent) and predicted (dependent) variables. Longitudinal designs, with repeated collections of data on the same variables, allow the researcher to test reverse effects. For example, the researcher might want to test if being dissatisfied causes participants to be absent, or if being absent leads to dissatisfaction. In that case, the researcher gathers repeated data on all variables at both Time 1 and Time 2 and tests for reciprocal relationships, using cross-lagged regression coefficients. Despite their ability to address issues of temporal precedence, in the absence of experimental control it is still difficult to draw strong inferences about causality from longitudinal field studies.

Valid and reliable measures used

Management researchers measure constructs/variables. Therefore, they need to utilise valid measures that measure the variables they say they measure (e.g., that a job satisfaction scale actually measures job satisfaction and not organisational commitment). A measure should also be reliable, meaning that it should not contain measurement error. These topics are covered in more detail in Chapter 8.

Samples chosen to answer the question

Sampling involves selecting members/units (e.g., individuals, pairs, groups, organisations) from a population so that they are representative of that population. If the sample is representative, the results of the study can be generalised to the population from which it was drawn. This is an important aspect of external validity. There are two broad types of sampling approaches – probability and non-probability sampling. The external validity of a study (generalisabilty) is much stronger when a probability sampling approach is adopted.

Probability sampling versus non-probability sampling approaches
In probability sampling approaches, each member of the population has a known, non-zero chance of being selected. In order to use probability sampling, the researcher will need an available list of all members of the population from which the sample can be drawn (a sampling frame). Probability sampling methods include simple random sampling, systematic sampling, and stratified sampling. Which method the researcher applies is contingent on a number of factors, such as the nature of the research question, the available sampling frame, and how dispersed the population is, as well as the time and expense considerations.

In a simple random sample, each member of the population is selected completely by chance; therefore, each member of the population is equally likely to be chosen. Additionally, with random sampling the choice of participants is independent, meaning that the selection of any given participant has no effect on the inclusion or exclusion from the sample of other members of the population. For a small random sample, the members' names may be drawn out of a hat; however, for a larger random sample, numbers may be assigned to each member using a random numbers table.

An alternative non-probability sampling approach is systematic sampling. Systematic sampling is similar to simple random sampling; however, instead of the researcher selecting random numbers from tables, he or she would work through the sampling frame and choose every nth name. For example, a researcher may wish to sample 500 public companies from a directory consisting of the names of 50 000 public companies. He or she would select every 100th public company named in the directory (total population size divided by the size of the required sample) for inclusion in the sample. This is the sampling interval. The researcher would start with a randomly selected number between 1 and 100, perhaps 57, and then choose the 157th, the 257th, and so on, until 500 names had been selected. Although it is not common in management research, there is the possibility of ordering bias. This may occur when the names in the list are arranged according to a pattern that matches or interferes with the sampling intervals. For example, the public companies in the directory may be listed according to size or profitability, and therefore starting with the 57th company and selecting every 100th thereafter may introduce sampling error.

In stratified sampling, the population is divided into mutually exclusive subgroups or strata (e.g., age, gender, occupation type, managerial level). The subjects for the study are then selected randomly from each stratum. Stratified sampling may be proportionate, in which case the size of the strata are commensurate with the size of the subgroups in the population. It can also be disproportionate, where certain subgroups are 'oversampled' in order to provide adequate numbers in each stratum. Stratified sampling is most appropriate when subjects within each stratum are homogeneous but are different from subjects in other strata.

Unlike probability sampling techniques, in non-probability sampling, the researcher does not know the probability of any particular member of a population being selected in the sample. Therefore, if a researcher uses non-probability sampling, as opposed to probability sampling, there is a greater chance of him or her selecting some members from the population for inclusion in the study than others. The main types of non-probability sampling techniques are convenience, quota, judgement, and snowball sampling.

In convenience sampling (sometimes called accidental or haphazard sampling), the researcher selects the subjects based on their availability (because they are convenient). While this sampling technique may provide a large sample at a low cost, the researcher should be aware that it is difficult to generalise beyond the sample as there is no way to guarantee that the sample is representative. Placing an ad in a newspaper inviting participation in a study, having students, colleagues, or friends complete a survey because they are available, or placing a survey on the internet, are all examples of convenience sampling. While it is a commonly used technique, it is best to use convenience sampling for exploratory purposes; for example, to pre-test or pilot a new measure.

Another non-probability sampling technique is quota sampling. In quota sampling, the researcher selects participants non-randomly until a predetermined quota is reached. Similar to proportional stratified sampling, quota sampling enables the researcher to ensure that his or her sample corresponds with the target population on particular characteristics. Thus the researcher initially identifies the strata or subgroups and their proportions as represented in the population. However, in quota sampling, unlike stratified sampling where the subjects are selected randomly from each stratum, convenience sampling is typically applied.

Judgement (purposive) sampling occurs when a researcher selects the sample on the basis of his or her judgement concerning a characteristic required of subjects that are included in the study. Therefore, in judgement sampling, the researcher (or experienced others) needs to be knowledgeable about the target population. Judgement sampling is most appropriate for use early in an exploratory study, or if the researcher needs to obtain a biased group for screening purposes (Cooper & Schindler, 2003).

In snowball sampling, the researcher begins by sampling a small number of people who satisfy the criteria for inclusion in the study (i.e., known members of the target population). The researcher then asks these initial respondents to identify other people who meet the criteria. These subsequent respondents, in turn, identify others, and so on. The intent is that the initial small sample will 'snowball' into a larger one. Snowball sampling is particularly appropriate when the target population is rare and inaccessible (i.e., difficult to locate and recruit).

Type
It is also true that some samples will not allow a researcher to test the relationship he or she is seeking. For example, if family roles influence men's and women's pay, the researcher would need to use the private sector rather than the public sector, as the former's pay levels are more able to be determined by the employer. The public sector has rigidly fixed pay scales. Also, it might be the case that the 'traditional family man' is awarded a higher salary if he is a manager, but not when a subordinate, because of social stereotypes. Consequently, a researcher would need a sample of managers, rather than employees in general.

Sample size
A researcher needs a large sample in order to determine the extent to which two or more variables are related. For example, a researcher may wish to test whether, as organisational commitment increases, intention to leave reduces. The study would need to include people with high organisational commitment and very low intention to leave, people with moderate organisational commitment and a little intention to

leave, people with fair organisational commitment and a reasonable intention to leave, and people with low organisational commitment and high intention to leave – and all the variations in-between along the continuum. Large samples have sufficient power to test quantitative relationships; small samples do not. Mone, Mueller, and Mauland (1996) concluded that small effect sizes are usually the norm in management and applied psychology research. The generally weak effect sizes in the social sciences means that large sample sizes are required to obtain sufficient power to detect a relationship. (See Chapter 10 for further discussion on sample size and statistical power.)

Valid types of data gathered

Objective, hard data versus subjective data

When conducting a correlational field study (survey), if the underyling variables are objective in nature, it is best if they are also measured objectively. Subjective data means that the measures are perceptions, whereas 'hard' data indicates that the variables are measured by objective means. If a researcher is measuring promotions, it is best to obtain these data from company records (if they are recorded and recorded accurately), rather than asking participants how often they have been promoted, especially via a rating scale (Krosnick, 1999; Schwarz, 1999). Alternatively, some variables (e.g., organisational commitment) can only be measured subjectively because they are attitudes, opinions, beliefs, and perceptions for which there are no objective measures.

For example, people's memories of their absences from work correlate weakly with their actual absences, as measured from company records. Absenteeism is a dependent variable that can be measured from company records, because organisations need to record all absences for pay purposes. Absence should thus be measured as objective data from company records, as people distort their self-reported absences.

There are many constructs that are measured by hard data. They include dependent variables such as organisational performance (obtainable from company reports), human resource management policies, promotion, managerial level, and salary (all obtainable from company records), organisational size or industry type (from accurate descriptions of the company obtainable from the company report), and so on. As organisational performance is an often studied dependent variable in management research, examples of how to measure it will be given here. Most annual reports, which are public documents (kept on a CD-Rom, obtainable from companies), provide measures of an organisation's performance (e.g., return on investment, return on assets, shareholders' equity, current ratio, and net margins). These must be accurate and are relatively easy to obtain.

Data on individual firms are also available from the stock exchange and other public sources (e.g., *Jobson's Online*, which is a subscription electronic database). However, difficulties often arise in measuring organisational performance, as shown by Agle, Sonnenfeld, and Srinivasan (2006). In their review of the charismatic leadership research, they identified that three different measures of organisational performance had been applied and argued that the use of different measures of this variable had contributed to the mixed findings in the prior research.

For example, Tosi, Misangyi, Fanelli, Waldman, and Yammarino (2004) measured firm performance using a market-based measure (shareholder return) and a financial-based measure (return on assets). Data were gathered over five years and the measures standardised for industry by year (converting the performance measures, for each firm in each year, to industry z-scores based on the means and standard deviations of all firms in each industry). The two measures of performance were analysed separately, as Tosi et al. argued that they do not always converge to represent the same construct of organisational performance.

Alternatively, Waldman, Ramirez, House, and Puranam (2001) measured organisational performance using industry-adjusted net profit margin (NPM). The authors obtained this measure by subtracting average industry NPM from firm-specific NPM (calculated as net income divided by sales). The industry-adjusted NPM data for each firm, collected over six years, was then averaged to yield a composite measure.

Finally, Waldman, Javidan, and Varella (2004) measured firm performance using industry-adjusted NPM, industry-adjusted return on equity (ROE; calculated by dividing net income by shareholders' equity), and industry-adjusted sales growth (measured in terms of the slope of sales measured over time). Both industry-adjusted NPM and industry-adjusted ROE for each firm were measured over five years and averaged to provide a more reliable measure. In this study the measures were not combined to form a composite, as each was analysed separately.

Same-source versus different-source data

It is best to have data that do not all come from the same source. It is especially useful to have the independent and dependent variables in a study measured from different sources. If they come from the same source, there is a tendency to make them consistent with each other (e.g., common-method variance discussed below), irrespective of how unconsciously the respondent does that. Ideally, researchers need to have data that are not all gathered from the same source; for example, individuals giving measures of both the independent and dependent variables on the same survey. At least if the study is longitudinal, it cannot be the same survey instrument measuring the independent variables at Time 1 and the dependent variables at Time 2, because the variables are separated in measurement temporally. As a consequence, the data are less likely to be subject to common-method variance.

Self-report versus others'-report

Data may be gathered from the persons themselves, called self-report (e.g., descriptions by managers of their leadership styles), or others may describe them (descriptions by subordinates of their supervisor's leadership style). Problems arise with the use of self-report measures, which are often caused by the way in which the questions are asked (Schwarz, 1999). Of course, some data are best collected by self-report. If the variable is quite introspective – for example, job satisfaction – then it is best measured via self-report, as only an individual can rate his or her own satisfaction.

Behaviours (e.g., leadership style) are often best described by others (others'-report), as they are visible to others (such as subordinates) and others can therefore provide an aggregate view. For example, supervisor behaviour should be measured by others' perceptions. It may be best not to have supervisors rate their own behaviour (at least as the only type of measure), but rather to have subordinates provide a rating, as well as each supervisor's peers. Even though these others'-reports are subjective, they are likely to be more accurate than self-reports. Organisational citizenship behaviour (OCB; i.e., out-of-role discretionary behaviour) is another variable best measured by others'-reports (supervisors or peers) rather than by self-report. Indeed, Organ and Ryan (1995), following their meta-analysis of the predictors of OCB, stated that, 'because ratings of OCB are inherently subjective, ratings of a person's own OCB are a poor substitute for independent judgements' (p. 779).

Alternatively, certain constructs may be best assessed by gathering both self-report and others'-report data. For example, when measuring the impact of a training program in first-line supervision skills on supervisors' leadership style, the impact can be measured both on subordinate and self-ratings of leadership style. There are some measures that have been developed which consist of a self-report version and an others'-report version. For example, the Job Diagnostic Survey (JDI: Hackman & Oldham, 1975) has a version whereby others, such as observers or supervisors, may rate a position for its job characteristics as well as the incumbent rating the job. The job characteristics measured by the JDI are: *skill variety, task identity, task significance, autonomy* and *feedback from the job.* Scores on these characteristics also combine into an overall motivating potential score for the job; that is, job complexity. Observer reports have been found to be related to self-reports of the five job characteristics and the overall motivating potential score (Fried & Ferris, 1987), suggesting that self-reports of job characteristics have at least some validity. Similarly, Spector (1992) found that perceptual measures of job characteristics reflected the objective environment. Therefore, self-report measures of objective job design characteristics can be said to have some accuracy.

Individual versus pair, versus group, versus organisational-level data
If the researcher believes that organisational variables or group variables affect an individual's responses, then they are best measured at those levels. For example, it may be that organisational training policies are influencing participation in training and development by individuals. The former variable is an organisational-level variable and may be best assessed from several of the organisation's executives who are asked to respond to measures examining the comprehensiveness of the training used across the organisation as a whole. As the dependent variable is individual participation, it would be best measured by company records detailing each individual's participation in training courses.

Data may be gathered from individuals (e.g., job satisfaction), from pairs, from groups/teams (e.g., work unit absenteeism, or team/self-managing group productivity), or from organisations (e.g., company records of profitability, executives' measures of strategy, human resource directors' views of their organisations' HR practices). The level from which data are gathered is contingent on the nature of the research question. The researcher therefore needs to determine whether the phenomenon he or she is attempting to explain occurs/exists at the individual level (e.g., self-esteem, work–family conflict), the group level (e.g., group cohesiveness, teamwork, absence culture), or the organisational level (e.g., business strategy, human resource management approaches). Thus, when deciding upon the unit of analysis it is important for the researcher to consider the level at which he or she seeks to make generalisations. If the researcher wishes to make generalisations about individuals, then the individual should be the unit of analysis. Researchers should be aware of the ecological fallacy, which holds that findings obtained from research conducted at a higher level (e.g., the group level) may not hold true at a lower level (e.g., the individual level of analysis). It is also a fallacy to assume that findings from a lower level (e.g., individuals) can be generalised to a higher level of analysis (e.g., groups).

Data may be gathered at the individual, pair, group, or larger unit levels of analysis, all within the one study if desired. At the individual level, each employee's response is a separate data source, such as individual measures of job satisfaction. At the dyad level, data gathered from two-person interactions, such as several supervisor–subordinate interactions, become the level of analysis. At the group level, data on phenomena such as group effectiveness (dependent variable) and group size or structure or cohesiveness (independent variable) become the unit of analysis. Even though data may be gathered from individuals, under appropriate circumstances, it can be aggregated at the group level. For example, individual-level responses are commonly aggregated to measure constructs such as organisational culture.

It is also possible to analyse data from several levels at once, to provide an overall answer to the research question. This is called multi-level research. For example, team characteristics could be used to predict individual team member performance outcomes. Specialised statistical techniques are now available to examine multi-level models (e.g., hierarchical linear modelling). Further discussion of multi-level research can be found in Klein and Kozlowski (2000).

Common method variance is reduced

Common method variance (see Mitchell, 1985; Williams & Brown, 1994) is the extent of the erroneous relationship that is measured between two (or more) variables that are measured in the same way (e.g., at the same time, on the same questionnaire, using the same rating scales). Common method variance is thus a very important issue in assessing the construct validity of research data. For example, respondents may develop a method set when items in a questionnaire have the same format or method, or it arises when respondents answer questions, unwittingly, in a similar way. Hence, if two or more variables are measured by the same method, the associated common method, or correlated measurement error variance, overestimates or inflates the relationship found between the two measures (Williams & Brown, 1994). Examples of method variance include halo effects in ratings and response sets in self-report questionnaires. Method variance, therefore, concerns variance in measurement attributed to the particular instrumentation, rather than to the construct of interest (Spector, 1987).

Method variance can be a cause of high relationships between variables, particularly when measured by self-report. Instrument- or method-specific bias accounts for method variance in that common bias sources will be correlated (Spector, 1987). As a consequence, the relationship between the variables of interest cannot be distinguished from the relationship between their methods.

The procedure for researchers to apply in order to overcome method variance is to not have all data collected from the same source, using the same method, at the same time. Despite these assertions, Spector's empirical study found that method variance was not a problem for scales measuring self-reported affect and perceptions of work. There did not seem to be method variance at the subscale or the item level (i.e., items or subscales related because they used the same method). In addition, correlations of bias measures (social desirability, acquiescence response set) with measures of the constructs of interest tended to be very small. However, Spector included only well-validated measures in his study. When he used single items, he found they did demonstrate some method variance. However, Williams, Cote and Buckley (1989) re-analysed Spector's (1987) data and found that method variance was present and that it explained about 25% of the variance in the measures examined.

Podsakoff, MacKenzie, Lee, and Podsakoff (2003) stated that common method biases constitute a significant problem, as they are one of the main sources of measurement error and have potentially serious effects on research findings. However, recently Spector (2006) has argued that problems associated with common method variance have been overstated and that it is incorrect to assume that the use of a single method automatically introduces systematic variance, causing inflated correlations. Instead, Spector has advocated that researchers consider each construct measure individually, in terms of the expected sources of variance, and then consider how different aspects of the method might control for them.

To overcome method effects, in addition to always using reliable and valid measures, researchers can use:

- longitudinal data (to measure the independent and dependent variables at different times so that they do not contaminate each other by being gathered simultaneously);
- subjective and objective data (so that the variables are usually not measured the same way);
- measures of the independent and dependent variables from different sources (e.g., company records for absence, job satisfaction from employees);
- counterbalancing of the question order;
- Harman's single-factor test (i.e., loading all of the variables into an exploratory factor analysis and examining the unrotated solution. If a single factor emerges, or a general factor accounts for the majority of the covariance among the measures, common method variance may be present);
- partial correlation or confirmatory factor analysis procedures (e.g., partialling out social desirability); and
- procedures that protect respondent anonymity and reduce evaluation apprehension.

Collecting better data and increasing return rates

The majority of correlational field studies (surveys) use mail (postal) questionnaires. The response (or return) rate is the percentage of members of a sample who respond to a questionnaire (or other instrument) from those eligible. As high a return rate as possible is needed as a means of reducing non-response error and increasing generalisability (Dillman, 1991). Baruch (1999) found that the average response rate from mailed surveys in 175 management studies published in 1975, 1985, and 1995 was 55.6% with a standard deviation (SD) of 19.7. Baruch also found some indication that response rates have declined over time, as the lowest average response rate was obtained in the most recent group of studies (an average of 48.4%, $SD = 20.1$ in 1995). In general, response rates were lower (average of 36.1% with a SD of 13.3) in studies where top management or organisational-level representatives were respondents. For other groups (employees, mid-level managers), the average was approximately 60% with a SD of 20. Recently, Cycyota and Harrison (2006) conducted a meta-analysis of response rate data from 231 studies that surveyed executives and were published in high-level management journals between 1992 and 2003. Consistent with Baruch's (1999) finding, Cycyota and Harrison found that mean response rates tended to decline over this period, with an average rate of 34% ($SD = 17$). It is useful for researchers, when reporting response rates in their studies, to refer to figures such as these in order to assess whether the rate is consistent with expectations for a particular population.

Harzing (1997) found that response rates in international mail surveys (e.g., mail surveys in more than one or two countries) varied considerably across 22 countries. Studies conducted in Japan (28.6%) had higher return rates than those conducted in Europe (22.9%), which in turn were higher than those undertaken in the United States (11.4%). Hong Kong had the lowest response rate (7.1%) of the countries overall. The study found that response rates appeared to be higher when:

- the geographical and cultural distance between the sender country and recipient was smaller;
- the country of location/origin of the recipient was rated lower on Hofstede's (1991) power distance index and was more internationally oriented;

- the recipient could be expected to have a higher English language capacity; and
- the recipient received a relatively small number of questionnaires.

Harzing (1997) concluded that a committee of recommendation (endorsement), a personal approach, and small non-monetary incentives might help to increase response rates.

Dillman (1991) reviewed the results of empirical studies designed solely to identify the factors that increase the return rates in mail-out surveys. Overall, in order of importance, with the first two the most (and always) important, are:

1. follow-up (e.g., reminders, postcards, a third follow-up letter);
2. financial/economic incentives (pre-paid, especially on the first contact);
3. prior notice (e.g., pre-contact by letter);
4. special postage/first-class;
5. a sponsor (e.g., government, association, or university sponsorship);
6. stamped return envelope/reply-paid postage;
7. personalisation;
8. interest salience (e.g., surveys sent to the appropriate people in the organisation, survey content addresses issues that are of personal interest, specific to the firm, or important to the industry); and
9. questionnaire length (though this has weak effects on the return rate).

Interestingly, what does not/may not seem to make a difference is the deadline date, promise of anonymity, nature of the cover letter, size, colour, and reproduction of the questionnaire, and the population surveyed. General factors that appear to be important include:

- reducing the perceived costs of filling out the questionnaire (making it look easier and less time-consuming to complete);
- increasing the perceived rewards (making the questionnaire interesting by adding interest-getting questions); and
- increasing trust (official stationery and sponsorship).

More specifically, Dillman (1991) has listed the procedures that researchers should follow where possible in order to obtain high return rates.

- All members of a population should have an opportunity to be sampled for inclusion (avoiding non-coverage).
- Random methods should be used for sampling (to reduce sampling error).
- Questions should be selected and phrased in ways that result in people providing accurate information (reducing measurement error).
- Attempt to ensure that everyone who is included in the sample responds (avoiding non-response error).

Similarly, Roth and BeVier (1998) summarised findings from studies conducted in marketing, sociology, and public opinion. They found that high response rates in consumer populations are associated with:

- advance notice;
- follow-up reminders;
- monetary incentives;
- issue salience; and
- length of the questionnaire (longer questionnaires reduce response rates).

They then analysed response rates from studies in human resource management/organisational behaviour, conducted from 1990 to 1994, to assess if the results for consumer populations held true for industrial samples (i.e., employees). They found that four variables were related to high response rates when controlling for several other variables in multiple regression analysis:

- advance notice, increasing response rates by 8% to 20%;
- identification numbers;
- follow-up reminders (only for mailed surveys), increasing response rates by about 10%; and
- issue salience (only for mailed surveys).

Cycyota and Harrison (2006) found, in studies sampling executives, that topical (issue) salience, consent pre-screening (advanced contact and pre-agreement to participate), and social networks (having a professional organisation or even a colleague of the executive request participation) were significant predictors of response rates. However, they found that advance notice, follow-up, and personalisation were not associated with higher response rates from senior managers.

It is also recommended that researchers check for non-response bias, which is bias that occurs when non-respondents differ in some way from those who do respond. Researchers can test for this by comparing non-respondents with respondents (e.g., conducting chi-square analyses on items measuring organisation type, size, etc.) on variables to see if the respondents represent the sample surveyed.

While high response rates are desirable, low response rates are not necessarily problematic. Certain demographic groups routinely have low response rates. For example, employees who are younger are less likely to respond than their older counterparts (Tharenou, 1999). Low response rates do not necessarily mean low representativeness, as those who do not respond may be special groups.

Increasingly, researchers are using web- and internet-based modalities for data collection in correlational field studies (surveys). Cook, Heath, and Thompson (2000) conducted a meta-analysis of response rates in 68 electronic surveys, reported in 49 studies, published in three journals (*Public Opinion Quarterly*, *Journal of Marketing Research*, and *American Sociological Review*), between 1994 and 1999. Cook et al. found that the mean response rate was 39.6% ($SD = 19.6\%$) and that the number of contacts, personalised contacts, and pre-contacts were the factors most associated with higher response rates in the electronic survey studies they analysed. Heerwegh, Vanhove, Matthijs, and Loosveldt (2005) used an experimental design to test the effects of personalisation on response rates in web-based surveys. They found that the response rate (49.1%) in the control condition (no-personalisation) was statistically significantly lower than the response rate (57.7%) in the experimental condition (personalisation).

Overcoming the problems in correlational field studies (surveys)

Although the correlational field study (survey) is one of the most popular research designs used in management, it has several problems. Creswell (2003) provided a checklist for setting up a correlational field study (survey) to ensure it is valid and the problems of interpretability can be overcome. The questions in the checklist are:

1. Is the purpose of the survey design stated?
2. Are the reasons for the design mentioned?

3. Is the nature of the survey – cross-sectional vs. longitudinal – identified? Longitudinal is better.
4. Are the population and size of the population mentioned?
5. Will the population be stratified? If so, how?
6. How many people will be in the sample? On what basis was this size chosen?
7. What will be the procedure for sampling these individuals (e.g., random, non-random)?
8. What are the content areas addressed in the survey? What are the scales (i.e., the measures of specific variables)?
9. Who developed the scales or single items?
10. What procedure will be used to pilot or field test the survey?
11. What is the time line for administering the survey?
12. What are the variables in the study?
13. How do these variables cross-reference the research questions and items on the survey?
14. What specific steps will be taken in data analysis to:
    (a) analyse returns;
    (b) check for response bias;
    (c) conduct a descriptive analysis;
    (d) collapse items into scales;
    (e) check for reliability of scales; and
    (f) run multivariate statistics to answer the research questions?

(*Source:* J.W. Creswell, *Research design – qualitative, quantitative and mixed methods approaches* (2nd ed.), p. 155. Copyright 2003 by Sage Publications, Inc. Reprinted by permission of Sage Publications, Inc.)

Conclusion

A correlational field study (survey) requires a well-justified and argued theoretical basis, clearly defined independent and dependent variables, control variables, and tests of mediator or moderator variable effects where the theory suggests them. Ideally, in a correlational field study (survey) it is best to use a longitudinal design and multiple measures of variables from different sources, including objective indicators where appropriate. Variables should be measured at the appropriate level using reliable and valid measures, and the sample should be representative of the population to which the researcher wishes to generalise the results. Correlational field studies (surveys) using probability sampling approaches (e.g., random, systematic, and stratified sampling) have stronger external validity (generalisability) than non-probabilistic approaches (e.g., convenience, quota, judgement, and snowball sampling). In a correlational field study (survey) it is also important that steps are taken to reduce method biases (e.g., robust designs, variables measured in different ways), to increase response rates (e.g., follow-up), and to test for non-response bias by comparing respondents with non-respondents.

References

Agle, B.R., Sonnenfeld, J.A., & Srinivasan, D. (2006). Does CEO charisma matter? An empirical analysis of the relationship among organizational performance, environmental uncertainty, and top management team perceptions of CEO charisma. *Academy of Management Journal*, *49*, 161–174.

Baruch, Y. (1999). Response rate in academic studies – a comparative analysis. *Human Relations*, *52*, 421–438.

Cook, C., Heath, F., & Thompson, R. (2000). A meta-analysis of response rates in web- or internet-based surveys. *Educational & Psychological Measurement*, *60*, 821–836.

Cooper, D.R. & Schindler, P.S. (2003). *Business research methods* (8th ed.). Boston: McGraw-Hill Irwin.

Creswell, J.W. (2003). *Research design – qualitative, quantitative and mixed methods approaches* (2nd ed.). Thousand Oaks, CA: Sage Publications.

Cycyota, C.S. & Harrison, D.A. (2006). What (not) to expect when surveying executives: A meta-analysis of top manager response rates and techniques over time. *Organizational Research Methods*, *9*, 133–160.

Dillman, D.A. (1991). The design and administration of mail surveys. *Annual Review of Sociology*, *17*, 224–249.

Fried,Y. & Ferris, G.R. (1987). The validity of the job characteristics model: A review and meta-analysis. *Personnel Psychology*, *40*, 287–332.

Hackman, J.R. & Oldham, G.R. (1975). Development of the Job Diagnostic Survey. *Journal of Applied Psychology*, *60*, 159–170.

Harzing, A.W. (1997). Response rates in international mail surveys: Results of a 22-country study. *International Business Review*, *6*, 641–665.

Heerwegh, D., Vanhove, T., Matthijs, K., & Loosveldt, G. (2005). The effect of personalization on response rates and data quality in web surveys. *International Journal of Social Research Methodology*, *8*, 85–99.

Hofstede, G. (1991). *Cultures and organizations: Software of the mind*. London: McGraw-Hill.

Jobson's Online. From http://jobsons.dnb.com.au/.

Klein, K.J. & Kozlowski, S.W. (2000). From micro to meso: Critical steps in conceptualizing and conducting multilevel research. *Organizational Research Methods, 3*, 211–236.

Krosnick, J.A. (1999). Survey research. *Annual Review of Psychology, 50*, 537–567.

Lindley, P. & Walker, S.N. (1993). Theoretical and methodological differentiation of moderation and mediation. *Nursing Research, 42*(5), 276–279.

Mitchell, T.R. (1985). An evaluation of the validity of correlational research conducted in organisations. *Academy of Management Review, 10*, 192–205.

Mone, M.A., Mueller, G.C., & Mauland, W. (1996). The perceptions and usage of statistical power in applied psychology and management research. *Personnel Psychology, 49*, 103–120.

Organ, D.W. & Ryan, K. (1995). A meta-analytic review of attitudinal and dispositional predictors of organizational citizenship behavior. *Personnel Psychology, 48*, 775–802.

Podsakoff, P.M., MacKenzie, S.B., Lee, J.Y., & Podsakoff, N.P. (2003). Common method biases in behavioural research: A critical review of the literature and recommended remedies. *Journal of Applied Psychology, 88*, 879–903.

Roth, P.L. & BeVier, C.A. (1998). Response rates in HRM/OB survey research: Norms and correlates, 1990–1994. *Journal of Management, 24*, 97–117.

Schwarz, N. (1999). Self-reports: How the questions shape the answers. *American Psychologist, 54*, 93–105.

Sekaran, U. (1992). *Research methods for business: A skill-building approach.* New York: John Wiley & Sons.

Spector, P.E. (1987). Method variance as an artifact in self-reported affect and perceptions at work: Myth or significant problem? *Journal of Applied Psychology, 72*, 438–443.

Spector, P.E. (1992). A consideration of the validity and meaning of self-report measures of job conditions. In C.L. Cooper and I.T. Robertson (eds.), *International review of industrial and organizational psychology* (pp. 123–151). Chichester, England: Wiley.

Spector, P.E. (2006). Method variance in organizational research: Truth or urban legend? *Organizational Research Methods, 9*, 221–232.

Tharenou, P. (1999). Is there a link between family structures and women's and men's managerial career advancement? *Journal of Organizational Behavior, 20*, 837–863.

Tosi, H.L., Misangyi, V.F., Fanelli, A., Waldman, D.A., & Yammarino, F.J. (2004). CEO charisma, compensation, and firm performance. *Leadership Quarterly, 15*, 405–421.

Waldman, D.A., Javidan, M., & Varella, P. (2004). Charismatic leadership at the strategic level: A new application of upper echelons theory. *Leadership Quarterly, 15*, 355–381.

Waldman, D.A., Ramirez, G.A., House, R.J., & Puranam, P. (2001). Does leadership matter? CEO leadership attributes and profitability under conditions of perceived environmental uncertainty. *Academy of Management Journal, 44*, 134–143.

Williams, L.J. & Brown, B.K. (1994). Method variance in organizational behavior and human resources research: Effects on correlations, path coefficients, and hypothesis testing. *Organizational Behavior and Human Decision Processes, 57*, 185–206.

Williams, L.J., Cote, J.A., & Buckley, M.R. (1989). Lack of method variance in self-reported affect and perceptions at work: Reality or artifact? *Journal of Applied Psychology, 74*, 462–468.

Chapter review questions

1   What is a correlational field study design?
2   When should researchers use a correlational field study design?
3   What are some of the problems with the correlational field study design?
4   How do researchers conduct correlational field studies?
5   Why are control variables used in correlational field studies? How are they dealt with and analysed?
6   Why are multiple independent variables usually measured in a correlational field study?
7   What is a mediator variable? What does it help to explain?
8   What is a moderator variable? What does it help to explain?
9   Why do researchers need to test mediator or moderator effects in correlational field studies?
10 Why do researchers need to carry out longitudinal correlation field study designs?
11 Why do researchers need a large sample size? What are the characteristics needed of a sample to help the validity of a correlational field study?
12 Why is it important to use not only subjective but also hard data in correlational field studies?
13 Why is it important to use different sources, not same-source data, in correlational field studies?
14 When do you need to gather data at different levels?
15 What is the problem with self-report data in correlational field studies?
16 Define 'common method variance'. How do you overcome its invalidating effect on survey/correlational field study results?
17 Using mail-out surveys, how do you collect better data and increase return rates?
18 How do researchers overcome the problems in correlational field research?
19 Overall, what are the characteristics of an interpretable correlational field study?

4 Case study research designs

Objectives

At the end of this chapter you will be able to:

- *describe case study research design;*
- *identify the advantages and disadvantages of case study research;*
- *determine when case study research design is suitable for use;*
- *describe the process for carrying out research using case study research design;*
- *identify the kinds of bias that may occur in case study research;*
- *address the difficulties linked to bias; and*
- *identify how to increase the reliability and validity of case study research designs.*

CONTENTS

Introduction	73
Case study research design	73
The research methodology used in case studies	78
Making case studies reliable and valid	80
How to conduct a case study	84
Conclusion	86
References	86
Chapter review questions	87

Introduction

The case study is one of the most common forms of research design in management research. Case studies that are developed for the purpose of conducting empirical research should not be confused with case studies developed for teaching or training purposes, such as those developed by Harvard University in the United States. A research case study is an empirical inquiry into a social or human problem. It begins with a research question and involves the collection of data to analyse and to answer that research question. Research case studies necessarily seek to *generate, elaborate, or test theory*. They enhance understanding through theory development that can occur within an in-depth investigation of one case situation, or across in-depth investigation of multiple cases. Conversely, the instruction case study (e.g., the Harvard-style case) involves no theoretical implication and enhances understanding through a rich and deep description within a single specific case situation (Lee, Mitchell, & Sablynski, 1999).

This chapter is an introduction to case study design. Researchers are also advised to review the seminal text on case study research by Yin (2003), as well as the chapter by Lee (1999) on this topic, as they are both highly instructive.

Case study research design

A case study is an in-depth, detailed investigation of a single instance or one setting, although more than one case at a time may be conducted (Sommer & Sommer, 1991). Yin (2003, p. 13) describes case studies as 'an empirical enquiry that investigates a contemporary phenomenon within its real-life context'. Case studies are *empirical inquiries* conducted to analyse and explain processes to do with units as small as individuals (e.g., medical case studies) or as large as countries (e.g., cultural case studies).

A case study's unit of analysis is the phenomenon under study (Lee, 1999). Deciding on the appropriate unit of analysis is central to a research study. According to Lee et al. (1999) a case can be persons, groups, organisations, or non-human objects (e.g., products, policies, or programs). Case studies can answer research questions; however, unlike experiments/quasi-experiments, the variables cannot be tightly controlled and manipulated. Typically, the case study's longitudinal, in-depth nature places emphasis on situationally dependent process variables and assumes that some level of causal inference can arise. In summary, then, a case study is an in-depth, empirical investigation of a single instance or setting to explain the processes of a phenomenon in context.

When to use case study research designs

In management research, cases have often been used to study events that are unusual, noteworthy, unfamiliar, and involve change (McCutcheon & Meredith, 1993). Case studies are useful when atypical or extreme situations need to be examined for their underlying processes, such as an organisational downsizing, merger, or acquisition. Multiple case studies of these types of events can also be carried out in order to understand their processes. Cases are commonly applied in context where there is a temporal dimension – where changes occur over time (Sommer & Sommer, 1991). The case study often focuses on the processes of change; therefore, it affords the researcher the opportunity to explore social processes as they unfold in organisations. The case study can allow process, contextual, and longitudinal analysis. These processes can be examined in-depth to develop a better understanding of particular phenomena. Therefore, case studies are used especially to understand social processes in their organisational and environmental context, which could be contemporary and/or historical. Case studies may also be useful when the researcher seeks a dynamic, as opposed to static, approach and seeks to explore informal, secret, illicit, or unusual processes (Hartley, 1994).

Case studies are particularly suited to the analysis of complex organisational processes. They are also an appropriate method for management research into unique situations, because case studies deal with process and multiple stakeholder considerations, by using longitudinal (dealing with processes) and multi-source data (Larsson, 1993). Cases are frequently used to explain the implementation of new methods and techniques, such as quality management (McCutcheon & Meredith,

1993). With these types of interventions there is often only one or a small number of situations; therefore, it is not possible to do statistical comparisons of large sample sizes. For example, a case study may be conducted using an exemplar site to provide the best example of a phenomenon (e.g., best practice); alternatively, it may focus on extreme examples of outcomes (e.g., successful vs. unsuccessful implementation of a strategy). Additionally, cases can be used to explain everyday practices that are affected by the culture in which they are embedded (e.g., absenteeism) and in cross-national research (e.g., cultural differences). Finally, exploratory case studies can be very useful for exploring new processes and behaviours, as they help to generate new hypotheses and build theories, which can then be tested in another setting (Hartley, 1994; Yin, 2003).

In summary, cases studies are often used in organisational research to study:

- unusual, extreme, or noteworthy events;
- unfamiliar events;
- events involving large-scale change, such as the implementation of new methods and techniques;
- everyday practices affected by the culture in which they are embedded;
- events involving change and time;
- events where processes unfold; and
- complex events.

In such circumstances, a case study approach is appropriate as there are insufficient numbers to conduct surveys and the events are complex and dynamic, benefiting from in-depth investigation.

Using case study designs as part of a mixed-method research design

In a research project, case studies may provide the predominant design, or may be part of a mixed-method design. For example, in terms of mixed-method designs, case studies can be used to develop an initial in-depth understanding of a phenomenon, using one or a small number of cases. The explanation/theory developed can then be tested through a large sample survey (see Larsson, 1993). The reverse sequence could also occur. Large-scale surveys could uncover relationships, and then case studies could be used to understand the specific processes underlying the relationship in context. Case studies provide illustrative examples by applying multiple methods (Sommer & Sommer, 1991). A case study can also humanise statistically based research by providing a real-life example that explains the underlying processes in-depth.

Importance of the context in case study research designs

In terms of social processes, a case study is a detailed investigation of one or more organisations, or groups within organisations, conducted to analyse the processes of a phenomenon within the context under study. In case studies, the emphasis is placed on understanding processes as they occur in their context (Hartley, 1994). The explanation of the phenomenon (e.g., a closure) is done within its context (e.g., the particular organisation that is closing down) and is of interest in relation to its context. Therefore, in conducting case studies, the emphasis is on understanding processes alongside their contexts. The case study explains not only the processes in a single or several situations, but also the development of theoretical explanations of the phenomenon of interest. Lee (1999) has suggested that researchers may be justified in drawing some level of causal inference from case studies due to their in-depth nature and their focus on situationally embedded processes.

Use of theory in case study research designs

Case studies are used in management research to generate theory and/or to test existing theory. The purpose of a case study is to understand *how or why events occur* and is best suited to the examination of *why and how contemporary real-life organisational phenomena occur*, under conditions where researchers have minimal control (Lee, 1999; Yin, 2003). The purpose of a research case study is not simply to describe a situation. Instead, the researcher assesses the conditions surrounding a phenomenon to build a plausible explanation or to discover a causal relationship that links the antecedents to the results (McCutcheon & Meredith, 1993). The description of the case is used only to substantiate the explanation provided.

Case studies often apply an inductive approach to theory building, deriving it from detailed observation of the situation. Other case studies may be used to test a well-established theory. Irrespective of the approach adopted, by the end of the case study, a theory/theoretical framework will have been developed. The theory allows the explanation of what is of general relevance and interest. Without a theory, a case study would be little more than a story about a unique situation. With a theory, however, case studies can explain fundamental organisational or other processes. Cases have unique features and generalisable principles, and the theory allows for the case not just to be descriptive, but to have wider meaning (Hartley, 1994).

Theory building occurs through the systematic piecing together of detailed evidence to generate theories of more general interest (Hartley, 1994). As a result, the analysis can be applicable to a wider basis than just the particular case(s). In theory building, the initial identification of research questions and the theoretical framework is usually tentative, and is then developed further as information is gathered and analysed. It is important, however, that cases not become what researchers 'want to find' (Hartley, 1994). In unfamiliar situations, such as the original accounts of firms' acquisition of flexible manufacturing systems, cases were used initially to describe and then explore a situation. Later accounts of the same phenomenon, using multiple case studies, were used to develop theoretical explanations of the major implementation decisions (McCutcheon & Meredith, 1993). Hence, new theories can be developed in unfamiliar situations.

Cases can also be applied in management research specifically to test a theory. A single instance is insufficient to support a theory, but a positive finding encourages confidence in a theory's predictive power (Sommer & Sommer, 1991). Therefore, case studies can be used to support, expand, or raise doubts concerning existing theories (McCutcheon & Meredith, 1993). Yin (2003) has referred to case studies designed to determine 'how' or 'why' events occur, as explanatory studies.

In summary, the purpose of a case study is to understand how or why events occur; that is, to provide explanation. A case study may be based on an initial theory that is modified by completion, or a theory may be induced by the end of the study. Therefore, a case study is not just a story or description; it is a theoretically based attempt to understand and explain complex phenomena, embedded in context.

The research methodology used in case studies

Case studies are often associated with a qualitative research design. However, case studies can be used with both qualitative and quantitative data (Eisenhardt, 1989; Yin, 2003). Moreover, a case study is not a particular method of data collection. Case studies can use a wide range of data collection methods. Case studies can include systematic application of:

- observations by the researcher;
- interviews (often unstructured and semi-structured) with key informants;
- questionnaires;
- documents to enable public records of information; or
- attendance at meetings.

A combination of methods is used because the phenomena studied are complex and multiple methods allow triangulation. Case studies also differ in terms of their duration and level of involvement (Hartley, 1994). McCutcheon and Meredith (1993) have suggested that case study research involves:

- one or more researchers gathering a large volume of data from within an organisation to develop the clearest possible picture of a phenomenon;
- data coming from:
  - primary sources, such as direct observations or interviews of people involved; and/or
  - secondary sources, such as documents or records;
- examination of a single situation or, with multiple case studies, several related situations;

- a focus on current conditions, using historical data primarily to understand or substantiate information gathered about the ongoing situation; and
- the researcher not having the capability to manipulate events.

Disentangling what is unique in a single case study, from what is common to other cases, is very difficult. Therefore, the researcher's understanding of the processes may be strengthened by the inclusion of additional cases. The researcher may examine up to a dozen cases and may carefully match pairs of cases. In this way, multiple case studies permit both within-case and cross-case analysis (Yin, 2003). Alternatively, contrasts can be developed within a particular case; for example, comparing groups or departments within a case to explain the same phenomenon (Hartley, 1994). Another option available to researchers involves combining case studies with other types of research design; for example, a survey of a large number of organisations, followed by in-depth case studies of a few (or vice versa) to explain the processes at different levels.

Lee (1999) has proposed that case studies are composed of the following five primary components:

1. *Research questions.* These usually focus on 'how' and 'why' organisational phenomena occur, rather than prevalence ('what' or 'how many' questions) as in survey studies, unless cross-case analysis occurs.
2. *Theoretical propositions.* Theory is either induced from the case study or tested. If tested, the tested theory should clarify the specific research questions asked, variables assessed, and the nature of the analysis.
3. *Units of analysis.* A study's unit of analysis is the phenomenon under study. In theory generation, one purpose of the study is to determine the most meaningful unit. With theory testing, the theory itself defines the most meaningful unit.
4. *Logic* linking data to these theoretical propositions.
5. The *criteria for evaluating* these propositions.

Cases may also utilise time-series designs in which organisational phenomena and the contexts in which they occur are tracked temporally. Patterns of organisational events, acts, circumstances, or variables are predicted. Data are collected (prospectively or retrospectively) and comparisons are made between the predicted and empirical patterns. In the simplest design, a variable is assessed over time to establish a base rate. An intervention will then occur, and the base rate, established in the pre-intervention period, and changes in the monitored variable can be compared before and after the intervention. Other more complicated designs – for example, an interrupted time-series design – also exist (Lee, 1999).

In summary, the research methodology of a case study can involve:

- multi-method, multi-source data;
- primary and secondary data sources;
- observation, interviews, questionnaires, documents, meetings;
- longitudinal data collection;
- one or more researchers; and
- one or more cases carefully chosen.

Making case studies reliable and valid

Reliability

In case studies, the question that researchers need to ask in relation to reliability is: to what extent would the data be duplicated if collected at another time or through another means, such as interviews versus surveys, or from different individuals? The accuracy of the information collected is increased in case study research by cross-checking. Cases always involve cross-checking information and descriptions; for example, from single observers. Multiple sources and techniques are required to allow cross-verification and to improve reliability (Sommer & Sommer, 1991). Some case studies occur after the fact and, therefore, respondents are recalling events. Unfortunately, memories are not infallible and, consequently, recollections are likely to be distorted (Sommer & Sommer, 1991).

One way for researchers to increase reliability is to employ a number of methods for measuring the same construct, as this provides convergence through triangulation. Reliability may also be increased in case study research through the use of more than one researcher, or tape recordings to independently code information (McCutcheon &

Meredith, 1993). In summary, in order to increase reliability, researchers need to cross-check information, apply multiple sources and verification, utilise different ways of measuring the same construct, and involve more than one researcher in the data collection, coding, and interpretation processes.

Validity

Internal validity

Internal validity is the extent to which the correct cause-and-effect relationships have been established (McCutcheon & Meredith, 1993). As there is no limit to the number of variables in case study research, and because they have not been manipulated with all other conditions controlled, it is possible to attribute causal relationships to the wrong causes (i.e., spurious relationships). These are called threats to internal validity and, because of these threats, other causes than those found may be true.

In case study research, a threat to internal validity arises through researchers' interpretations. As in all research, these interpretations threaten validity as researchers' interpretations of the case data may be influenced by their own biases and assumptions (Neck, Godwin, & Spencer, 1996). This is referred to as projection, and it occurs when the researcher's own values and experiences are projected on to the case. Cases always require an explanation of the processes under investigation and to do so, researchers need to fill in the gaps. Additionally, case researchers determine whether information is salient according to their pre-existing cognitive structures, which represents another source of bias (Neck et al., 1996). In summary, researchers need to categorise and interpret the information in a case, which may lead to error, especially through projection.

Data triangulation, through use of multiple sources and methods, will assist researchers in establishing defensible, cause–effect relationships. In addition, multiple researchers may be used, with specific roles (interviewer, note taker, devil's advocate). In case studies conducted by multiple researchers, it may be decided that all researchers will be present at each site, for the benefit of consistency, or that some will stay behind to allow fresh insights (McCutcheon & Meredith, 1993).

External validity

External validity is the extent to which findings drawn from one group are generalisable or applicable to other groups or settings (McCutcheon & Meredith, 1993). It is often difficult to generalise from case studies to other situations. In fact, the event may have been selected *because* it was atypical. Therefore, while it is appropriate to draw conclusions from case study data, the findings may not be generalisable to other instances of the phenomenon (Sommer & Sommer, 1991). One way for researchers to increase generalisability is to undertake multiple case studies of the phenomena of interest (Sommer & Sommer, 1991).

The logic underlying case studies is that detailed examination of processes in a context can reveal processes that can be proposed as general or as peculiar to the organisation. An understanding of the processes and their context allows the researcher to stipulate the expected conditions under which the behaviour occurs. Therefore, in case study research, generalisation has to do with extrapolation to theoretical propositions and not to populations. Case studies seek analytic generalisation rather than statistical generalisation (Yin, 2003). As a result, the emphasis in a case study is not on how typical the organisation is, but rather on the existence of particular processes. Case researchers need to write with a clear conceptual framework in mind and use the existing literature to check the generalisability of the findings (Hartley, 1994). While cases are generally weak in terms of their generalisability and breadth, they compensate for these short-fallings by providing the researcher with an in-depth analysis of a phenomenon (Sommer & Sommer, 1991).

For case studies, results can be tested by *replication* (McCutcheon & Meredith, 1993), in which other cases are conducted in contexts where the results should be comparable. Thus, the researcher would only select those cases for replication where the theory would propose similar results, or alternatively, those cases where the theory suggests different, but predictable, results (Yin, in McCutcheon & Meredith, 1993). The validation should not result in a small sample of cases. Rather, the theory developed from the situation is extended to other contexts where the conditions appear to be similar in terms of the salient characteristics (McCutcheon & Meredith, 1993). It may be appropriate to choose future cases which differ maximally from the first from which the theory was developed. Confidence is gained by the case researcher if the theory is still applicable to the subsequent cases.

Ways have been developed to summarise the results of many case studies when case studies dominate an area of research, such as in mergers or strikes. As a number of studies of the one phenomenon are collectively analysed, generalisability is possible. An example of this is the case survey methodology, which involves a summary of many cases, on the same topic, at the same unit of analysis (i.e., the unit may be the organisation level). Relevant case studies are pooled into data sets large enough for statistical testing of relationships. According to Larsson (1993), researchers wishing to apply the case survey methodology are required to:

1. select a group of existing case studies relevant to the chosen research question; that is, that examine a *common research question* – e.g., 'What leads to/helps the implementation of quality management to be successful?';
2. *design a coding scheme* for systematic conversion of the qualitative case descriptions into quantified variables;
3. use multiple raters to *code the cases* and measure their inter-rater reliability; and
4. *statistically analyse* the coded data (e.g., correlations, multiple regression – the dependent variable could be extent of success, and the independent variables the variables identified linked to success vs. lack of success in the coding scheme devised).

The reliability of the coding can be measured by using multiple independent raters to code the same published cases and by assessing the extent to which they correspond. By summing and averaging the results in this manner, the case researcher is able to examine cross-sectional patterns and to generalise to large populations (Larsson, 1993).

In summary, to increase validity in case study research, researchers need to increase internal validity through the use of multiple methods and sources. They can, if they wish, increase external validity by the use of multiple case studies or replication. Researchers can also use the case survey methodology to arrive at overall/average findings from cases on the same topic.

How to conduct a case study

Hartley (1994) has outlined the following eight steps that researchers should follow when conducting a case study.

1. *Choose the case study organisation(s)*
   Considerations need to be given to, for example:
   (a) whether a typical or extreme example of the phenomenon to be studied is warranted;
   (b) if more than one case is chosen, how the cases might contrast with each other; and
   (c) what is the population of cases from which you might draw.
2. *Gain and maintain access*
   A third party can arrange an initial contact instead of cold calling. Interviews can then be conducted with prospective suitable organisations (e.g., with the human resources manager) to see which organisations are suitable. Further approaches need to be made through organisational gatekeepers; that is, those who would allow access. After sanction is given, a working party can oversee the research and allow for inclusion of stakeholders and regular reporting-back mechanisms to maintain access.
3. *Choose an initial theoretical framework*
   Hartley (1994) recommends the use of a theoretical framework at the beginning of the research, although it may change as the research progresses. A theoretical framework, no matter how tentative, is needed to structure the study, so as not to be overwhelmed by the amount of data and not end up just in a descriptive narrative.
4. *Collect systematic data*
   There are two main steps to data collection:
   (a) Collect data that gain a general overview of the structure and functioning of the organisation through, for example, half a dozen orientation interviews, an organisation chart, walking around, etc.
   (b) Plan the people and groups to talk to and the research methods to use. Triangulated methods are needed; that is, testing of the theory from evidence gained in different ways, from different groups, in different situations, and by different researchers. The broad array of evidence should take into account disconfirming as well

as confirming data. The data collection needs to be systematic, not ad hoc. Interviews and observations need to be set up so that appropriate sampling has occurred of enough informants; other data need to be collected that may not support current hypotheses, and other people interviewed who might give a different picture.

5. *Manage the data collection*

    The researcher will have to decide when to stop gathering data – in terms of whether further collection will add significantly to what is known, allow the testing of tentative ideas, allow further disconfirming evidence to be gathered, etc. The data need to be recorded, usually by notebook. There are usually observation notes, method notes, and theoretical notes. Notes of interviews and impressions need to be written up without delay.

6. *Analyse the data*

    Synthesis and analysis is about putting the information together from various sources into a coherent whole (Sommer & Sommer, 1991). The end of the case study is a synthesis and explanation, with evidence presented to justify each conclusion in the case.

    Data analysis and collection are done together in an iterative process. The first part of the analysis is careful description of the data and development of the categories in which to place information. The data can be organised around certain topics, key themes, or central questions. Then the data need to be examined to see how much they fail to fit the expected categories. Tables can be set up to help search for patterns or groupings of similar topics. The categories may need refining. The presence of disconfirming data needs to be taken into account. The final explanation should be an accurate rendition of the facts of the case, include some consideration of possible alternative explanations of these facts, and should draw conclusions based on a single explanation that appears most congruent with the facts. More detail on analysing case studies can be found in Chapter 12.

7. *Write up*

    The write-up should include enough evidence for each aspect to allow readers to make their own assessment of the fit. The case should not be written up as a descriptive narrative, but the wider implications of the case should be drawn. Hence, wider themes are of interest, and not just the particular circumstances of the case written up.

To increase the internal validity:

(a) the constructs and theory derived need to be checked against the evidence;

(b) a number of researchers need to be used to help with similarities and contrasts in the data and to act as devil's advocates; and

(c) reference needs to be made to the existing literature in order to raise questions about the findings, especially differences from the literature.

8. *Leave the case*

Decisions need to be made about how to report the findings to the organisation.

Conclusion

A case study is an in-depth investigation of a single instance. Cases are suited to explaining complex situations as an integrated whole and in terms of processes that unfold temporally. Generalisability is weak in single case study research, but may be increased by using more than one case, thereby increasing external validity. Cases provide an explanation of processes; however, they require a theoretical framework in order to do so. Finally, case researchers need to be mindful of reliability and validity, which may be improved through cross-verification, and using multiple sources and multiple methods of data collection.

References

Eisenhardt, K.M. (1989). Building theories from case study research. *The Academy of Management Review*, *14*, 532–550.

Hartley, J.F. (1994). Case studies in organizational research. In C. Cassell & G. Symon (eds.), *Qualitative methods in organizational research* (pp. 208–229). Newbury Park, CA: Sage Publications.

Larsson, R. (1993). Case survey methodology: Quantitative analysis of patterns across case studies. *Academy of Management Journal*, *36*, 1515–1546.

Lee, T.W. (1999). *Using qualitative methods in organizational research*. Thousand Oaks, CA: Sage Publications.

Lee, T.W., Mitchell, T.R., & Sablynski, C.J. (1999). Qualitative research in organizational and vocational psychology, 1979–1999. *Journal of Vocational Behavior*, *55*, 161–187.

McCutcheon, D.M. & Meredith, J.R. (1993). Conducting case study research in operations management. *Journal of Operations Management*, *11*, 239–256.

Neck, C.P., Godwin, J.L., & Spencer, E.S. (1996). Understanding researcher projection in interpreting case study data: The South Canyon Fir Tragedy. *Journal of Applied Behavioral Science*, *32*, 48–61.

Sommer, B. & Sommer, R. (1991). *A practical guide to behavioral research: Tools and techniques*. New York: Oxford University Press.

Yin, R.K. (2003). *Case study research: Design and methods* (3rd ed.). Thousand Oaks, CA: Sage Publications.

Chapter review questions

1 What is a case study research design?
2 When do you use case study research design?
3 How could a case study be used as part of a mixed-method research design?
4 Why is the context important in case study research design?
5 How do you use theory in the case study research design?
6 What is the research methodology used in case studies?
7 How do you make case study research designs reliable and valid?
8 How do you carry out a case study research design? Compare the approaches of Hartley (1994) and McCutcheon and Meredith (1993).

5 Action research designs

Objectives

At the end of this chapter you will be able to:

- *explain the philosophy underlying action research;*
- *outline the general principles underlying action research;*
- *decide when action research should be used to answer research questions;*
- *outline how to overcome the problems with action research;*
- *outline how to increase rigour in action research;*
- *explain the characteristics that differentiate participatory action research and appreciative inquiry from action research; and*
- *understand the stages of appreciative inquiry.*

CONTENTS

Introduction	89
The main characteristics of action research	89
Principles of action research	91
Characteristics of research design in action research	92
The ten stages of action research	94
Participatory action research and appreciative inquiry	96
Conclusion	97
References	97
Chapter review questions	98

Introduction

Action research is a design that simultaneously combines *action* (e.g., interventions) to bring about change in a setting (e.g., an organisation or a community) and *research* (e.g., diagnosis) to increase and/or develop understanding on the part of the researcher, client group, etc. about that social system in order to develop knowledge. Action research is concurrently focused on learning and bringing about change in a social system. In action research, learning is applied to bring about change. Simultaneously, what is sought is an understanding of a social system and an opportunity to change that system. The knowledge gained from action research is contingent on the particular kind of system examined and can relate to:

- action research methodology;
- understanding the client system; and
- change to the client system.

In action research, a deeper understanding of system processes is sought, as well as comprehension of what was not understood before, in order to contribute to knowledge. Chisholm and Elden (1993) and Elden and Chisholm (1993) have provided excellent summaries of the action research approach.

The main characteristics of action research

Cyclical or spiral process

Action research is a process that can be thought of as spiral, in which there are brief cycles usually of action and then reflection or understanding in the form of: Plan, Act, Observe, and Reflect (Kolb, 1984). There are iterations of repeated cycles until there is convergence on understanding and actions for change. Through these iterations, the researcher gradually refines his or her understanding of the situation under examination. The researcher lets the data decide, at each step, what the next step is and uses the information so far available to determine the next step. Each turn of the spiral involves the integration of both theory and practice. The researcher develops interpretations as he or she proceeds and, in turn, understanding or action informs the next stage of the process. Later cycles can challenge information and interpretations from earlier stages.

Collaborative/participative in diagnosis, analysis, action, evaluation, and reflection

In an action research project, the researcher and the client are in partnership, with the process carried out by the client, rather than being passive subjects. This allows the client to be an informed source, which means there are better chances of the client disclosing what they know and what they need. Hence, the system is a self-maintaining system because clients are empowered to conduct the process themselves. There is an empowering process in which the participants develop competent strategies for coping with problem situations. The consultant/researcher role is thus not that of an expert but of a participant. Throughout this process, the consultative mechanisms need to be maintained. The consultant has a negotiator role and there is also a steering committee that oversees the project. Consultative mechanisms include seeking regular sanctions from the steering committee, conducting ongoing evaluation of the research, and responding to organisational issues that are raised.

Action-oriented and contributes to positive system development

The aim is the generation of a self-maintaining system. This is thought to be likely because the solution to the problem is generated from the source itself through client participation. There is generation and use of valid information about the system through a self-inquiry process about how the system is currently functioning to provide incremental improvement. A fundamental requirement of action research is learning about changing one's own system.

Principles of action research

Responsiveness to client group

Action research is responsive to the local situation, rather than being interested in the project's results being able to be replicated. Hence, action research is interested in local relevance, not global relevance or generalisability.

Starts with an idea – a fuzzy question/a general question – then specific questions are developed as research progresses

In action research, the researcher begins with a general question or focus. As the project progresses, the researcher, in concert with the client group, develops questions about the current state and the desired state sought. This is done as the situation is known and the client group is interacted with. Hence, there is a fuzzy question that results in fuzzy methods, which arrive at fuzzy answers. Therefore, in action research there is convergence towards precision.

Flexibility in the process

Action research cannot be planned and directed along particular trajectories, as each stage depends on the preceding stage. As a consequence, the researcher needs to relinquish his or her old and new theories. The action researcher also needs to negotiate flexibility into his or her role, as slavishly following a predetermined process can create problems in this type of research.

Gradual integration of theory and practice, understanding, and action

The aim of action research is to integrate theory and practice. Action is what is sought, but sometimes there is considerable data gathering and understanding, but no application. Hence, in these circumstances there is theory and diagnosis, but no practice or action. Action research is very focused on local relevance, and on attempting to change the system in line with the understanding gained. The intent in action research is for practice to inform theory, as well as theory to inform practice. Action is critical, and the researcher needs to question whether he or she has achieved the desired outcomes. A problem in action research is that practice is never really attained. There will also be a content area and research literature on the research problem; however, with action research it may not be used to inform practice/action.

Characteristics of research design in action research

Choice of data collection techniques: Qualitative, or qualitative and quantitative complementary

A qualitative approach is almost invariably used, because researchers believe it is more responsive and generates more understanding than a quantitative approach. In action research, the requirement is for the researcher to establish a dialectic. The aim is to match the research method with the particular applied problem or theoretical question. If quantitative research is applied, it is done in a metric that the client can follow. The quantitative approach needs to be set up beforehand, because the language is often difficult for the client to comprehend. In some action research projects both approaches are used, however the quantitative approach is the less dominant, is applied in a complementary manner, and is used to inform decisions.

Rigour in data collection and interpretation to give valid information

'Rigour' refers to validity in which the correct interpretations of the data are made. There needs to be an assurance about the quality of the data being gathered and the interpretation of it, as it is important to establish validity in action research. The action researcher therefore needs to test his or her assumptions. Any agreement about understanding from the data can be tested by seeking to find exceptions and explaining any disagreements. Thus, in action research, considerable emphasis is placed on seeking disconfirmatory evidence. In order to attain rigour with this approach, researchers should attempt to:

- use a cyclical process (plan, act, observe, reflect). Information from the previous cycle informs future cycles until there is convergence. There is gradual refinement of the idea;
- work with multiple sources of data, multiple information sources, different times of data collection, different research methodologies, different models/theories, and different researchers. There is then a natural dialectic or comparison of the processes. Similarities and differences from the data sources set up the dialectic; and
- test interpretations formed from earlier cycles in later cycles to see if there is convergence. There is evaluation, reflecting, and testing of assumptions, so that there is public testing and reflection of these ideas. For example, preliminary reports can be circulated to the organisation for comment.

Includes consideration of overall methodology before starting, and, if necessary, the specific methodology

Information is needed prior to settling on a choice about the paradigm/methodology/method used in action research. This information may be obtained initially in the entry and contracting stage. A common methodology is participative action research, but other options are available to the researcher, such as action science, soft systems, or evaluation techniques. Researchers need to ensure that they undertake preliminary reading of the action research literature to ensure that the most appropriate approach is selected.

Systematic reflection

Reflection in action research includes recalling what was already understood and confirming what was previously learnt, or deciding that the learning was inadequate. In action research, investigators are required to reflect on the problem faced by the client group and also on themselves (e.g., their own biases).

Researcher/consultant has diagnostic and intervention skills

The skills required of action research include interviewing (e.g., convergent interviewing), diagnostic techniques (e.g., interviews or surveys), participant observation, conducting planning sessions, group facilitation techniques, conflict management/mediation, the Delphi technique, the nominal group technique, group feedback analysis, and focus groups.

Data used to decide what happens at each step

Interpretations are developed as part of, and from, the data collection. In action research, later interventions differ from earlier interventions, and similarly later data collections are different from earlier interventions. Brief cycles are used to provide accurate iterations.

The ten stages of action research

Action research may involve the following ten possible stages:

1. **Entry and contracting**
   Entry to the client system needs to be negotiated, and there should be negotiation of the original topic at all levels. The negotiation needs to arrive at something mutually beneficial to the researcher and the client system. Researchers need to negotiate flexibility in their role in the different contexts in the organisation. Action research starts with an idea and then tests the idea. Relationships need to be formed to enable high-quality data to be obtained and to meet the client's needs.

   Consultative mechanisms need to be maintained throughout the research. A structure needs to be created for participation, so that there is a partnership between the researcher and the client group. Consideration needs to be given to whether consultation is with all stakeholders, or a sample of maximum diversity, or with just informants, or all those involved (i.e., participation). As many views need to be included as possible. There also needs to be regular liaison with those who can sanction the research, through progress being reviewed. Additionally, ongoing evaluation of the research, not just through survey evaluation but also through personal contact, should be undertaken. There needs to be responsiveness to client issues raised in the data evaluation and a presentation of choices. The relationship of the steering committee with the researcher/consultant needs to be clear, so that their roles are outlined. A process needs to be agreed on that the consultant/researcher and steering committee will use together and it needs to be flexible.

FIRST PHASE OF THE CYCLE

Steps 2, 3, and 4 are analysing, fact-finding, and conceptualisation.

2. **Analysing, fact-finding, and conceptualisation – information collection and analysis of first data collection**
   Brief cycles are used to provide adequate iteration, and interpretations are developed and reported as part of the data collection right from the start. Each cycle has data collection, interpretation, literature search, and reporting. Additional iterations and more cycles are then undertaken to test the data thoroughly. Each cycle is smaller and develops plans for change.

3. **Testing the rigour of the information collection through other ways of collecting information**
   There are multiple data sources to provide a dialectic. Exceptions are sought to agreement and explanations sought for disagreements. Ideas are generated and responses are sought to summary reports provided along the course of the project. The researcher seeks to find confirming results for his or her interpretations.

4. **Testing emerging themes against other research**
   In steps 2, 3, and 4, the researcher/consultant's interpretations are recorded along with data relevant to confirming and disconfirming the interpretation(s). More detailed information is sought in later cycles and supersedes earlier data.

5. **Feeding back information: Communicating information (valid) – e.g., to client group about current functioning**
   The information that is fed back is that with the greatest relevance for action. The feedback can be through the steering committee or by group feedback analysis to relevant groups within the organisation.

6. **Reflection about information – theorising**

7. **Planning of action programs in partnership with or by the client group**
8. **Executing action programs – usually practical problem-solving**
9. **Observation and evaluation, reflection**
   More fact-finding is often undertaken at this stage. It may have to be determined why interventions are having unexpected effects.

SECOND PHASE OF THE CYCLE
10. **The next cycle begins, with the next stage being more focused, relevant, and refined**
    The process is refined and adjusted in the next cycle.

Participatory action research and appreciative inquiry

Participatory action research and appreciative inquiry are two recent adaptations to action research that are increasingly being used by consultants and reported more frequently in journals. In participative action research, greater emphasis is placed on the participation of members of the client system in all aspects and iterations of the research process, than is the case in action research. For example, in a participatory action research project, designed to help Aboriginal health workers attain greater autonomy and responsibility, the health workers were involved in all aspects of the research. This included co-authoring a report on the project with the principal researcher. Additionally, in participative action research there is more importance placed on empowering and emancipating disadvantaged groups, as it originated in studies in developing countries and also has its foundations in both liberationist ideology and community psychology (Kidd & Karl, 2005).

Appreciative inquiry is similar to participatory action research in that it places greater emphasis on stakeholder participation than does action research. However, appreciative inquiry also adopts a more positive stance than action research. Thus, in contrast to the problem correction orientation of action research, the focus of appreciative inquiry is on identifying and improving the capabilities and strengths of the organisation (Egan & Lancaster, 2005). Van der Haar and Hosking (2004) stated that appreciative inquiry preferably involves the whole organisation and comprises four stages. In the first stage, *discovering*, the strengths of the organisation are identified through positive stories representing peak experiences. During the second stage, *dreaming*, stakeholders attempt to envision the organisation's ideal future, using data collected in the first stage. The purpose of the third stage, *designing*, is to create the organisational structures, policies, practices, and procedures required to facilitate the realisation of the vision developed in the previous stage. In the final stage, *destiny*, the focus is on maintaining the improvements and innovations of the research by instilling a sense of destiny. Consistent with action research, the process is iterative as new strengths are 'discovered' in the destiny stage and therefore the cycle continues.

Conclusion

Action research is an approach which involves combining the consultant approach with research design. The aim of action research is to change the client system and at the same time generate new knowledge regarding it. The process works in a cycle, with enough data gathered and analysed at each stage to derive action and understanding for that stage only. Understanding leads to action; and once action has taken place, new data are generated for analysis to generate the next lot of action. Reflection is used in each stage of the process to consider what has occurred at each step. The process is cyclical, with each cycle resulting in a new cycle. The short cycles are Plan, Act, Observe, and Reflect, after which the process begins again. The knowledge gained may relate to action research methodology, the nature of that specific system, and/or how to change the client system. Participatory action research and appreciative inquiry are two contemporary adaptations of action research. Participation and emancipation are features of participatory action research, while appreciative inquiry is characterised by its positive strengths-based focus.

References

Chisholm, R.F. & Elden, M. (1993). Features of emerging action research. *Human Relations*, 46, 275–298.

Egan, T.M. & Lancaster, C.M. (2005). Comparing appreciative inquiry to action research: OD practitioner perspectives. *Organization Development Journal, 23,* 29–49.

Elden, M. & Chisholm, R.F. (1993). Emerging varieties of action research. *Human Relations, 46,* 121–142.

Kidd, S.A. & Karl, M.J. (2005). Practicing participatory action research. *Journal of Counseling Psychology, 52,* 187–195.

Kolb, D. (1984). *Experiential learning: Experience as the source of learning and development.* Englewood Cliffs, NJ: Prentice-Hall.

Van der Haar, D. & Hosking, D.M. (2004). Evaluating appreciative inquiry: A relational constructionist perspective. *Human Relations, 57,* 1017–1036.

Chapter review questions

1 What is action research?
2 What are the main characteristics of action research?
3 Discuss the principles of action research.
4 List and discuss the characteristics of research design in action research.
5 Describe the ten possible stages in the process of action research.
6 What features distinguish participatory action research from action research?
7 What distinguishes appreciative inquiry from action research?
8 What are the stages of appreciative inquiry?

Methods of data collection

6 Asking questions: Questionnaires and interviews

Objectives

At the end of this chapter you will be able to:

- *understand the different types of questions used in interviews and questionnaires;*
- *explain the purpose of different types of questions used in interviews and questionnaires;*
- *design questions for interviews and questionnaires;*
- *understand the problems and errors that can occur in designing research interview questions;*
- *design questions to reduce or overcome the errors and problems that can occur; and*
- *understand how to record answers in questionnaires and interviews.*

CONTENTS ·

Asking questions: Questionnaires and interviews	102
The main categories of interviews	103
When to use questionnaires and interviews	106
Problems with questionnaire and interview data	108
The design of questions	111
Recording the answers in questionnaires and interviews	119
Conclusion	120
References	121
Chapter review questions	122

Asking questions: Questionnaires and interviews

Questionnaires and interviews are usually conducted for the purpose of asking questions to ascertain people's thoughts about, and feelings towards, issues, events, behaviours, and so on. There are a number of important issues that the researcher needs to consider when choosing questionnaires and interviews as data collection techniques and these issues are covered in this chapter. Questionnaires and interviews can be used in any research design (e.g., experiment, correlational field study, case study). They may be the main data collection technique, or they may be used as part of a mixed-method design, either as an equal part, or as a minor or major part.

Questionnaires are instruments completed by the respondents themselves (Bryman, 2004). They are often referred to as self-administered questionnaires. Questionnaires are the most frequently used method of data collection in management research. They are relatively easy to use, inexpensive, and are often the most plausible alternative for measuring unobservable constructs such as attitudes, values and preferences, intentions, and personalities (Moorman & Podsakoff, 1992).

As discussed in Chapter 3, questionnaires are commonly associated with correlational field study (survey) designs, of which the mail (postal) questionnaire is the most popular. Questionnaires can also be administered by hand or conducted on-line or by email. Questionnaires are highly structured instruments composed of pre-set standardised questions. Due to their highly structured format, questionnaires are used where the aim is to generate quantitative data from a large sample to test research questions and/or hypotheses.

Management research uses interviews only second in frequency to questionnaires for data collection. Interviews can yield both qualitative and quantitative data. The overall aim of interviews is to elicit the interviewee's information (e.g., their thoughts and feelings) about a topic, rather than the interviewer influencing them. Interviews are typically conducted face-to-face, but telephone interviews are also common. Interviews often follow questionnaire surveys to explore issues in-depth, or precede them to help design surveys. Interviews are well suited when the researcher wants to see the topic from the perspective of the interviewee and understand how and why he or she comes to have this particular perspective (King, 1994).

The main categories of interviews

Interviews fall along a continuum in terms of their formality and rigidity, and *structured interviews* lie at the end of that continuum. Structured interviews are composed of completely pre-set standardised questions, normally closed-ended (fixed alternative) (Seidman, 2006). Many field surveys are administered through structured interviews, including telephone interviews, rather than as mail-out surveys. In structured interviews, questions are read aloud to the interviewee and the interviewer records the responses. It is essential for the interviewer to ensure that the interviewee understands the questions and that the responses are reliably given. The respondents' answers are written down, and everyone is asked the same questions in the same manner.

Lee (1999) described structured interviews as being essentially questionnaires that are administered verbally with immutable response options. Crabtree and Miller (1992) have also conceived structured interviews as being analogous to spoken questionnaires, with a rigidly structured interview schedule directing the interview. For example, a researcher may wish to measure organisational human resource management strategy and may have a number of different scenarios that he or she wishes to present to human resource managers that represent different strategies. By presenting them in an interview, the respondents can broadly discuss the scenarios with the interviewer until they are clear in meaning, and then choose the appropriate scenario for their organisation. If the scenarios were administered in a questionnaire, there would be no opportunity for discussion and correct classification. Interviews provide the respondent with the opportunity to talk through the issues. Additionally, they provide the interviewer with the ability to ensure that all of the questions are understood.

Unstructured interviews lie at the other end of the continuum. In this type of interviewing, the questions are open-ended (free answer) and the interview is conducted in a manner that is similar to a friendly conversation (Seidman, 2006), with no predetermined order of questions or specified wording to the questions. Unstructured interviews include in-depth interviews and oral or life history interviews. Usually, initially, only broad open-ended questions are asked. For example, the *critical incident technique* might be used and two opposite questions asked. The first question might be, 'What do you most like about working here?' The second might be, 'What do you least like about working here?'

Answers to these broad questions usually lead to the more specific topics that may be asked.

Miller and Crabtree (1992) give everyday conversation and interviews with key informants as examples of unstructured interviews. The interview has one or more topic areas that are probed. The data gathered from unstructured interviews are usually qualitative (data in the form of words). They are suited to research questions where a descriptive account of a topic is required, without formal hypothesis-testing (King, 1994). Unstructured interviews are also useful where the nature and range of the participants' likely opinions about the research topic are not known and cannot be easily quantified.

At the middle of the continuum fall *semi-structured interviews*. According to Lee (1999), semi-structured interviews have an overall topic, general themes, targeted issues, and specific questions. They are more flexible than structured interviews, but have more focus than unstructured interviews. As in the unstructured interview, the interviewer is free to pursue matters as the situation dictates (Lee, 1999, p. 62). Miller and Crabtree (1992) have stated that semi-structured interviews are guided, concentrated, focused, and open-ended communication events that are co-created by the interviewer and interviewee and occur outside of the stream of everyday life. The questions, probes, and prompts are written in the form of a flexible interview guide or schedule.

The semi-structured interview, like the unstructured interview, requires strong interviewer skills. Under the rubric of semi-structured interviews, Miller and Crabtree (1992) have included in-depth/focused interviews that intensively explore a particular topic (both individual interviews and group interviews), life histories (they reveal personal biography), critical incidents techniques, and free listing (projective techniques that expose personality).

Group interviews

Interviews may also be conducted of groups (e.g., three to five people), such as in focus groups. A group is interviewed when the unit of analysis is the group (Crabtree & Miller, 1992), and group interviews are not equivalent to individual interviews with the same people. Who is interviewed depends on whom the researcher wishes to make inferences about (i.e., individuals or groups). Therefore, sometimes the researcher's interest is in the views of a group. For example, the researcher may be interested in how functional areas of an organisation see particular issues. The researcher may be conducting a training-needs analysis of middle managers and may assemble them into functional groups, because this might give an indication of different needs. In this example, the researcher might take all the middle managers and classify them as operations managers, accounting managers, marketing managers, administration, etc. The researcher would then assemble groups of similar functions and interview each of these groups. It is best to have multiple groups (three) from each function, and the groups' answers from that functional area can then be averaged. Typically, this will identify differences between the functional areas on the variables. In order to do this, the researcher must utilise a highly structured interview format. In this example, the researcher may ask middle managers in their group to record answers to the question as to how they see the performance of the area they manage; what they envisage the ideal performance to be, and how they would see the interventions for bridging that gap. The researcher would then code themes in each of these questions and use the discrepancy between the current and desired performance to arrive at the training needs of middle managers as a group (not individuals) and in different functions. Subsequently, the researcher would use the solutions presented to try to discern what are not training needs and to identify other issues.

The structured format here should include individuals answering questions individually and then joining together with their group to pool their responses and arrive at a combined answer to record. The answer is arrived at by counting the number who contribute each response, rather than by consensus, when dominant people may control the group's responses. The group members then vote for the top-priority items (e.g., raising two hands for first choice, one hand for second choice), so that those issues emerging as most representing the group can be equally influenced, through voting by all members of the group. This also results in the information having been coded and ranked in each group. That information is then combined for all the groups and further voted on for all the groups (e.g., subgroups of operations managers) that are being interviewed at the same time and in the same location. Overall, in order to stop individuals dominating the group and to gain the group's opinion, individuals are first asked for their views, which are then combined for the group; voting may then be used to gain an overall view for a functional area.

Focus groups are a special kind of group interview consisting of individuals who have some personal experience with the phenomenon being researched (Morgan, 1996). The interview focuses on the respondents' impressions, interpretations, and opinions (Schmitt & Klimoski, 1991). Focus groups are often used in marketing research to determine consumer needs and preferences and how they will respond to new products. Focus groups may be useful to help determine the content and wording of surveys; alternatively, they may be used to provide generalisations from the information generated by the group.

Another interviewing technique for group or aggregate-level data is *convergent interviewing*. In this approach, after interviewing several people using open-ended questions and some follow-up probes, the themes may be consistent across people and clear. After several interviews, the interviewers (usually two) compare notes and determine the themes. In subsequent interviews of more people, the researcher asks questions that are specifically related to validating those themes, as well as questions probing those areas on which there has not yet been agreement. In this way, part of the data analysis is conducted along the way (by coding for the major themes by the two interviewers, whose inter-rater reliability can be established), while later interviews probe those themes and explore other possible themes.

When to use questionnaires and interviews

The use of questionnaires and interviews is linked to the nature of the research question being asked. Researchers are advised to avoid using structured (standardised) interviews and questionnaires in exploratory studies, due to their rigidity. Instead, researchers should consider employing non-standardised interviews (i.e., semi-structured or unstructured), as their focus is exploratory (Fowler & Mangione, 1990). Unstructured interviews are typically used in interpretive and inductive (i.e., deriving theory from the data and the context) research.

If a researcher is testing a theory (usually there will be hypotheses) and requires self- or others' report data, then a questionnaire or structured interview is the method of choice. The topics and questions are specified, and often rating scales are used for the answers; however, this does not preclude the researcher also asking open-ended questions to gain further information or to allow a respondent to provide an explanation. One of the benefits of a structured interview over a questionnaire is that the former allows opportunity for discussion and probing of responses, to enable clarification. According to Lee (1999), structured interviews are also useful when respondents do not have sufficient verbal skills or tolerance for written materials to undertake less structured interviews. Telephone interviews are another option for gathering structured data. The advantages of collecting data through telephone interviews are the lower costs and increased speed of data collection when compared with face-to-face interviews. Although self-administered questionnaires are relatively inexpensive to administer compared with interview studies, it is important to note that response rates for postal questionnaires are typically lower compared with interviews (Bryman, 2004). More information on response rates is found in Chapter 3.

Interviews may be used for many purposes. Here are three examples:

1. If the interview is being used to gather information to assist in choosing questionnaire items, then specific persons may be targeted who are known to possess that kind of information. This may include informal (opinion) leaders (because they have well-developed and articulated views), more senior people (a historical perspective), new hires (a more objective view), the dissatisfied, those leaving, etc.
2. The interview may be of groups that are called opportunity samples (Schmitt & Klimoski, 1991) if they have the kind of knowledge or experience that is of interest. These opportunity samples may be intact groups, such as work groups. In this case, the interview would often utilise the main data analytic technique.
3. Key informants are often used for reasons of efficiency, because it is not possible to interview everyone and because they provide access to information, individuals, and sponsorship. Informants are individuals who provide information through formal interviews and informal verbal interchanges or conversations. The informant may also provide a picture or map and introductions and interpretations. Key informants often have a special position in the culture/organisation and may have a relationship of longer duration with the researcher. Key informants are individuals who can teach

the researcher. The reasons for this are that key informants possess special knowledge, status, or communication skills, are willing to share their knowledge and skills with the researcher, and have access to perspectives or observations denied to the researcher (Gilchrist, 1992). Key informants are chosen who provide representative pictures of information or knowledge, distributed within the study population.

Problems with questionnaire and interview data

Questionnaire and interview data can often be of dubious validity and reliability. Foddy (1993, pp. 2–9, 66, 151) reviewed empirical evidence to highlight common problems of research interviews. These problems are:

- some respondents answer factual questions (e.g., age) incorrectly;
- what people say they do and what they actually do may differ;
- respondents' answers can be unstable;
- small changes in wording sometimes produce major changes in the distribution of responses;
- respondents commonly misinterpret questions;
- answers to earlier questions can affect answers to later questions;
- changing the order in which response options are presented sometimes affects answers;
- respondents' answers are sometimes affected by the question format per se;
- respondents often answer questions even when they appear to know little about the topic;
- the cultural context in which a question is presented may affect the way respondents answer questions;
- respondents have a psychological need to be consistent; and
- open and closed versions of the same questions give different response distributions for the answers and it is not obvious which type produces the most valid data.

(*Source:* W. Foddy, *Constructing questions for interviews and questionnaires*, pp. 2–9, 66, 151. Copyright 1993 by Cambridge University Press. Reprinted by permission of Cambridge University Press.)

Reducing problems in questionnaires and interviews

Foddy (1993) has developed a number of suggestions based on empirical evidence that should ameliorate potential difficulties in questionnaires and interviews. These suggestions are summarised below. Researchers are advised to:

1. clearly define the topic about which information is required and be clear about what information you want;
2. clearly conceptualise what is being measured;
3. have an adequate theoretical explanation of assumed links between the constructs;
4. conduct a pilot. Pre-test the interview for respondent understanding and appropriate response categories;
5. tape the interview to be able to go back over interpretations;
6. ensure respondents have the information the researcher requires;
7. ensure the applicability of the questions to the respondents;
8. ensure the respondents are capable of verbalising the information the researcher wants under the conditions of the research situation;
9. phrase the questions so that they are understood as the researcher intends them to be understood. Consider the context, relative difficulty of words, lack of referents, unintended nuances, number of words, complex grammar, use of negatives (bad) and addition of clauses, phrases, and instructions;
10. ensure respondents are willing to give the required information to the researcher;
11. ensure you understand the respondent's answer;
12. use an appropriate sequence of questions:
    - general question to find out if respondents have information;
    - open question to get respondents' general perceptions about that topic;
    - dichotomous question to elicit perceptions about a specific aspect of the topic;
    - open question to get at reasons for responses to the specific topic; and
    - a rating question to indicate strength of the responses towards the specific topic.

13. phrase threatening questions in an unthreatening way;
14. clearly define the topic in specific concrete terms to the intervie-wee before asking the question and spell out the reason for asking;
15. give the frame of reference. Respondents need to know *what sort of answer* they should give; for example, type, level of generality, standards of comparison; and
16. use a mix of open and closed questions.

(*Source*: W. Foddy, *Constructing questions for interviews and question-naires*, pp. 184–185. Copyright 1993 by Cambridge University Press. Reprinted by permission of Cambridge University Press.)

In terms of conducting a structured or standardised inter-view, Fowler and Mangione (1990, pp. 136–139) have advised that researchers:

1. train interviewers using an interview manual, lectures, demonstra-tions, supervised practice, and by monitoring and evaluating their performance and giving feedback;
2. fully script questions so that the questions as written fully prepare a respondent to provide the answer;
3. ensure the questions mean the same thing to everybody;
4. communicate the kinds of answers that constitute an appropriate response to the questions to all respondents;
5. test the questions through laboratory techniques, focus groups, and coding of pre-test interviews to provide feedback on questions;
6. read questions exactly as worded;
7. provide a model to respondents;
8. provide consistent instructions to the respondent before and dur-ing the interview to reinforce desired behaviour;
9. ask respondents for commitment to a specific level of perfor-mance; and
10. select interviewers carefully on ability, reading skills, and pleasant personality.

Seidman (2006, pp. 78–92) has recommended a number of broad principles for researchers to follow when conducting in-depth, unstruc-tured research interviews. According to these principles, the inter-viewer should:

- focus more on listening, less on talking;
- follow up on information provided by the participant;
- ask questions for clarification;
- enquire more about the subject if necessary;
- explore issues, but try to avoid probing;
- ask genuine questions – ones that the researcher does not know the answer to;
- not use leading questions;
- use open-ended questions;
- not interrupt the interviewee;
- ask participants to imagine the interviewer is someone else that they are more familiar with to put them at ease;
- encourage participants to tell a story;
- ensure participants remain focused and try to elicit concrete details;
- share his/her own experiences when appropriate;
- encourage participants to reconstruct (what happened? what was such and such like?) rather than to remember, as memory is unreliable;
- avoid positively or negatively reinforcing the interviewee's answers;
- explore laughter;
- follow his or her intuitions; and
- learn to tolerate pauses and silences.

The design of questions

One approach to constructing interview and survey questions is referred to as the TAP procedure (Foddy, 1993). Given that 'tapping' valid, reliable, respondent information is the primary aim underlying the use of questions, the 'TAP' acronym is a useful reminder of the three issues that researchers should keep in mind when constructing questions for interviews and questionnaires. The TAP acronym stands for:

- *Topic:* The topic should be properly defined so that each respondent clearly understands what is being talked about.
- *Applicability:* The applicability of the question to each respondent should be established. Respondents should not be asked to give information that they do not have.

- *Perspective:* The perspective that respondents should adopt, when answering the question, should be specified so that each respondent gives the same kind of answer.

Foddy (1993, pp. 184–185) has summarised the general principles that should be used in designing interviews and questionnaires that take this approach. For each question, the researcher should:

1. make sure that the topic has been clearly defined;
2. be clear both about the information that is required about the topic and the reason for wanting this information;
3. make sure that the topic has been defined properly for the respondents by:
   - avoiding the use of 'blab' words (i.e., words that are so abstract or general that they lack specific empirical referents); and
   - avoiding words that are unlikely to be understood by all respondents either because they are rarely used in everyday life, or are specialist (i.e., jargon) words.
4. make sure that the question is relevant to respondents by:
   - using an appropriate filter;
   - avoiding asking for information respondents are likely to have forgotten; and
   - avoiding hypothetical issues.
5. make sure that the question is not biased by:
   - ensuring balance in the introduction to the question (e.g., 'Some people like X and some people dislike X. Do you like X or dislike X?');
   - ensuring that sets of response options are complete;
   - ensuring that sets of response options are balanced; and
   - avoiding using words that are likely to invoke stereotypical reactions.
6. eliminate complexities that prevent respondents from easily assimilating the meaning of the question by:
   - avoiding asking two or more questions at once;
   - avoiding the use of words that have several meanings;
   - checking whether the question has been worded as simply as possible;
   - avoiding the use of too many 'meaningful' words in the one question;

- avoiding the use of qualifying clauses and phrases and the addition of complicating instructions, which cause respondents to start to answer, before they have been exposed to the whole question – if qualifying clauses and phrases have to be used, they should be placed at the beginning rather than at the end of the question;
- making sure that the question is as short as possible; and
- avoiding the use of both negatives and double negatives.
7. ensure that respondents understand what kind of answer is required by:
   - setting the question in context;
   - informing respondents why the question is being asked;
   - informing respondents what will be done with the information they give; and
   - specifying the perspective that respondents should adopt.

(*Source:* W. Foddy, *Constructing questions for interviews and questionnaires*, pp. 184–185. Copyright 1993 by Cambridge University Press. Reprinted by permission of Cambridge University Press.)

Open and closed questions

An important distinction is made between open-ended and closed-ended questions. A closed-ended question is one where the response alternatives are fixed or pre-specified. For example, Likert items are closed-ended. Closed-ended questions are typically used in questionnaires and structured interviews. They are suitable for purposes of standardisation and can be efficiently processed for statistical analysis.

Open questions have no fixed alternatives. Open-ended questions are particularly used during in-depth interviews (unstructured and semi-structured). They establish the territory to be explored while allowing the participant to take any direction he or she wants (Seidman, 1991). Hickman and Longman (1994) have provided a number of examples of open questions in their text. These open questions relate to business strategy; however, irrespective of the topic, the style of questioning remains consistent. The examples of open questions are:

- In your own words, what is the essence of the business as you see it?
- What is the purpose of your business? What does it exist for?

- What are you trying to achieve? What are your aims and objectives?
- How do you measure your company's success?
- What are your biggest strengths, weaknesses, and opportunities, and the biggest threats to your business?
- If you had to give us some key things to remember so that we could do your job tomorrow, what would they be?
- Describe the competitive situation in the industry at the moment.
- In what way do you expect the business to change in the future?
- What are the most critical factors in running this company?
- Can you give me an example of that?
- What happens when things go wrong?
- What would happen if you stopped doing 'xyz' activity?
- Take us through a typical day in your job.
- What happens next, after 'xyz' activity?

Avoiding asking difficult/faulty questions

Researchers should refrain from asking highly complex questions in questionnaires and interviews, as they create confusion for the informant/respondent and may yield inaccurate responses. Foddy (1993, p. 51) has presented a modified list of Belson's (1981) 16 types of difficult questions to be avoided. The types, arranged in order of decreasing frequency of occurrence, are:

1. *two questions presented as one* (e.g., 'Which brand do you use or do you change brands frequently?');
2. *questions with a lot of meaningful words* (e.g., 'How many of each sized packet have you bought?');
3. questions that include *qualifying phrases or clauses* (e.g., 'Have you bought any chocolate in the last seven days, not counting today?');
4. questions with *multiple ideas or subjects* (e.g., 'Which store have you heard of or shopped at?');
5. questions that contain difficult or unfamiliar words;
6. questions that contain *one or more instructions* (e.g., 'Do not include "X" in your answer');
7. questions that start with words that are meant to soften them (e.g., 'Would you mind . . . ?');
8. questions with difficult phrases;
9. hypothetical questions;

10. questions that are *dependent upon prior questions for meaning* (e.g., question 1: 'Did you buy a copy of X?' followed by question 2: 'Where is it now?');
11. questions with negative elements;
12. *inverted questions* (e.g., 'The ones you bought last time – what were they?');
13. questions including *either 'if any' or 'if at all'* (e.g., 'Which of these, if any, have you bought?');
14. questions that are *too long*;
15. questions that include *both present and past tenses*; and
16. questions in which *singular and plural cases* are used.

(*Source:* W. Foddy, *Constructing questions for interviews and questionnaires*, p. 51. Copyright 1993 by Cambridge University Press. Reprinted by permission of Cambridge University Press.)

Avoiding bias from preceding questions

Foddy (1993, p. 62) has developed a method for asking questions regarding the same topic in such a way so that the preceding questions have the least biasing influence. Foddy's plan for formulating questions pertaining to the same topic requires that researchers have:

1. a general question to establish whether respondents have the required information concerning the topic.
   * For example:
     Have you heard of X?
       yes __
       no __
2. an open question to get at respondents' general perceptions or feelings about the topic.
   * For example:
     What are your views about X?
3. a dichotomous question to elicit perceptions or feelings about a specific aspect of the topic.
   * For example:
     Do you favour or not favour X?
       favour __
       not favour __

4. an open question to get at reasons for responses towards the aspect of the topic specified in step 3.
   - For example:
     Why do you favour (not favour) X?
5. a rating question to allow respondents to indicate the strength of their responses towards the aspect of the topic specified in step 3.
   - For example:
     How strongly do you feel about this?
        very strongly ___
        fairly strongly ___
        not at all strongly ___

(*Source:* W. Foddy, *Constructing questions for interviews and questionnaires,* p. 62. Copyright 1993 by Cambridge University Press. Reprinted by permission of Cambridge University Press.)

Leading questions

It is important for researchers to avoid asking leading questions in questionnaires and interviews. A leading question is one that influences the direction the response will take. For example, the question 'How satisfied were you with your supervisor?' is somewhat leading, as it directs the informant/respondent towards the issue of satisfaction. A far less directive question would be, 'What is your supervisor like?'

Different types of interview questions

Kvale (1996, pp. 133–135) has outlined nine interrelated types of questions applicable to semi- and unstructured interviews. They are as follows:

- *introductory questions* start off the theme and help frame subsequent questions. 'Can you tell me about . . . ?', 'What happened when . . . ?', 'Have you experienced . . . ?';
- *follow-up questions*;
- *probing questions* are used to seek new information without necessarily stating the theme the interviewer wishes to pursue. 'Could you

say more about that . . . ?', 'Can you give me an example to help clarify . . . ?', 'What did you mean by . . . ?';

- *specifying questions* move towards greater specificity and follow more general questions. 'What did you actually do at that moment?', 'Did you have a physical as well as an emotional reaction?', 'Has this, or anything like this, ever happened before?';
- *direct questions* introduce new topics and themes. Direct questions can be very threatening so have to be handled carefully. 'Have you ever stolen anything worth more than $10 from work?' 'When dealing with your former boss, did you ever behave towards her in a mean-spirited fashion?';
- *indirect questions* concern specific topics but allow for either specific or general responses and may be personal or about the general group. 'What are the typical reasons people quit their jobs here?', 'What do you believe is the general morale around here?';
- *structured questions* are pre-written items that are used to shift conversation to a new topic when a current topic is unlikely to generate any more discussion. 'I'd like to move to a new topic';
- *interpretative questions* involve restating, rephrasing, summarising, or paraphrasing the interviewee's remarks. They often serve to facilitate conversation, redirect discussion, and avoid misunderstanding. 'Let me see if I understand you – did you mean to say . . . ?', 'If I heard you correctly, you're saying . . . ?', 'Let me summarise what you've said . . . '; and
- *silence* is a well-placed pause and can be effective at eliciting comments.

(*Source:* S. Kvale, *Interviews: An introduction to qualitative research interviewing*, pp. 133–135. Copyright 1996 by Sage Publications, Inc. Reprinted by permission of Sage Publications, Inc.)

Story-telling and probing questions in in-depth interviews

Minichiello, Aroni, Timewell, and Alexander (1995, pp. 89–94) have classified questions for in-depth research interviews (thus, semi-structured or unstructured and not stuctured) as either story-telling or probing. Story-telling questions are those in which the interviewer attempts to encourage the interviewee to tell a story. With this style of questioning, the interviewer asks for a description of something, which is then followed up with further questions in order to explain or elaborate. Probing questions are those used to elicit information more fully than the original questions that introduced a topic. Original or primary questions start the interview or begin new topics, whereas probing questions are follow-up questions that are used to clarify and gain more detail. The types of probing questions are:

- very simple probes. For example, *'Tell me more'*; *'Oh, really'*; *'Go on'*; *'And then . . . '*; *'I see . . . '*; *'Please continue'*; and *'What happened then?'*;
- more complex probes to obtain clearer and deeper answers. For example, *'Tell me a little more about . . . ?'*; *'Why did you . . . ?'*; *'What did you have in mind when you said?'*; *'Just how . . . was . . . ?'*; *'What happened after . . . ?'*; and *'I'm not sure I understand your point . . . '*;
- probes to explore a feeling or attitude. For example, *'How did you react?'*; *'What did you think and feel about that?'*; and *'Why do you think and feel that way?'*;
- probes to help correctly understand answers. For example, *'You meant such and such . . . ?'*; and *'Am I correct in assuming . . . ?'*;
- reflective probing mirrors what is said. For example, *'Let me see if I have this straight?'*; *'So to summarise your situation . . . ?'*; and *'It is my understanding that . . . ?'*;
- cross-checks, to check for consistency by checking with other information given, or confronting with contradictions; and
- devil's advocate questions. These types of questions may also be used as probes (what opponents might say), hypothetical questions (suggesting plausible scenarios or occurrences and asking the interviewee about their responses to them), or posing the ideal (asks interviewee to describe the most ideal situation that they could conceive).

Issues to watch out for in piloting questions

It is recommended to pilot a questionnaire or interview schedule before administration. The number of respondents involved in a pilot study may be up to 30, but a minimum of five is recommended. Foddy (1993, p. 185) has provided a process that can be used to determine whether piloted questions need modifying or deleting. According to this process, people involved in piloting the interview/questionnaire should be systematically asked:

- Did any of the questions seem to make respondents uncomfortable?
- Did you have to repeat any questions?
- Did the respondents misinterpret any questions?
- Which questions were the most difficult or awkward for you to read?
- Have you come to dislike any specific questions? Why?
- Did any sections seem to drag?
- Were there any sections in which you felt that the respondents would have liked the opportunity to say more?

(*Source:* W. Foddy, *Constructing questions for interviews and questionnaires*, p. 185. Copyright 1993 by Cambridge University Press. Reprinted by permission of Cambridge University Press.)

How to organise the questions in interview schedules

The structure or sequencing of questions in an interview schedule can impact on the accuracy of the information provided and the flow of the interview process. Consequently, it is advisable that when conducting interviews, researchers:

- have strategies to start the interview, including establishing rapport and explaining clearly the purpose of the interview;
- divide the interview into sections to cover topics;
- in a section, use the funnelling technique, whereby the interviewer starts a section with questions of a broad and general nature, then asks more specific questions about particular issues within that topic;
- develop transition statements to move from one section to another; and
- are able to wrap up the interview, including giving the interviewee an opportunity to add any more information he or she wishes.

Recording the answers in questionnaires and interviews

Questionnaires usually use closed-ended questions and so the answers given for questions can be ticked or circled on the form. In this way, the responses are pre-coded (Bryman, 2004). Similarly, structured interviews provide *response categories* for closed-ended questions for the interviewer to record as they go along. Even where the questions are open-ended, they are specific, providing *spaces on the form* to note the answer.

Semi- and unstructured interviews are usually recorded using audiotape (with permission, completely voluntary on the part of the interviewee) and field notes. The field notes should be transcribed within 24 hours in order to accurately record the interview while it is still fresh in the interviewer's mind. Tape recorders often fail (e.g., the interview was not recorded when the researcher thought it was, part of the interview did not get recorded, or the machine malfunctioned) and therefore cannot be relied on. Researchers are advised to practise with the machine beforehand, take a back-up recorder, check that the machine is recording, and place the microphone carefully. With semi-structured or structured interviews, a *precise transcript* is required. *Verbatim responses* are those written down exactly as they are spoken, whereas *paraphrased responses* are the interviewer's impressions of what the respondent said (Sommer & Sommer, 1991).

Finally, it is best not to interview people who are not committed to a research interview. However, researchers will invariably encounter an informant at some stage who has agreed to the interview, but subsequently becomes reticent, bored, or tired. In order to reduce recalcitrance on the part of interviewees, researchers should confirm the informant's availability, confirm coverage of topics, reframe questions, use probing questions, work from real examples, and engage in non-biasing phrases and summarising (Hickman & Longman, 1994).

Conclusion

Questionnaires and interviews are a commonly used method of gathering data for research purposes. They may be used as a research technique singly, or they may form part of a larger mixed-method research design, such as in case studies, to achieve triangulation. Due to their highly structured format, questionnaires are used where the aim is to generate quantitative data to test research questions and/or hypotheses from a large sample. Interviews range from unstructured through semi-structured to structured, and vary in their purpose. Unstructured interviews are typically naturalistic, interpretive, and inductive, whereas structured interviews are used for testing theory. Choice of method is therefore linked to the nature of the research question being asked. The design of questions needs to be based on the theoretical framework underlying the research question, and the purpose of each question needs to be clear. Designing questions for structured interviews requires skills akin to those used in questionnaire item design. Alternatively, in order to conduct effective non-standardised interviews, the skills associated with establishing and maintaining complex interpersonal dialogues are required.

References

Belson, W.A. (1981). *The design and understanding of research questions*. Aldershot: Gower.

Bryman, A. (2004). *Social research methods*. Oxford: Oxford University Press.

Crabtree, B.F. & Miller, W.L. (1992). *Doing qualitative research*. Newbury Park, CA: Sage Publications.

Foddy, W. (1993). *Constructing questions for interviews and questionnaires*. New York: Cambridge University Press.

Fowler, F.J. & Mangione, T.W. (1990). *Standardized survey interviewing: Minimizing interviewer-related error*. Newbury Park, CA: Sage Publications.

Gilchrist, V.J. (1992). Key informant interviews. In B.F. Crabtree & W.L. Miller (eds.), *Doing qualitative research* (pp. 70–89). Newbury Park, CA: Sage Publications.

Hickman, L. & Longman, C. (1994). *Case method*. Wokingham, England: Oracle.

King, N. (1994). The qualitative research interview. In C. Cassell & G. Symon (eds.), *Qualitative methods in organizational research* (pp. 14–36). London: Sage Publications.

Kvale, S. (1996). *Interviews: An introduction to qualitative research interviewing*. Thousand Oaks, CA: Sage Publications.

Lee, T.W. (1999). *Using qualitative methods in organizational research*. Thousand Oaks, CA: Sage Publications.

Miller, W.L. & Crabtree, B.F. (1992). Primary care research: A multimethod typology and qualitative road map. In B.F. Crabtree & W.L. Miller (eds.), *Doing qualitative research* (pp. 3–30). Newbury Park, CA: Sage Publications.

Minichiello, V., Aroni, R., Timewell, E., & Alexander, L. (1995). *In-depth interviewing*. Melbourne: Longman.

Moorman, R.H. & Podsakoff, P.M. (1992). A meta-analytic review and empirical test of the potential confounding effects of social desirability response sets in organizational behaviour research. *Journal of Occupational and Organizational Psychology, 65,* 131–149.

Morgan, D.L. (1996). Focus groups. *Annual Review of Sociology, 22,* 129–152.

Schmitt, N.W. & Klimoski, R.J. (1991). *Research methods in human resource management.* Cincinnati, OH: South-Western Publishing Company.

Seidman, I.E. (2006). *Interviewing as qualitative research: A guide for researchers in education and the social sciences* (3rd ed.). New York: Teacher College Process.

Sommer, B. & Sommer, R. (1991). *A practical guide to behavioral research: Tools and techniques.* New York: Oxford University Press.

Chapter review questions

1   What are the main broad categories of interviews?
2   When are group (focus group) interviews appropriate?
3   How is theory dealt with in interviews and questionnaires?
4   What are the problems with interview and questionnaire data?
5   What are ways for reducing problems with interviews and questionnaires?
6   What is the TAP procedure for constructing questions?
7   What are the general principles for designing questions using the TAP approach?
8   When should you use (a) open-ended questions and (b) closed-ended questions?
9   How can you avoid difficult questions?
10   How can you avoid bias from preceding questions?
11   What are leading questions, and why should they be avoided?
12   What are different types of interview questions?
13   What are story-telling and probing questions?
14   What are the issues to watch out for in piloting questions?
15   How should you organise the questions in an interview schedule?
16   How should answers be recorded in questionnaires and interviews?

7 Documentation and observation

At the end of this chapter you will be able to:

- *discuss documentation as a method of data collection;*
- *list the kinds of documentation that are used in research;*
- *identify when documentation can be used as the main research method;*
- *identify the problems in using documentation as the main method of data collection;*
- *outline the process of using documentation in research;*
- *define what historical research is and when it should be used;*
- *identify the primary steps in applying the historical method;*
- *identify the common difficulties associated with each step in the historical method and explain how to overcome them;*
- *describe how observation is used as a method of research;*
- *describe the main types of observation used in research design;*
- *identify when observation is suitable as a research method;*
- *compare the advantages and disadvantages of using observation as a research method;*
- *describe participant observation research and explain when it should be used;*
- *identify the problems in using observation as a method of research data collection and explain how to overcome the problems; and*
- *recognise how to analyse the data gained from observation to answer research questions.*

CONTENTS

Introduction   124
Documentation as a method of data collection   124
Observation as a method of data collection   134
Conclusion   142
References   143
Chapter review questions   144

Introduction

Documentation and observation as techniques of data collection are often used for the purpose of studying natural behaviour. The techniques of observation and documentation analysis may be used singly, as primary sources of data in their own right, or as part of a multi-method study. Observation and documentation can be used in any research design, including correlational field studies (surveys) and experiments. Case studies typically include observation and analysis of documentation as parts of their research design.

Documentation as a method of data collection

Documentation when used for research purposes

Document analysis involves the study of public and private documents such as the minutes of meetings, newspapers and personal journals, diaries, and letters. According to Lee (1999), document construction and analysis includes archival searches of documents (e.g., official and unofficial company documents, journals or logs, personal letters, and diaries). It can also include the construction of such documents through narratives and life histories. Documentation usually involves analysis of verbal text, but can include quantitative data in the form of archival records.

The use of documentation as a research technique

Documentation may be used for many research purposes. As this documentation has already been collected, it does not involve active intervention, such as conducting interviews, administering questionnaires, or carrying out experiments where primary data are gathered. Documentation is unobtrusive and non-reactive. It can also be used for triangulation of data, helping to counteract the biases of other methods and supplement sources of information. The varied documentary records constitute insights into different employee and group interpretations of organisational life, because they are one of the principal by-products of the interactions and communications of individuals and groups at all levels in organisations (Forster, 1994). The documents allow the researcher to obtain the language and words of informants. Documents represent data that are important and thoughtful, as the organisation has allocated resources and informants have given time for their compilation (Creswell, 2003).

When documentation can be used in organisational research

Documentation may be used, as outlined by Forster (1994), to:

- tell researchers about the *kind of image and culture a company is trying to present* internally to its own employees and externally to customers or potential competitors; and
- look at *historical processes and developments* in organisations and help informants in the rewriting of history in later verbal accounts.

Documentation may be used as a preliminary to a study using primary data (e.g., interviews) or as research data in their own right (Forster, 1994). Although documentation often yields data suitable for qualitative analysis, it is also used in studies that seek to quantify relationships. For example, company documentation may be coded for business strategy. It can then be used as the independent variable in a design considering its effects on dependent variables (e.g., staffing and appraising). In this design the variables could be measured by questionnaires, perhaps distributed to executives in the organisation. By applying this design, the relationship, articulated in Schuler's (1989) theory, between the business strategy and the types of specific human resource management practices can be determined. The research question is therefore testing Schuler's theory.

Main types of documentation

Forster (1994) has delineated the main types of organisational documentation that may be used in research. These types of documentation are:

- company annual reports (they provide hard data such as profitability and can also be coded for qualitative data such as organisation mission and vision or human resource management approach);
- public relations material and press releases;
- account statements (hard data);
- corporate mission statements (used to assess business strategy);
- policies on marketing strategy;
- formal charters and legal documents;
- policies on rules and procedures;
- human resource management policies;
- policy directives on training, career management, job mobility, and relocation management (e.g., the training policy gives the organisation's training strategy and information on training programs; career management policies provide career development policies; and information is available on succession planning systems);
- formal memos between different groups and departments; and
- informal and private correspondence between staff and correspondence between respondents and researchers.

There are also documents such as human resource managers' files of complaints or of exit interviews with employees who have left the organisation, which can be used to analyse, perhaps, staff morale or causes of employee turnover. As an example, data may be gathered to understand organisation policies for employee participation in training and development. The documents sought for coding would include: the company annual report, the corporate mission statement, formal documents on the operation of the human resource function in the organisation, the training policy, the staff development policy, the staff recruitment policy, any training plans or documents on training budgets, any memos in relation to training, any information collected to give to government departments on training expenditure, career development policies, performance appraisal policy and procedure, policy and forms for appraisal for different types of staff, succession planning policy, assistance for training attendance, and relocation policy.

The documents can also be obtained at two levels:

1. the macro organisation view, relating to the entire organisation; that is, the intention of policies about training and development of staff; and
2. the region/department/more micro view, relating to management of staff within regions or departments; that is, the implementation of the broader policies.

Creswell (2003) has provided an alternative way of classifying documentation. According to Creswell, there are:

*   public documents, such as minutes of meetings and newspapers; and
*   private documents, such as journals, diaries, letters, or emails.

For example, diaries may already exist, but may also be derived for the purposes of the research (Sommer & Sommer, 1991). For the specific purposes of research, respondents are usually asked to keep diaries or daily journals on specific activities for time units/periods indicated during the day (e.g., managers' tasks each day). These are primary data. There are also secondary data. Published diaries, journals, letters, and autobiographies can be used to assemble life histories of types of individuals, where there are sufficient numbers of these to conduct systematic analyses and to form generalisations. These methods are also useful to illustrate the findings from other techniques; however, they need to be chosen based on internal validity (similar statements occur elsewhere in the same diary) and external validity (similar statements occur in other people's journals).

Archival measures in general are those that are public records and documents, collected by governments and industries (reporting on several organisations), or other documents reporting across organisations. They are a rich source of both qualitative and quantitative data. For example, several sources exist for data on Australian companies that can be coded for research (e.g., organisation size, age, industry, ownership, headquarters, revenue, turnover, line of business, international operations, etc.). These sources include: *Kompass Australia* (Australian Chamber of Commerce, Associated Chambers of Manufacturers of Australia, & Metal Trades Industry Association of Australia, 2006), *Australia's top 500 companies* (Business Who's Who of Australia, 2005), and *Jobson's Online*, as well as companies' annual reports. Moreover, published data are given on other variables useful in research, such as the economic performance of variance countries in the *Human Development Report* (United Nations Development Programme, 2005). Similarly, the Australian Bureau of Statistics has a wealth of official statistics.

Some numerical information, such as affirmative action information (e.g., representation of women in management at different levels by the major organisations in an industry), may be analysed to provide conclusions about groups (e.g., senior women managers in banking). The Equal Opportunity for Women in the Workplace Agency (EOWA) provides reports of quantitative and qualitative data (Equal Opportunity for Women in the Workplace Agency, 2004–2005). Where the publications, either by government, industries, or organisations, provide numerical data, they are often useful for comparing trends temporally (Sommer & Sommer, 1991). Researchers should be mindful that underreporting may be an issue in some secondary data sources and therefore needs to be taken into account.

Advantages and disadvantages of the use of documentation

There are several problems that can arise in the use of documents. Difficulties may occur in gaining access to the information. The documentation may be protected and unavailable to public or private access. It may also be difficult to find. Additionally, the materials may be incomplete and the documents may not be authentic or accurate. A major problem with archival measures is that the data were originally gathered for another purpose and may not contain the variables of interest (Payne, Finch, & Tremble, 2003).

Forster (1994) has outlined problems with organisational documentation as research data. The records may be difficult to use to generalise about kinds of organisations. They may not be representative of the life of a particular organisation. It is also the case that documents are political and subjective and may be used for ulterior motives. Therefore, company documentation, or other forms of documentation, needs to be checked, interpreted, and triangulated with other data sources. According to Forster (1994), documents should be regarded as data that are context-specific and must be contextualised with other forms of research.

Despite these potential problems, the strengths of using documentation in a research design include the opportunity the researcher has to examine texts written in the participant's own words and often with substantial care, its unobtrusiveness, and the need for relatively little transcription. Further, an enormous amount of useful information for research purposes is stored in archives, both qualitative and quantitative (Lee, 1999).

Steps in using documentation

Presented below are the steps or procedures that might be followed in conducting document analysis, especially if the researcher is gathering information within one organisation.

1. Obtain as many kinds of documentation as possible linked to the research question.
2. Develop a protocol for (a) recording the different documents and (b) the key categories being looked for.
3. Search for themes within each document and within clusters of documents (parts and the whole) to arrive at sub-themes and any central theme(s).
4. Compare themes with other sources of data – interviews, questionnaires, observation – to obtain triangulation.
5. Determine relationships (e.g., between variables) against the research question.
6. Develop a deductive understanding of the whole.

Analysing the data from documentation

Documentation often has text, for example, from annual reports, public relations and press material, mission statements, policies on rules and procedures, human resource management strategies, and policy directives (e.g., on training). This makes the data appropriate for a qualitative analysis of the content or meaning of textual materials. For instance, the meanings which people attribute to situations in which they find themselves are the basic units of research, rather than causal variables. 'Understanding', rather than 'hypothesis-testing', becomes the key methodological issue to be resolved (Forster, 1994, p. 150). The meaning is said not to be reducible to a few independent and dependent variables. The organisation is also conceptualised from within, rather than as a detached observer. The meaning of disparate and sometimes contradictory texts is determined through analysing the meaning of individual texts, relating them to the totality of the worlds from which they originate, and re-interpreting the separate texts anew (Forster, 1994).

Throughout the process, there needs to be a way of recording documents. A protocol for recording information can be established that identifies (a) information about the document or material, and (b) key categories that the researcher is looking for in the source of information (Creswell, 2003). It should also be noted whether the information has been obtained from a primary source (information directly from the people or situation being studied), or from a secondary source (second-hand accounts of the people or situation).

Steps in the process and how to improve reliability and validity

Forster (1994) has described the process for analysing documentation from a single organisation, as well as the techniques that can be applied to improve both validity and reliability. These steps are presented below.

1. *The researcher coming to understand the meaning of the individual texts through searching for themes within each document and then within clusters of documents.*

The process is a continuous one back and forth between the parts and the whole. Initially, the researcher has a vague and unclear understanding of the documents. The initial task is to search for themes within each document and then within clusters of documents. The focus of attention is on meanings, not analysis. The themes and sub-themes are identified. Sub-themes may be references to units of relevant meaning, such as culture, people management, communication, and power relationships (Forster, 1994). The actual number of times the units of relevant meaning occur is noted to indicate significance and how important particular issues are perceived to be within the context of the document (Forster, 1994). Hence, themes emerge from the grounded knowledge. The themes emerge from examining each individual unit of meaning (e.g., culture), its occurrence in documents, and then understanding its meaning given the wider context(s) in which it exists. The link to other contexts needs to be understood.

2. *Identifying sub-themes.*
   The different themes are then related to each other to see if there is a central theme that provides a higher-order level of understanding of contradictory themes.

3. *Identifying thematic clusters by relating these sub-themes with each other to see if there are central themes.*
   Groupings of text are made that have a unity and commonality of meaning. Documents can then be clustered according to their inner cohesion and logic. These can be tested by comparing them with texts produced by the same author (of the original documents), with interviews, and with texts by other authors. Hence, clusters of 'meaning' have been elicited (Forster, 1994).

4. *Triangulating documentary data by comparing with other texts and other forms of data, or by comparing them with research questions.*
   The meanings can then be compared to the research questions of the study. This is done by considering all of the texts and other forms of data at once, rather than analysing a segment of text in its own right against the research questions. The meaning of individual text segments can be different from that of the entire document being the unit of analysis or when all the data are employed. It is usually impossible to take into account the full range and quantity of documents in an organisation.

5. *Employing reliability and validity checks.*
   Reliability checks can be done by training other researchers in the method in order to verify the findings. The other researchers can check the general rigour of the study and the representativeness of the documents. Different researchers may also arrive at differences in interpretations of the same text, providing validity problems. Company documents must not be used on their own, in order to provide reliability and validity checks.
6. *Contextualising documentary data by examining them within the broader organisational context and processes.*
   Documents can only be understood within broader organisational contexts and processes and with reference to other forms of data.
7. *Using representative written material as quotations or illustrations in the final report.*
   Documents need to be sampled and used as the illustrative materials (examples) in the report of the study.

Historical analysis

Historical analysis is a constructivist approach that is commonly applied in areas such as industrial relations. Historical analysis results in new knowledge about history (what has occurred in the past). The focus of historical analysis is the manner in which humans in the past constructed their unique reality. Hence, historical analysis is appropriate for questions relating to the past, what was happening at that time, and the manner in which people create their reality (Bedolla, 1992). The aim of historical analysis is to learn how past intentions were related to phenomena and events, due to their meaning and their value. Hence, historical analysis provides a method for understanding how culture emerges and develops.

History (the past) is a succession of actions, interactions, events, and situations; it is not an historical record. The accounts produced by historical researchers are never exact accounts of what has happened in the past. Despite attempts on the part of the historical researcher to be rigorous and exhaustive in his or her inquiry, the final account will be a subjective and ideological construct. Also, with the passing of time and as new information, insights, and paradigms emerge, the construct (the account) will change (Andrews, 2001).

The historical method begins with a question that arises from historical data. The historical data from which the question emerged need to be examined and then new data analysed. Insights emerge for the researcher as tentative answers to the question, and those insights need to be verified (Bedolla, 1992). If all the existing data are explained, the historian is in possession of knowledge that answers the questions correctly. However, only part of the data may be explained.

Steps involved in the historical method
Mason, McKenney, and Copeland (1997a, b) and Patemore (1998) provide descriptions of the historical research method and the steps required. They are:

1. research on the remnants of the past that are available in the present;
2. interpretation of the results of the research;
3. judgement of the correctness of the interpretation; and
4. communication of the interpretation judged to be correct.

In historical analysis, it is important that the researcher applies both external and internal criticism. With external criticism, the researcher attempts to provide criticism of historical written material. With internal criticism, however, the researcher seeks to reproduce the psychological states of the author to determine what the author meant or intended, whether the author believed what he or she said, and whether this belief or commitment was justified. Historical data need to be reliable. The information has to be understood, and the understanding has to be judged correct in order to progress from experience to knowledge. Having obtained the data and determined their reliability, the historian then undertakes an interpretive process in which he or she pieces together the data that have been gathered and then critically evaluates them (Bedolla, 1992).

Bedolla (1992) has provided a general description of the historical method which states that it is an:

- investigation;
- interpretation;
- historical judgement; and
- judgement and the communication of history.

Observation as a method of data collection

When observation is used in research

Observational studies can be used to comprehend complex issues through direct observation and then, possibly, asking questions to seek clarification on certain issues (Sekaran, 1992). Data may be gathered by observing people in their natural work environment and recording their behaviours. For example, the nature of work undertaken by managers can be determined by observing managers, day to day, in their work settings and recording what they actually do and the reasons why. Observation is often used for studying unusual events, such as strikes in industrial relations research (Whitfield & Strauss, 1998).

Sommer and Sommer (1991) have highlighted the difference between observational research and merely 'looking'. Observation, unlike casual and unguided 'looking':

- serves a specified research purpose;
- is planned systematically;
- is recorded systematically and related to more general propositions, rather than simply being presented as an interesting set of curiosities; and
- is subjected to checks and controls on validity and reliability.

Types of observation research

Observation may be described along two continua (Miller & Crabtree, 1992). The first is the *degree to which the researcher participates* in the scene being observed (e.g., a quiet note-taker in the background versus keeping notes as one is doing the actual job). The researcher can either be a non-participant observer or a participant observer (Sekaran, 1992). A non-participant observer merely observes and may do so for extended periods of time (e.g., all day for three months). A participant observer becomes part of the group or immerses him or herself in the setting of interest (e.g., workplace, organisation).

The second continuum refers to the *degree of structure in the observations* themselves. Observational studies may also be structured or unstructured (Sekaran, 1992). Structured observation requires a pre-determined set of categories of activities of the phenomenon to be studied, and observations of behaviour are specifically recorded against the categories. Structured observation yields data suitable for quantitative analysis. With unstructured observation, everything that is observed is recorded. Unstructured approaches to observation tend to place more emphasis on detailed personal description, and less emphasis on pre-determined categories and quantification, than structured observation techniques (Sommer & Sommer, 1991). Qualitative techniques are usually employed with participant observation and ethnography. (The latter is applied to the study of specific people and places – for example, societies, courtrooms, or banks.)

Participant observation research

The most commonly known variant of observation in research is participant observation. Participant observation has been defined as research characterised by a prolonged period of intense social interaction between the researcher and the subjects, in the setting of the latter, during which time data in the form of field notes are unobtrusively and systematically collected (Bogdewic, 1992). Waddington (1994) has defined participant observation as the observer being able to study first-hand the day-to-day experience and behaviour of subjects in particular situations and, if necessary, to talk to them about their feelings and interpretations. Participant observation is intended to understand the experience of people – the way they think, feel, and act – and, as such, to gain that information by sharing that experience. Participant observers often use observation to research a culture internally, rather than operate as objective observers who approach a culture externally.

When participant observation should be used

Participant observation research is typically used where the observer needs to explore meanings, interpretations, and motives (Waddington, 1994). Bogdewic (1992) has recommended using participant observation when the activities and interactions of a setting give meaning to certain behaviours or beliefs. The inhabitants of any culture are influenced by any assumptions they take for granted. Differences between real and verbal behaviour are made apparent through participant observation. The sequence and connectedness of events that contribute to the meaning of a phenomenon can be identified, with the context being observed as it unfolds in real life.

Participant observation is said to be best suited to research projects (Waddington, 1994):

- which emphasise the importance of human meanings, interpretations, and interactions;
- when the phenomenon under investigation is generally obscured from public view;
- where it is controversial; and
- where it is little understood and therefore an insider perspective may enhance knowledge.

Participant observation, however, should not be conducted where it would be considered an intrusion to have a complete stranger witness and record the situation of interest, where the situation of interest is obscured or completely hidden from the public, or where the inhabitants appear to have significantly different views than outsiders (Bogdewic, 1992). According to Waddington (1994), the researcher requires: (a) reasonable access; (b) the research problem to be observable and capable of being addressed by qualitative data; and (c) the research setting to be sufficiently limited in size and location for it to be effectively observed.

There are four main ways in which participant observers can immerse themselves in the experience and activities of people. According to Creswell (2003), the researcher can be:

1. a *complete participant*, where he or she conceals his or her role (covert);
2. a *participant as observer*, where the observation role is secondary to the participant role;
3. an *observer as participant*, where his or her role is known (overt); or
4. a *complete observer*, where he or she observes without participating.

Advantages and disadvantages of participant observation

The primary advantage of participation and observation derives from the first-hand knowledge gained about organisational phenomena as they occur (a) in a real-world context, (b) in real time, and (c) without the prompting of potential distortions from post hoc verbal descriptions. The main disadvantage stems from the potential for conflict between researchers' efforts to establish trust and their possible observation of unethical situations and acts (Lee, 1999). As Waddington (1994) has pointed out, ethical issues may arise because, in the course of participant observation, observers know of actions that are being taken that may be illegal or potentially dangerous (e.g., by strikers). The researcher's presence may have an impact on the reality being observed. This is known as reactivity. Finally, there is also the possibility of 'going native' – that is, where the researcher over-identifies with the people he or she is studying (Bryman, 2004).

The steps in participant observation research

Waddington (1994) has described the process for a research study based on participant observation. The steps are:

1. *Entering the field.* The initial approach should guarantee confidentiality and privacy, emphasise that the researcher's interests are not confined to any one setting or group of people, and give a truthful but broad general summary of the research procedures and objectives, to reduce defensive or self-conscious behaviour.
2. *Conduct in the field.* A positive and non-threatening self-image must be maintained. Observers must emphasise features they have in common with respondents and not require them to depart from their usual behaviour.
3. *Recording data.* Participant observation is concerned with the observation and recording of human activity. An initial period of acclimatisation is needed to ensure sufficient knowledge of what is being done (where one should be, making sense of the activity). Note-taking is required, but may need to be done when not in the field. Note-taking should include descriptions of people, events, and

conversations, as well as the observer's actions, feelings, and working hypotheses. The setting and timing are described in detail, with everything recorded that can possibly be. Triangulation is needed by making use of more than one source of data collection, such as the addition of documentation (e.g., diaries, minutes, letters, memos) and discussions with respondents (e.g., casual conversations through to tape-recorded interviews and surveys).

4. *Analysing data.* The analysis is usually inductive:
   - data are assembled into units or themes, which are then subsequently analysed for patterns or relationships, often in connection with existing theories or with hypotheses that have emerged during fieldwork;
   - the data are then re-assembled, providing an interpretation or explanation of a question or particular problem;
   - the synthesis is then evaluated and critically examined and may be rejected or accepted with modifications; and
   - the entire process may then be repeated to test further theoretical conceptions, or to expand its generality.

5. *Leaving the field.* When there are no major new insights being gained, participant observation should stop. Easing off relationships without terminating them too abruptly is advised. Informants should be advised of the results of the research.

An example of participant observation

Currall, Hammer, Baggett and Doniger (1999) provide an example of participant observation used as a data collection method. The research aim in this study was to examine group processes within a corporate board of directors. Interestingly, this study combined both qualitative and quantitative techniques. The steps undertaken by the researchers in conducting the study are detailed below.

1. An observer was asked to be a director on a board and agreed, provided she could study the board as a participant observer. Hence, the observer had a 'participant-as-observer' role.
2. The participant observer collected field notes on group processes within the corporate board.

3. The field notes were transcribed into verbatim scripts of who said what to whom inside the boardroom. The verbatim transcripts of directors' verbal behaviours were cross-checked with the board secretary throughout the five-year data collection period.
4. Content analysis of the transcripts was used to code board members' verbal behaviours on the basis of exhaustive and mutually exclusive categories. Fifteen iterations of the content analysis scheme were done to ensure the coding categories were exhaustive and mutually exclusive.
5. Inter-rater reliability was assessed. There were inter-rater reliability indices across three raters.
6. The transcripts were quantified by recording counts of different types of verbal behaviours elicited by board members. These were counts of verbal behaviours of board members.
7. Based on counts of directors' verbal behaviours, hypotheses about group processes were tested using statistical techniques appropriate for count data. These gave a measure of a change in a single variable over time, a bivariate relationship between two variables, and a multivariate analysis that used statistical control to eliminate the potential effects of confounding variables.

In this study, theory was developed concerning the subtleties of conflict, power struggles, and interest group advocacy displayed by board members inside the boardroom. Currall et al. (1999) found that:

- The overall activity level of new outside directors, but not worker directors, increased over time.
- Executive directors were more dominant in board discussion, debate, and argumentation than pre-existent outside, new outside, or worker directors, particularly on topics that required firm-specific knowledge. Worker directors were the least dominant of the sub-groups.
- There were no significant amounts of interest group arguments and conflict in the board's deliberations concerning another firm's procurement. Conflict was due not only to interest group arguments, but also to criticisms of management decisions by outside (both pre-existent and new) directors.

Currall et al. (1999) highlighted the strengths of qualitative observation for investigating group processes. These strengths are:

- Observation data are rich in detail about group member behaviour and interactions.
- An observer obtains an intimate knowledge of group history and norms to use as an interpretive framework with which to decipher the actions of group members.
- Observation allows the researcher to collect data on a group as it unfolds over time, making it possible to conduct a longitudinal investigation.

In this study, the researchers also noted the methodological disadvantages associated with this particular technique. The problems related to:

- cognitive information processing limitations of an observer (some behaviour goes unrecorded);
- other researchers not being able to determine how the observer made interpretations from field notes; and
- field notes not used to test hypotheses using statistical inference techniques, just used as rich description of events and behaviours.

Conducting structured observation as a research technique

Structured (also called systematic) observation requires the use of a scoring system and prearranged categories that are applied consistently in the recording of observed behaviour. Consequently, an observation checklist is required on which information is recorded under headings. Categories in the checklist include those items of behaviour that occur naturally in the situation and can be observed and recorded. Casual observation is often needed initially to determine the categories used for observation. More than one observer can be used, and then the agreement between two or more observers is calculated to establish inter-rater reliability. At least two independent observers are advised in the early stages of a research project until reliability has been established. The observers must also have a location from which behaviour can be recorded. The steps for systematic observation research (Sommer & Sommer, 1991) are:

1. Specify the questions of interest for the study.
2. Conduct casual observations, distinguishing between observation (the actual behaviours) and inference (interpretation).
3. Describe the observational categories clearly.
4. Design the measurement instruments (e.g., checklists, categories, coding systems).
5. Design the study so that it will be valid; that is, it measures what it is supposed to measure and it has some generalisability.
6. Train observers in the use of the instruments.
7. Conduct a pilot test:
   • test the actual observation procedure; and
   • check reliability of the categories using at least two independent observers. Statistics that measure degree of agreement, such as Kappa, can be calculated to establish inter-rater reliability (see Chapter 12 for details).
8. Revise the procedure and instruments. If there are substantial changes, do another pilot test.
9. Collect data.
10. Compile, analyse, and interpret the results.

There are difficulties in inferring people's attitudes, beliefs, or opinions from structured observations of behaviour. Individual attitudes, beliefs, and opinions should be assessed directly through interviews or questionnaires. Alternatively, participant observation research can be used where the observer wishes to explore meanings, interpretations, and motives within a social context.

Problems with observation as a research method

There are a number of pitfalls for researchers to avoid when conducting observational research, whether participant or structured (Sommer & Sommer, 1991). These potential problems include:

1. *Reactive effects* from being observed (self-consciousness, accommodating behaviour, etc.).

Participant observation is particularly useful for investigating cultural groups. As the observer is there longer, inhabitants are less likely to change their behaviour in his or her presence and the observer is accommodated rather than reacted to (Bogdewic, 1992).

2. *Observer error* (unclear and unreliable observational categories, observer bias, changes in observational periods during the study, etc.).

In participant observation, the participant observer may find it difficult to maintain a passive role. Observer biases may also occur, as well as fatigue or boredom. Observers can be given training in how to observe and what to record (Sekaran, 1992). If there are several observers, inter-observer reliability can be calculated.

The field notes of a participant observer can lack reliability and the observer may change the behaviour of those being observed, or be biased, or over-identify with the participants. Another way of overcoming these problems is triangulation, or the use of more than one method, observer (a team), other site(s), and public or private records to provide additional checks on a single observer (Sommer & Sommer, 1991). Hence, different vantage points or methods can be used to pinpoint aspects of the same phenomenon.

3. *Sampling error* (observed people not representative of groups to which the results will be generalised, inadequate time periods, bias due to location, day, etc.).

Conclusion

Analysis of documentation involves developing an inductive understanding of clusters of company documents through to a deductive understanding of the whole. The documents may not be able to be taken at face value. They cannot be analysed in isolation and can only be understood within the context of a holistic view of the organisation and in relation to other types of analyses. One of the advantages of documentation analysis is that it can highlight the interactions between different subgroups and the politics of organisational life.

Observation is applied to answer research questions concerning natural behaviour. Casual observation does not use prearranged categories or a scoring system and may be most useful at the early stages of research. Structured observation employs detailed categories and a scoring system. There are sources of error from structured observation, such as reactive effects, observer error, and biased sampling. Reliability can be calculated by having two or more observers in the early stages of a study. Participant observation is where the observer becomes part of the events being studied; however, there may be problems of reliability and generalisability. In participant observation, triangulation can be used to check on reliability and more than one method, observer, or site can be used to provide additional checks on observers' accounts.

References

Andrews, J. (2001). Group work's place in social work: A historical analysis. *Journal of Sociology and Social Welfare*, *28*, 45–65.

Australian Chamber of Commerce, Associated Chambers of Manufacturers of Australia, & Metal Trades Industry Association of Australia (2006). *Kompass Australia* (35th ed.). Prahran: Isaacson Publications.

Bedolla, M. (1992). Historical method: A brief introduction. In B.F. Crabtree & W.L. Miller (eds.), *Doing qualitative research* (pp. 163–173). Newbury Park, CA: Sage Publications.

Bogdewic, S.P. (1992). Participant observation. In B.F. Crabtree & W.L. Miller (eds.), *Doing qualitative research* (pp. 45–69). Newbury Park, CA: Sage Publications.

Bryman, A. (2004). *Social research methods*. Oxford: Oxford University Press.

Business Who's Who of Australia (2005). *Australia's top 500 companies* (19th ed.). Chatswood: Dun & Bradstreet.

Creswell, J.W. (2003). *Research design – qualitative, quantitative, and mixed-method approaches* (2nd ed.). Thousand Oaks, CA: Sage Publications.

Currall, S.C., Hammer, T.H., Baggett, L.C., & Doniger, G.M. (1999). Combining qualitative and quantitative methodologies to study group processes. *Organizational Research Methods*, *2*, 5–36.

Equal Opportunity for Women in the Workplace Agency (2004–2005). *Equal Opportunity for Women in the Workplace Agency Annual Report*. Canberra: Australian Government Publishing Service.

Forster, N. (1994). The analysis of company documentation. In C. Cassell & G. Symon (eds.), *Qualitative methods in organizational research* (pp. 147–166). London: Sage Publications.

Lee, T.W. (1999). *Using qualitative methods in organizational research*. Thousand Oaks, CA: Sage Publications.

Mason, R.O., McKenney, J.L., & Copeland, D.G. (1997a). Developing an historical tradition in MIS research. *MIS Quarterly*, *21*, 257–278.

Mason, R.O., McKenney, J.L., & Copeland, D.G. (1997b). An historical method for MIS research. *MIS Quarterly*, *21*, 307–320.

Miller, W.L. & Crabtree, B.F. (1992). Primary care research: A multimethod typology and qualitative road map. In B.F. Crabtree & W.L. Miller (eds.), *Doing qualitative research* (pp. 3–30). Newbury Park, CA: Sage Publications.

Patemore, G. (1998). Digging up the past: Historical methods in industrial relations research. In K.W. Whitfield & G. Strauss (eds.), *Researching the world of work: Strategies and methods in studying industrial relations* (pp. 213–227). Ithaca, NY: Cornell University Press.

Payne, S.C., Finch, J.F., & Tremble, T.R., Jr. (2003). Validating surrogate measures of psychological constructs: The application of construct equivalence to archival data. *Organizational Research Methods*, *6*, 363–382.

Schuler, R. (1989), Strategic human resource management. *Human Relations*, *42*(2), 157–184.

Sekaran, U. (1992). *Research methods for business: A skill-building approach*. New York: John Wiley & Sons.

Sommer, B. & Sommer, R. (1991). *A practical guide to behavioral research: Tools and techniques*. New York: Oxford University Press.

United Nations Development Programme (2005). *Human development report*. New York: Oxford University Press.

Waddington, D. (1994). Participant observation. In C. Cassell & G. Symon (eds.), *Qualitative methods in organizational research* (pp. 107–123). London: Sage Publications.

Whitfield, K.W. & Strauss, G. (1998). *Researching the world of work: Strategies and methods in studying industrial relations*. Ithaca, NY: Cornell University Press.

Chapter review questions

1 What is documentation when used as a method of research?
2 When can documentation be used in research design?
3 What are the main types of documentation used in research?
4 What are problems with the use of documentation?
5 What are the strengths of using documentation?
6 What are the steps in using documentation in research design?
7 How can documentation be analysed?
8 What are the steps in a typical documentation study (e.g., Forster's [1994] study)?
9 What is observation research?
10 What are the main types of observation used in research design?

11   What is participant observation research?

12   When is participant observation used in research design?

13   What are the advantages and disadvantages of participant observation as a data collection method?

14   What are the steps in participant observation?

15   How is structured observation carried out?

16   What are the problems with observation?

Part 4

Measurement

8 Reliability and validity

Objectives

At the end of this chapter you will be able to:

- *explain what reliability is;*
- *define validity;*
- *distinguish reliability from validity;*
- *describe internal consistency and stability reliability;*
- *compare the types of validity: construct, content, and criterion-related validity;*
- *describe how to measure reliability;*
- *describe how to measure validity;*
- *explain how to increase reliability; and*
- *explain how to increase validity.*

CONTENTS

Improving the quality of the study: Reliability and validity of measures	150
Types of reliability	152
Types of validity	155
Conclusion	157
References	158
Chapter review questions	158

Improving the quality of the study: Reliability and validity of measures

Constructs and measures

This chapter begins by defining some key terms. Following Edwards and Bagozzi (2000), a construct is a conceptual term for a phenomenon of theoretical interest. Constructs are thus concepts that exist as part of a theoretical language. Examples of constructs used in management research are 'total quality management', 'transformational leadership', and 'emotional intelligence'. Most constructs of interest to researchers are conceptualised as variables; that is, they can take on different values or states, whether qualitative or quantitative in nature. For this reason, constructs are often called latent or unobserved variables. Because constructs are abstractions, researchers need to be able to operationalise or measure them in an empirical study. A measure is defined here as a score or observed value that is taken to empirically represent a construct (Edwards & Bagozzi, 2000). Measures may be gathered through methods of data collection such as questionnaires, documentation, and observation. We can thus speak of measured or observed variables as *indicators* of their respective latent constructs. However, no measure is a perfect representation of the underlying construct. An important part of empirical research is to maximise the reliability and validity of measures.

Reliability and validity of measures

'Reliability' refers to the extent to which a measure is free of random measurement error (Smithson, 2005). A perfectly reliable measure has no random measurement error. Reliability can be defined as the ratio of the true score variance to the observed score variance (the variance is the mean of the squared deviations from the mean, and the standard deviation is the square root of the variance), because each observed (i.e., measured) score is composed of a 'true' score and measurement error. If there is random measurement error, the measure has less-than-perfect reliability. Of course, most measures used in research are imperfect. However, if a measure's reliability is too low, it cannot be used in research. Note that reliability is a property of the scores (i.e., the measures) and not of the instrument or procedure used to gather the data. Therefore, reliability must be tested each time an instrument is used to generate scores for a sample.

Validity is whether the researcher is measuring the construct he or she purports to be measuring. In other words, it is the extent to which a measure measures what it is supposed to measure. For example, if a researcher examines a measure of self-esteem, he or she needs to ask whether it really measures self-esteem, or whether in fact it measures self-confidence (a similar self-evaluation), or lack of depression, or lack of anxiety, or life satisfaction (other measures of positive affect/attitudes that are highly related to self-esteem).

Validity is the degree of confidence that a researcher can have in inferences drawn from scores, and the confidence that a researcher can have in the meaning attached to scores. It is important to understand that a measure cannot be valid unless it is reliable, but a measure can be reliable but not valid. Reliability is thus a necessary but not sufficient condition for validity. Reliability and validity apply to both qualitative and quantitative data. Often, it is easier to assess reliability and validity with quantitative data; however, in our opinion, they are equally important with qualitative data.

The necessity for reliability and validity

Studies that use measures with poor reliability and validity produce data, both quantitative and qualitative, that lack rigour. Consequently, the researcher cannot justify the use of these measures because other interpretations could be drawn from the data.

For example, statistics such as correlation coefficients are attenuated (reduced in size) due to the presence of measurement error. Researchers often measure relationships between variables (e.g., between intentions to leave a job and actual labour turnover). If a researcher has measures with low reliability, he or she is less likely to detect the associations between variables when they are in fact related. The reason for this is that, when a measure has low reliability, it weakens the effect size and thereby limits statistical power to detect relationships with another variable.

If a researcher was to compose a measure of a construct and it appeared as if it measured that construct (i.e., it has face validity), this would not constitute sufficient evidence that it really does. For example, measures of intelligence may actually capture how well an individual is able to answer written tests (which he or she may be well practised in as a result of being highly educated), rather than his or her innate intelligence, as reflected in genetic inheritance. Therefore, in this example, instead of measuring intelligence (innate ability), the researcher is really also measuring years of schooling and grade point average. Those individuals with higher educational levels thus score higher on this measure than those with lower educational levels. As a consequence, the scores are not a valid measure of intelligence, as they actually reflect education.

Before initiating a research project, researchers need to establish that they are using reliable and valid measures. In some areas, researchers will find that measures of the variable have already been developed and they are advised to use these. In other areas, there may not be established measures and therefore researchers have to establish their reliability and validity.

Types of reliability

We have defined reliability as the extent to which a measure is free of random measurement error. The measures can be single-item or multi-item (i.e., summed or averaged across several items) scores. The development and validation of multi-item scales is discussed in more detail in Chapter 9. The following is a discussion of various ways of estimating reliability of scores.

Internal consistency reliability

Internal consistency reliability is used for multi-item measures. If a multi-item measure has little random measurement error, the researcher would expect the items to be consistent with each other. Internal consistency reliability is typically measured by a statistic called Cronbach's alpha coefficient (see Cortina, 1993). An alpha coefficient measures how correlated each item is with each other item in the scale. It is a measure of consistency because if the items in the scale are related to each other, it is an internally consistent measure.

Alpha coefficients are calculated using the average correlation among the items. So at least two items are required in order to calculate an alpha coefficient. An alpha coefficient ranges from 0 to 1. It is not possible to obtain a negative alpha coefficient, unless the researcher has made a computational error (e.g., failed to reverse score negatively worded items), or the scale is extremely unreliable. In general, measures that are highly reliable have alpha coefficients of .90 or greater, while scales that have alphas below .70 can be said to have less than fair reliability (although alphas of .60 or higher are acceptable for newly developed scales) (Nunnally, 1978). It is important to understand that Cronbach's alpha does not indicate that the scale is unidimensional or valid. It also needs to be remembered that as a researcher increases the number of items, Cronbach's alpha coefficient will also increase. Unless the items have a high average intercorrelation, it may be difficult to get acceptable internal consistency reliability for scales with a small number of items (e.g., two or three items).

Test–retest reliability

Test–retest reliability is the extent to which a measure gives the same result on two (or more) repeated administrations. If a measure is perfectly reliable, it should provide the same score on repeated administrations. For example, if a researcher measures an individual's intelligence one week, he or she could obtain an estimate of test–retest reliability by re-measuring intelligence two weeks later using the same test. If the measure is reliable, the test scores should be similar. Similarly, if a researcher measures an employee's job satisfaction or intentions to leave on one day, the employee's satisfaction and intentions to leave should be approximately the same two weeks later. This type of reliability is referred to as stability. The error associated with test–retest reliability is anything that yields different scores on repeated administrations. The length of time between measures is an important consideration; a shorter interval will typically yield a higher correlation. Test–retest reliability is often used to measure reliability in single-item measures, provided the underlying construct is not expected to change substantively over time.

Test–retest reliability is measured via a correlation coefficient (e.g., Pearson's correlation coefficient). To obtain this coefficient, the researcher merely correlates scores on the first administration of the measure with their matched scores on the second administration. It does imply that researchers require longitudinal data and need to match up scores from the first administration to the second administration. The correlation coefficient should be positive and as high as possible. Test–retest (i.e., stability) coefficients are usually lower than estimates of internal consistency reliabilities. According to Corcoran and Fischer's (1987) criteria, a test–retest coefficient above .80 indicates strong stability; a coefficient above .71 implies good stability; and a coefficient above .51 denotes fair stability.

Inter-rater reliability

Data are often gathered through observation. With observational data, one researcher's observations might differ from another researcher's observations. A similar issue arises with analysis of qualitative (textual) data. Usually with qualitative data, the researcher wants to determine whether there are identifiable themes in the text. Again, one researcher's interpretation might differ from another researcher's interpretation. In these types of situations, inter-rater (or inter-observer) reliability statistics can be calculated. In order to assess inter-rater reliability, two (or more) researchers should provide ratings or scores for each of the variables in the data. There are many statistics for calculating inter-rater reliability, including per cent agreement and coefficients such as Kappa. In general, inter-rater reliability should be .80 or greater in order for the researchers to conclude that they are rating consistently.

Other measures of reliability

There are several other measures of reliability. Instead of alpha coefficients, researchers can apply *split-half reliabilities* to measure the internal consistency of a multi-item scale. In order to do this, the researcher can split the items of a measure into the odd (e.g., first, third, fifth items) and even (second, fourth, sixth) items, and then estimate a coefficient that indicates how related the odd scores are with the even scores. If a measure assesses what it is supposed to measure, then it should be internally consistent. Consequently, the test is split into two halves and the total score for odd items is arrived at, as well as the total score for even items for each respondent. Then, for the whole sample, the correlation of odd with even scores is estimated.

Other forms of reliability are estimated by developing parallel forms of the measure. They measure the same construct or phenomenon, with very similar, but not identical, items. The correlation coefficient is calculated by administering the two measures to the same sample. This procedure is referred to as *parallel forms*.

Types of validity

There are several types of validity, and researchers should be familiar with them all when searching for published and/or established measures in order to make an informed decision about whether the measure assesses what it purports to measure. It is difficult to establish validity for 'home-grown' measures (those developed by the researcher for the study), as large sample sizes and multiple measures are required. More information on validating multi-item measures or scales can be found in Chapter 12.

Construct validity

Essentially, construct validity refers to whether a measure relates to other measures in ways predicted by an underlying theory of the construct. Construct validity is comprised of two subtypes: convergent and divergent validity. If a measure captures what it really is supposed to measure, scores on that measure should be more related to scores on other similar constructs (convergent validity) and not, or less, related to scores on dissimilar constructs (discriminant validity). For example, if a measure of managerial level actually assesses managerial level, it should be more related to constructs closely associated with managerial level (e.g., salary, the number of managerial promotions, and the number of subordinates responsible to that person) than to other constructs that may be spuriously related to advancement. The latter could be age, the number of years employed in full-time work, the number of levels in the organisation, and the organisation's size. Thus, if the managerial level item was valid, it would be more highly correlated with the former constructs (convergent validity), and not related or less highly related to the latter constructs (discriminant validity). In other words, the convergent and divergent validity of a measure is assessed by determining whether the pattern of relationships in the empirical data match those in the nomological network (i.e., the expected theoretical relationships between the construct the measure is capturing and other constructs) (Schwab, 2005). Another approach to examining construct validity is through the use of both exploratory and confirmatory factor analysis to determine evidence of convergent and discriminant validity.

Criterion-related validity

If a measure is valid, it should predict something that the researcher is interested in. For example, if a selection interview or a selection test is a valid measure for choosing future staff, it should predict their performance on the job. Criterion-related validity means that the measure predicts a relevant criterion. In other words, it attempts to answer the question, 'Does it matter?' Criterion-related validity is practical and pragmatic. However, the choice of the criterion variable is critical. Smithson (2005) notes that the criterion measure should be known to be reliable and valid already.

Criterion-related validity may be predictive or concurrent, depending on how it is measured. Predictive validity is the extent to which a measure predicts subsequent performance or behaviour. For example, scores may be obtained in a selection interview (e.g., supervisory ability), subsequently people are hired (for research purposes, it would be best to hire everyone to avoid range restriction problems), and their job performance is measured a year later. Predictive validity is determined by the strength of the correlation (called a validity coefficient) between supervisory ability, measured at selection, and job performance, measured a year later. Alternatively, the researcher could measure the current staff on supervisory ability, using the interview, and then take their job performance scores and correlate the two. This is referred to as concurrent validity, as the measure (supervisory skills measured via interview) is correlated with a criterion (job performance) that is measured at the same point in time. In order for validity coefficients to have criterion-related validity, the coefficient should be as high as possible. One rule of thumb is that a relationship may be considered weak if the validity coefficient is .10, medium if .30, and strong if .50 (Cohen, 1988).

Content validity

Content validity refers to whether the items designed for the measure adequately cover the domain of interest. For example, an exam with content validity would have questions covering all of the content that had been covered in the course. Thus, content validity is focused on the extent to which the content of a measure is representative of a wider body of material that it is trying to assess. Content validity is often estimated by a thorough review of the relevant literature and consultation with subject matter experts, to determine whether the items in the measure have adequately sampled the domain.

Face validity

Measures that have face validity appear, at face value, as if they measure what they say they measure. Face validity is subjective. Nevertheless, all measures must have face validity. However, just because a measure appears to measure what it claims to measure, there is no guarantee that it does. The measure has face validity, but not empirically demonstrated validity.

Conclusion

Measures used in research need to be reliable and valid. If they are not valid and reliable, the researcher cannot be confident about the conclusions drawn from the study. This applies to interpreting both qualitative and quantitative data. Irrespective of the type of data collected, it needs to be reliable. The measure also needs to be valid. In other words, it needs to measure what it is supposed to measure, predict relevant criteria, cover the content underlying the construct, be similar to similar constructs and dissimilar from different constructs, and not be contaminated by method factors such as social desirability. This may require the use of published measures, which have been through rigorous reliability and validity checks. Alternatively, researchers may use hard data (e.g., number of sales for measuring performance), the validity of which can be more easily demonstrated. Often it is best for researchers to use multiple measures, which allows them to determine if a number of the measures converge for evidence of construct validity.

References

Cohen, J. (1988). *Statistical power analysis for the behavioral sciences* (2nd ed.). Hillsdale, NJ: Lawrence Erlbaum Associates.

Corcoran, K. & Fischer, J. (1987). *Measures for clinical practice: A sourcebook*. New York: Free Press.

Cortina, J.M. (1993). What is coefficient alpha? *Journal of Applied Psychology, 78*, 98–104.

Edwards, J.R. & Bagozzi, R.P. (2000). On the nature and direction of relationships between constructs and measures. *Psychological Methods, 5*, 155–174.

Nunnally, J.C. (1978). *Psychometric theory* (2nd ed.). New York: McGraw-Hill.

Schwab, D.P. (2005). *Research methods for organizational studies*. Hillsdale, NJ: Lawrence Erlbaum Associates.

Smithson, M. (2005). *Statistics with confidence*. Thousand Oaks, CA: Sage Publications.

Chapter review questions

1 What is reliability?
2 What is validity?
3 Are there any differences in the need for reliability and validity in qualitative and quantitative data?
4 What is internal consistency reliability?

5   What is test–retest reliability?
6   How do internal consistency reliability and test–retest reliability differ?
7   What is inter-rater reliability?
8   How is inter-rater reliability calculated?
9   What are construct, content, and criterion-related validity?
10   How do the various measures of validity differ?

9 Scale development

Objectives

At the end of this chapter you will be able to:

- *identify what a multi-item scale is;*
- *develop a new multi-item scale to measure a construct;*
- *describe the main steps involved in developing a multi-item scale;*
- *describe the reason behind each step and why it is needed;*
- *outline the problems to overcome in developing a reliable and valid measure;*
- *apply the methods needed at each step to produce a reliable, valid measure; and*
- *explain how to tell if the measure designed was reliable and valid.*

CONTENTS

Multi-item measures	161
Problems with measures used in management research	161
Social desirability and acquiescence response set	171
Conclusion	173
References	174
Chapter review questions	175
Appendix A: Sources of organisational, social psychology, and community measuring instruments	176
Appendix B: Standard, conventional item stems and their response categories	179

Multi-item measures

Management researchers will often use multi-item scales in their studies. In fact, multi-item measures are the most commonly used measurement device in management research. They are typically used to measure complex unobservable constructs such as attitudes, values, and beliefs, and form a major part of data collection instruments such as questionnaires. As discussed in the previous chapter, a single indicator is unlikely to capture an underlying construct. A *scale* is defined here as a measure consisting of two or more items designed to measure a construct. Each item (e.g., question) is an indicator of the construct. One of the most common uses of a scale is to generate a composite score (sum/average of the items) that operationalises the construct of interest – for example, job satisfaction, charismatic leadership style, job involvement, motivation, and so on. Constructs can be unidimensional or multidimensional. A single-scale score is only designed to measure a unidimensional construct. Multidimensional constructs consist of two or more dimensions. For multidimensional constructs, each dimension (or facet) will require the development of subscales.

There are numerous benefits in using multi-item measures in research:

- Multi-item measures usually have superior reliability and validity compared with single-item measures.
- Multi-item measures can be more easily tested for evidence of reliability than single-item measures.
- A composite (average/sum) score comprised of two or more items can be used to represent the construct of interest, thereby simplifying quantitative analysis.
- The relationship between multi-item measures and their underlying constructs can be modelled using factor analytic procedures.

Problems with measures used in management research

Schriesheim, Powers, Scandura, Gardiner, and Lankau (1993) reviewed the management literature and identified several problems in the development and use of measures. The problems included reliance on single-item measures, lack of reporting of the measure's reliability, shortened measures of full scales, modified items or instructions to the original scale, changed response categories from the original, and missing or incorrect specifications of the measure. These issues are elaborated on below.

- Single-item measures are used without demonstrating inter-rater or test–retest reliability. Also, single-item measures usually cannot adequately cover a construct.
- Lack of reporting of the measure's reliability indicates that measurement error was not calculated. Reliability is also a precursor to validity (though it is not validity). Reliability needs to be reported from past studies and also calculated for the present study. This is because reliability is a property of a sample (belongs to the scores for the particular sample used) and not a property of the data collection instrument itself.
- Employment of shortened measures of full scales without justifying item selection, at least, by recalculating reliability or checking against content validity and adequacy – does the measure still cover the construct?
- Employment of modified items or instructions to the original scale without justifying, at least, by recalculating reliability or checking that the measure is still adequate.
- Employment of different response categories to the original, without justification.
- Not specifying the version used of the measure and often reporting the wrong version.

Some further comment on single-item measures is warranted. It is believed that single-item measures are more appropriate for concrete and easily measured constructs. For example, single-item measures are commonly used in questionnaires (and interviews) for measuring factual-type data such as age, occupation, and so on. Large-scale surveys – for example, the Gallup poll – use single items to measure public opinion. They have had many years of designing questionnaire items and have trialled them several times, including in pilots. Researchers may use those items because they have usually been well developed.

In some areas of investigation, researchers have objective, 'hard' data measuring what they seek to measure. These are often single measures, such as those for financial performance (e.g., return on investment, current ratio, net margin) and are more valid than other subjective, 'soft' data. However, it is always best to use multiple measures of hard data, because each single measure may be tapping into only one facet of the overall construct.

Wanous, Reichers, and Hudy (1997, p. 247) argued that single-item measures may be appropriate provided the construct is 'sufficiently narrow and unambiguous'. For example, global job satisfaction is often measured with a single question (e.g., 'How satisfied are you with your job?'). Similarly, training or teaching effectiveness is often measured using a single item (e.g., 'Overall, how effective was the training/teaching in this program?'). Wanous and Hudy (2001) have described two methods for calculating single-item reliability (correction for attenuation formula and factor analysis). Additionally, following a meta-analytic study, Wanous and Hudy concluded that a minimum estimate of .70 for single-item reliability is acceptable for individual-level data, while a minimum reliability estimate of .80 is reasonable for group-level data.

Published measures

Generally, it is an unwise practice for researchers to make up their own measures. It is best to use published or established measures for which the reliability and validity data are reported in journals. There are books of published measures for the behavioural and social sciences that usually provide a researcher with an evaluation of the quality of the measure of that construct – for example, in terms of validity and reliability. Appendix A presents some of the books that are used in organisational behaviour. They also provide several measures of the same construct so that the researcher can make a choice, depending on his or her need. Any measure that is published in a book held in a library is usually not copyright and may be used as long as its author is cited. The top journals (e.g., *Academy of Management Journal, Journal of Applied Psychology, Journal of Management, Journal of Vocational Behavior, Personnel Psychology*) usually ensure authors place their measures, if new, in an appendix to the paper and they may be used without copyright problems. Looking through those journals, electronically or by hand, will often give the researcher the exact measure he or she requires, in full detail. A researcher can obtain measures, and their scoring, from the article or write to the authors for them.

Developing a new scale

The construction of a new multi-item measure is a highly complex process. Several steps are required to develop a multi-item scale to measure a construct. The researcher needs to:

1. apply a theoretical basis to develop the items;
2. design the individual items;
3. conduct an item analysis to eliminate poor items (ambiguous, no variation);
4. determine the construct validity of the measure using factor analysis;
5. determine the convergent validity of the measure;
6. determine the divergent validity (discriminant validity, including method effects); and
7. assess its reliability.

Both Hinkin (1995) and DeVellis (2003) have reviewed the practices used to develop scales, and they have developed a series of steps that researchers should follow when constructing scales. A summary of these steps is presented below.

Establishing what the scale should measure

As a first step to scale development, the researcher should carefully examine the extant theory relating to the construct he or she wishes to measure. Theory can provide a guide in terms of developing the conceptual formulations required for operationalisation. Examining theory helps to establish the parameters of the construct to ensure that the content of the scale is focused on the actual domain of interest, rather than unrelated areas. The researcher also needs to determine the level of specificity required of the scale. This will largely be determined by the research question, as the level of specificity of the scale should align with the level of specificity of the research question and the other constructs it will be compared with (DeVellis, 2003).

Item generation: Use a theoretical basis

The researcher should develop the items from a theory of the construct (latent variable) so that they are consistent with it. If there is a theoretical basis for this construct, it can be defined and the type of relationships it has with other constructs can be predicted. For example, self-esteem is represented by feelings of approval or disapproval towards oneself and is an evaluation of the self, indicating whether one feels worthy, successful, significant, or important. High self-esteem should be related to feelings of positive affect in general, such as self-confidence and lack of depression and anxiety. However, it is different from ability and intelligence, and is also different from affect measures in relation to work, such as job satisfaction, organisational commitment, and intentions to leave.

After the construct has been defined and its relationships with other constructs established, items are written to measure it from the theory. An item is simply a single question or statement. Redundancy needs to be a feature of the initial item pool, as some items will be deleted in the final scale. It is also worth noting that there should be overlapping and seemingly redundant items in the final scale, as the common aspects of the items will be summated or aggregated across the items and the irrelevant aspects will be negated (DeVellis, 2003). There is no established convention for determining the number of items that should be included in the initial item pool. However, DeVellis has suggested that there should be three or four times as many items in the initial item pool than the number of items anticipated in the final scale. Therefore, an eight-item scale might begin from an initial item pool of 32.

When writing the actual items, researchers should ensure that they are relatively brief and that the language used is not too complex, in order to avoid confusion. Additionally, double-negative (e.g., 'I am not concerned when my supervisor fails to recognise my achievements') and double-barrelled (e.g., 'I am committed to my organisation because I am satisfied in my job') items should be avoided.

Researchers may also develop negatively, as well as positively (regularly), worded items. This is to avoid an acquiescence response set where, when items are all positively worded, people are more likely to agree, because they are in the positive direction. However, some authors strongly advocate, based on empirical data, that negative items should not be developed (Schriesheim & Eisenbach, 1995).

Another issue is the optimal number of response categories for an item. The most commonly used response formats are five- or seven-point Likert scales (e.g., strongly disagree, disagree, neither agree nor disagree, agree, strongly agree). Hinkin (1995) concluded that five to seven response categories is adequate for most items. An alternative to Likert-type scales is the semantic differential. The semantic differential is used to measure attitudes using bipolar scales defined with contrasting adjectives at each end. Appendix B provides some commonly used item stems and response categories for Likert scales.

Hinkin's (1995) review of the management literature identified that item generation was the most important component of developing sound measures. He found that measures frequently lacked content validity (the adequacy with which a measure assesses the domain of interest). Schriesheim, Cogliser, Scandura, Lankau, and Powers (1999) have argued that content validity should be the initial psychometric property of a scale to be assessed. If the content validity of a measure is not acceptable, one cannot be certain that it will reflect the theoretical definition of the construct the scale purports to assess (i.e., construct validity). They suggest that if a newly developed measure lacks content validity, subsequent assessment of its construct validity may be redundant, at least until its content adequacy is improved.

Hinkin (1995) concluded that it is necessary to develop a clear link between items and their theoretical domain. This can be accomplished by employing a robust sorting process that matches items to construct definitions.

Use an expert panel for content validation

Once the researcher has generated the initial pool of items, the next step involves having a panel of subject-matter experts review the items in terms of content adequacy. These experts should be provided with construct definitions and instructed to sort the items according to these definitions, to determine whether their sort aligns with the scale developer's conceptualisations. Those items that are not correctly sorted can be dropped, replaced, or modified. Typically, this is a relatively inexpensive process. Schriesheim et al. (1993) have also recommended that the panel rate the content adequacy of items, which are then averaged. Specifically, each item is rated for the achievement of some specific objective/subdomain (e.g., part of the construct's definition). Thus, the panel of judges separately rates specific items for their adequacy in representing the construct. Schriesheim et al. suggested that the panel's ratings of each item's theoretical relevance should then be factor analysed. The factor analysis will indicate the dimensionality of the items and the distinctiveness of the content categories (see Chapter 11). Schriesheim et al. developed an exemplar of a rating questionnaire to provide to judges. Researchers may modify this judges' rating questionnaire for use in their own studies. Overall, the method is relatively quick, easy to score, and simple to analyse.

Design of the developmental study: Conduct an item analysis

An initial item analysis is undertaken to determine whether the items are ambiguous or are skewed (participants tending to respond very similarly to the items). A basic item analysis usually involves obtaining data from a developmental sample to remove ambiguous items, and calculating basic statistics, such as means and standard deviations and frequencies, to remove skewed items. Researchers should not retain items that fail to discriminate among respondents. Therefore, items need to survive an item analysis. Measures of other theoretically relevant constructs should also be administered to the developmental sample. The researcher can then examine the pattern of relationships between the new scale and these other relevant constructs in order to assess the validity of the new scale (DeVellis, 2003).

Hinkin (1995) found that to examine the psychometric properties of a new measure, it should be made clear why the specific sample was chosen. The developmental sample should be representative of the population for which the scale was intended. DeVellis (2003) has argued that sample size for a developmental study should take into account the number of items and number of scales to be extracted. Hinkin has advocated, as a minimum, a sample of 150 for scale development procedures. He has also stated that there should be careful examination of factor loadings to determine whether negatively worded items are problematic, and their impact on consistency reliability should be assessed. He found that both long and short measures have potential negative effects on results. According to Hinkin, five or six items that utilise five- or seven-point Likert scales are adequate for most organisational measures.

Scale construction: Determine the construct validity of the measure

The next step involves conducting an exploratory factor analysis on the remaining items. The method usually applied in this context is principal components analysis (Hinkin, 1995). The purpose of an exploratory factor analysis is to analyse scores on several items to see if they can be reduced to underlying dimensions. Those items that are highly related to each other will load on one factor. Their loadings on the factor (how much they are related to the factor) should be .30 or .40 (Kim & Mueller, 1978) or greater (the loadings can range from −1.00 to +1.00). If a researcher is developing a measure of global (overall) self-esteem, he or she would expect only one factor to emerge from the analysis. Sometimes researchers will want more than one factor because they are developing measures of different constructs or have different components (e.g., task variety, autonomy, job feedback, significance, task identity) of an overlying construct (e.g., job complexity). The items that are measuring one construct should load on one factor and those measuring another construct should load on a different factor. Analyses that yield no clear factors or one factor (for a unidimensional scale) are problematic. Additionally, the factor analysis should explain a substantial amount of the variance in the scores. Based on these factor loadings, the researcher needs to decide which items from the scale should be retained or deleted.

Hinkin (1995) has advocated the use of confirmatory factor analysis (using LISREL, AMOS, or EQS), rather than principal components factor analysis, in scale construction to examine the stability of the factor structure and provide information to help refine a new measure. He advocates confirmatory techniques because they allow the researcher more precision than exploratory techniques (i.e., principal components analysis) in evaluating the measurement model. Confirmatory factor analysis assumes that there is a theoretical model underlying the measure and that the fit of the overall model to the data (i.e., the covariances) and of the item loadings is tested. For example, Job Characteristics Theory states that jobs have five core dimensions: skill variety, task identity, significance, autonomy, and feedback of results. The Job Diagnostic Survey measures each of these dimensions using three items, and the theory states that they should be related. Hence, a five-factor oblique (allowing interrelationships) model is tested for best fit to the data and compared to the fit of other rival models that could exist: a five-factor orthogonal model (job characteristics not related), a one-factor model (job complexity), and a null model, in which all 15 items load on separate factors. The model with the best fit to the data is used. What is being looked for is the five-factor, oblique model to be confirmed, because that is consistent with the theoretical model.

DeVellis (2003) has also stated that confirmatory techniques provide more flexibility than exploratory approaches, such as allowing the researcher to vary the independence of the error terms and to incorporate uncorrelated and correlated factors in the same model. However, he has also cautioned that slavishly applying the statistical criterion for how well the data fit specified model confirmatory techniques can lead to overfactoring. Additionally, DeVellis has suggested that if the practice of testing competing models and comparing how they fit the data is undertaken injudiciously, it can result in improved model fit; however, the model specifications may be theoretically inexplicable.

The appropriate approach is the one suggested by Kelloway (1998), where exploratory factor analysis is used in the initial stages of research, followed by confirmatory factor analyses as the state of knowledge on particular topics increases. Finally, Hinkin (1995) has warned that scales should not be derived post hoc, based only on the results of the factor analysis. Items that load on the same factor do not necessarily measure the same theoretical construct.

Reliability assessment

Having examined the factor structure, these items then need to be subjected to a reliability check. Reliability is an essential issue in scale development and refers to the amount of variance attributable to the true score of the latent construct (DeVellis, 2003). One form of reliability, internal consistency, is determined by calculating coefficient alpha. This coefficient should be as high as possible. If not, items contributing to low reliability (low item to total correlations) need to be dropped and new items developed. Reliability is a necessary pre-condition for validity. Hinkin (1995) stated that relying exclusively on internal consistency reliabilities is not adequate. Multiple methods of reliability assessment are ideally required. While alpha coefficients of .70 and above are required of established scales, internal consistency coefficients of .60 or better are acceptable for a newly developed scale (Nunnally, 1978). Problems with reliability appear to occur because of lack of attention by researchers at the item development stage. Reliability, in terms of stability of the measure in the form of a test–retest correlation, should only be calculated if the construct under examination is not expected to change over time. An alternative method of obtaining multiple measures of reliability is to calculate another internal consistency reliability coefficient by administering the measure to an additional sample (Hinkin, 1995). DeVellis has argued that reliable scales provide greater statistical power, for any given sample size, when compared with less reliable scales. The reason for this is that reliable scales introduce less error to statistical analyses, relative to less reliable measures.

Scale evaluation: Validity

It should be noted that establishing that a scale is reliable does not ensure that the latent variable assessed by the items is in fact the construct the scale developer intended them to measure (DeVellis, 2003). The researcher also needs to determine the convergent and the divergent validity (discriminant validity, including method effects) of their measures. Specifically, he or she needs to check that there are no plausible alternative explanations for what the scale measures. In order to do this, the researcher would obtain measures of the scale from a sample from whom he or she also obtained measures of constructs the scale should be related to, including alternative measures of the construct of interest (*convergent validity*), and of constructs the scale should not be related to (*divergent validity*). These relationships are calculated by correlation coefficients (e.g., a Pearson product moment correlation coefficient – see Chapter 10). The variables the scale should not be related to may include method effects, such as acquiescence response set and social desirability, for which there are measures (see Robinson, Shaver, & Wrightsman, 1991). If there are not the appropriately sized convergent (moderate to high) and divergent (zero to low) validity correlations, then items need to be examined in the scale in terms of what alternatives they may be measuring, other than this construct, and then additional items need to be added. Following this, a criterion-related study should be conducted, where the measure is used to predict what it should predict (e.g., sales ability with sales performance). Data are gathered from respondents on the construct, as well as on a criterion (or criteria) it should predict, and a correlation coefficient(s) is calculated.

Hinkin (1995) concluded that construct validation is essential for the development of quality measures. His review of the scale construction literature in management identified a reliance on factor analysis to infer the existence of construct validity. Criterion-related validity is required; however, it must be noted that large sample sizes will yield statistically significant relationships because of their increased power. Indeed, Hinkin (1995) found that the majority of the criterion-related relationships had very small magnitude, meaning they were of little practical significance. If, having completed the above procedures, the final version of the scale contains the appropriate number of dimensions and it is related to what it is supposed to be related to and not related to what it is not supposed to be related to, it can be deemed to have construct validity.

Social desirability and acquiescence response set

In designing scales, researchers need to ensure that the items are not socially desirable. In addition, researchers need to give consideration to the issue of acquiescence response set. Each of these method problems is discussed in more detail below.

Social desirability

Social desirability (see Moorman & Podsakoff, 1992; Paulhus, 1991; Richman, Kiesler, Weisband, & Drasgow, 1999; Spector, 1987) is the tendency for a respondent to choose the socially desirable response, regardless of whether it is true or not, and to present themselves in a favourable light, regardless of their true feelings about an issue or topic. The tendency is seen to be a problem because of its potential to bias the answers of respondents, and also because it can mask relationships between two or more variables, or produce spurious relationships. Respondents who score high on social desirability scales are said to be 'faking good' and would contaminate the results of any data obtained from them (Moorman & Podsakoff, 1992).

Often the problem can be reduced by originally developing measures low in social desirability. This is achieved by administering to a sample the newly developed scale, in addition to a scale that measures social desirability, and then removing items that correlate highly with the social desirability scale. Moorman and Podsakoff's (1992) review of empirical studies indicated that social desirability was related to locus of control (external), general job satisfaction, role conflict and role ambiguity (both negatively), and organisational commitment, although the magnitude of the relationships was weak.

Acquiescence response set

Acquiescence response set (also called agreement response set) occurs when respondents are asked positively phrased questions and are likely to answer positively. Acquiescence response set is thus the tendency for a respondent to agree with items, regardless of their content (Spector, 1987). It is the tendency to agree or acquiesce, although it also occurs when a respondent disagrees with all of the items, irrespective of their content. One method for reducing acquiescence is to include negatively worded items, as well as positively worded items, in a multi-item scale. Although developing negatively worded items may reduce acquiescence, their inclusion often leads to misinterpretation by respondents. Indeed, Schriesheim and Eisenbach

(1995) have argued that negatively worded items cause measurement error in scales, citing evidence for several well-known scales including the Job Diagnostic Survey and the usual measures of role conflict and ambiguity. Schriesheim and Eisenbach differentiated between negatively worded items, which usually include the word 'not' (e.g., 'I am not happy') and polar opposite items, which are natural negatives (e.g., 'I am sad'). For example, a negated item on the most popular Organisational Commitment Survey is, 'There's not too much to be gained by sticking with this organisation indefinitely'. A polar opposite item is, 'Often, I find it difficult to agree with this organisation's policies on important matters relating to its employees.'

It appears that factor analysis of a scale may place the positively worded items on one factor and the negative items on another. The negative factor often has a low internal consistency reliability (i.e., an alpha coefficient). Schriesheim and Eisenbach (1995) pointed out that the negative factor is likely to be a method factor (they are all negative items) and increase measurement error in the full scale. In their empirical test, Schriesheim and Eisenbach demonstrated that positively worded items were superior in all ways, including lower levels of error and method effects and higher reliability, than the negative factors. Thus, designing negatively worded items may not be necessary and, indeed, may be problematic. If negatively worded items are included in a scale, the alpha coefficients should be checked for the total scale both with, and without, the negatively worded items, to determine when the error is highest (i.e., the lowest alpha).

Conclusion

There are a number of important steps required in order to design a new multi-item measure or scale. First, the construct needs to be defined. Substantial attention needs to be given to the way in which the items are created. There must be strong and clear links between the items and a theory or theories. Sufficient items must be developed in order to allow for the later deletion of those deemed to be redundant. Deletion may arise because validity is poor (assessed through factor analysis, or judgements by others) or because criterion-related tests and/or reliability are low. A sorting process that groups the items reliably into the constructs they are supposed to measure is a minimum requirement. The scale should have minimum response bias and sufficient length to ensure adequate sampling of the domain of the construct. Factor analytic techniques should be used to assess the underlying factor structure. Internal consistency reliability (i.e., coefficient alpha) should be calculated, remembering that reliability does not ensure validity. Stability over time (i.e., test–retest correlations) should be used if the construct is not expected to change temporally. Scale development seeks ultimately to demonstrate construct validity. This can be attained by using within-measure factor analysis, but also by calculating relationships with criterion variables. The scale will then need to be modified, with a new scale presented. The use of multiple tests/analyses (confirmatory factor analysis, criterion-related validity) and multiple samples (to obtain more than one alpha coefficient) are necessary.

References

DeVellis, R.F. (2003). *Scale development: Theory and application* (2nd ed.). Thousand Oaks, CA: Sage Publications.

Hinkin, T.R. (1995). A review of scale development practices in the study of organisations. *Journal of Management, 21*, 967–988.

Kelloway, E.K. (1998). *Using LISREL for structural equation modeling*. Thousand Oaks, CA: Sage Publications.

Kim, J.O. & Mueller, C.W. (1978). *Factor analysis*. Beverly Hills, CA: Sage Publications.

Moorman, R.H. & Podsakoff, P.M. (1992). A meta-analytical review and empirical test of the potential confounding effects of social desirability response sets in organizational behaviour research. *Journal of Occupational and Organizational Psychology, 65*, 131–149.

Nunnally, J.C. (1978). *Psychometric theory*. New York: McGraw-Hill.

Paulhus, D.L. (1991). Measurement and control of response bias. In J.P. Robinson, P.R. Shaver, & L.S. Wrightsman (eds.), *Measures of personality and social psychological attitudes* (pp. 17–60). New York: Academic Press.

Richman, W.L., Kiesler, S., Weisband, S., & Drasgow, F. (1999). A meta-analytic study of social desirability distortion in computer-administered questionnaires. *Journal of Applied Psychology, 84*, 754–775.

Robinson, J.P., Shaver, P.R., & Wrightsman, L.S. (1991). *Measures of personality and social psychological attitudes*. San Diego, CA: Academic Press.

Schriesheim, C.A., Cogliser, C.C., Scandura, T.A., Lankau, M.J., & Powers, K.J. (1999). An empirical comparison of approaches for quantitatively assessing the content adequacy of paper-and-pencil measurement instruments. *Organizational Research Methods, 2*, 140–156.

Schriesheim, C.A. & Eisenbach, R.J. (1995). An exploratory and confirmatory factor-analytic investigation of item wording effects on the obtained factor structures of survey questionnaire methods. *Journal of Management, 21*, 1177–1193.

Schriesheim, C.A., Powers, K.J., Scandura, T.A., Gardiner, C.G., & Lankau, M.J. (1993). Improving construct measurement in management research. *Journal of Management, 19*, 385–417.

Spector, P.E. (1987). Method variance as an artifact in self-reported affect and perceptions at work: Myth or significant problem? *Journal of Applied Psychology, 72*, 438–443.

Wanous, J.P. & Hudy, M.J. (2001). Single-item reliability: A replication and extension. *Organizational Research Methods, 4*, 361–375.

Wanous, J.P., Reichers, A.E., & Hudy, M.J. (1997). Overall job satisfaction: How good are single-item measures? *Journal of Applied Psychology, 82*, 247–252.

Chapter review questions

1 What problems are found in the development of measures in management research?

2 What are published measures? Where do you find them?

3 What are the five main steps in developing a multi-item measure?

4 How do you generate items? Why do you do it that way?

5 What is an item analysis? How do you do an item analysis, and why do you do it that way?

6 How do you assess the construct validity of a measure?

7 How do you assess a measure's reliability? What is internal consistency reliability (i.e., alpha reliability)? What is test–retest/stability reliability? What is inter-rater reliability?

8 How do you evaluate the new scale/measure?

9 What is convergent validity?

10 What is discriminant validity?

11 What is social desirability error? What can you do about it?

12 What is acquiescence response set? What can you do about it?

13 What is the rationale for each of the principles that can be used to overcome problems with measures in correlation field studies (survey) research?

Appendix A: Sources of organisational, social psychology, and community measuring instruments

Beere, C.A. (1992). *Gender roles: A handbook of tests and measures*. New York: Greenwood Press.

This book gives a description and evaluation of many measures used in the area of gender roles, including sex role stereotypes, attitudes towards women and gender roles, work–family role measures, gender roles, employee roles, multiple roles, and family measures.

British Telecom (1984). *Survey item bank. Volume 1: Measures of satisfaction*. Bradford, England: MCB University Press.

This volume contains scales covering global job satisfaction, extrinsic job satisfaction, intrinsic job satisfaction, and internal needs and drives. It breaks down into three sections:

1. Extrinsic satisfiers, which are those aspects of satisfaction that are not an integral part of the job itself – such as pay, promotion prospects, supervision, co-workers, other staff, the firm, physical working conditions, job security, social status, and the work itself.
2. Intrinsic satisfiers, which are those aspects of satisfaction that arise naturally from the nature of the work performed – variety, autonomy, and responsibility. This section finishes by describing each of the scales of Hackman and Oldham's Job Diagnostic Survey.
3. Internal motivations focus on the motivations of workers. This section describes a work involvement scale, measures of the need for extrinsic satisfiers (pay, security, esteem, etc.), and intrinsic satisfiers (the need for autonomy, growth opportunities, etc.). Full copies of all scales are given.

British Telecom (1984). *Survey item bank. Volume 2: Measures of organizational characteristics*. Bradford, England: MCB University Press.

This volume deals with measures of organisations under five headings:

1. Context of the organization.
2. Structure of the organization.
3. Processes used by the organization (planning, organizing, various aspects of staffing, decision making, and control).
4. The organization's physical environment.
5. The organization's values and norms concerning people, innovation and risk, ideas and research, rules, and work.

Full copies of all scales are given. In both volume 1 and 2 the Survey Item Bank provides information for each scale. Most of the scales are scored by simply adding the scores on the individual items. Whenever possible, percentile norms are also given for each scale in the Survey Item Bank.

Buros, O.K. (various editions). *Tests in prints.* **Highland Park, NJ: Gryphon Press.**

All psychological tests are evaluated for reliability and validity in this series.

Cook, J.D., Hepworth, S.J., Wall, T.D., & Warr, P.R. (1981). *The experience of work.* **London: Academic Press.**

This is the best source of scales and evidence on their validity and reliability. It contains 249 scales measuring overall job satisfaction, specific satisfactions, alienation, commitment, occupational health and ill health, job involvement, job motivation, work values, beliefs and needs, job characteristics, the organisational climate, leadership style, and others. It also provides the definition of the construct, reliability and validity evidence, and many references where the scale has been used. In addition, the book includes a copy of the complete scale and the scoring procedures. The scales must be assembled for use.

De Bello, T.C. (1990). Comparison of eleven major learning styles models. *Reading, Writing and Learning Disabilities,* **6, 203–222.**

This article reviews and critiques 11 measures of learning styles, including the Kolb inventory. It does not give the measures but gives their sources.

Furnham, A. & Gunter, B. (1993). *Corporate assessment: Auditing a company's personality.* **London: Routledge.**

Included in this source are measures of organisational culture, climate, ideology, employee participation, communication audits, customer audits, people systems audits, including human resource management practices, and organisational commitment. It also provides several of the full measures, and it reviews the measures of organisational culture and climate and, where it does not provide the full measure, gives the underlying dimensions and examples of them.

Greenbaum, H.H., Clamputt, P., & Willihaganz, S. (1988). Organizational communication: An examination of four instruments. *Management Communication Quarterly,* **2, 245–282.**

This article evaluates and describes four measures of organisational communication.

Hackman, J.K. & Oldham, G.R. (1980). *Work redesign.* **Reading, MA: Addison Wesley Publishing Co.**

Contains the Job Diagnostic Survey, which is the most used measure of job characteristics.

Kline, P. (1993). *The handbook of psychological testing*. New York: Routledge.

This book gives reliability and validity evidence for specific psychological tests used in industry in the areas of intelligence, ability, aptitude and attainment, personality, projective tests, motivation and interest tests, attitudes, and others. It does not give each specific test but describes the measure in detail and gives test administration information and reliability and validity. It also includes a conclusion on whether the measure is suitable for use.

Miller, D.C. (1991). *Handbook of research design and social measurement*. London: Sage Publications.

This source includes descriptions of measures of social status, group structure, organisational structure, community, social participation, leadership in work organisations, morale and job satisfaction, family and marriage, personality, and attitudes. In addition, it provides reliability and validity evidence and the utility of the measures. It may often include the full scales.

Pfeiffer, J.W., Heslin, R., & Jones, J.E. (1976). *Instrumentation in human relations training*. La Jolla, CA: University Associates Inc.

Included in this publication are scales with an individual focus (personality), those with an interpersonal focus (general, marriage, family, and group dynamics), and those with an organisational focus (organisational climate, management/leadership style, and supervisor–subordinate relations). It does not provide the scale, but gives a description of it and the positive and negative features.

Pfeiffer, J.W. & Jones, J.E. (1970–1981). *Annual handbook for group facilitators*. La Jolla, CA: University Associates Inc.

Pfeiffer, J.W. (1981 to present). *The annual: Developing human resources*. San Diego, CA: Pfeiffer and Company.

This series includes scales on communication, consulting/facilitation including training/learning style, groups/teams, management/leadership including attitudes, organisations including diagnosis, employee attitudes and values/culture, personal factors including conflict/stress, life planning/career management, values/sexual issues, personality, organisation development and climate, group processes and behaviour, leadership, communication, motivation, and supervision, in the instrumentation section in each year's handbook or annual. The purpose of each scale, a description of suggested uses, references, and sometimes a copy of the complete scale and scoring are also provided.

Price, J.L. (1997). Handbook of organizational measurement. *International Journal of Manpower*, 18(4/5/6), 303–558.

Price, J.L. & Mueller, C.W. (1986). *Handbook of organizational measurement*. Marshfield, MA: Pitman.

The article by Price (1997) is a revised version of the Price and Mueller (1986) text. Scales cover 32 organisational topics – absenteeism, administrative intensity, autonomy, centralisation, communication, complexity, motivation, commitment, general training, need strength, satisfaction, formalisation, standardisation, routinisation, mechanisation, effectiveness, coordination, distributive justice, departmentalisation, productivity, pay stratification, bases of power, organisational size, ideology, innovation, violence of conflict, turnover, work load, work group cohesion, etc. It gives a definition of the topic and how it is measured, followed by a description of the scale, scoring validity, reliability, and references. It usually has a number of scales for measuring the one topic and includes sample items but not the whole scale.

Robinson, J.R.P. & Shaver, P.R. (1975). *Measures of social psychological attitudes.* Ann Arbor, MI: Institute for Social Research.

This source covers life satisfaction, self-esteem, locus of control, social desirability, and other topics. It gives a comprehensive review of each of these areas and indicates which of the scales within each topic is/are the best. In addition, a description of the scale, reliability and validity, references, scoring, administration, and a complete copy of each scale are included.

Robinson, J.P., Shaver, P.R., & Wrightsman, L.S. (1991). *Measures of personality and social psychological attitudes.* New York: Academic Press.

This is widely regarded as the best book of social psychology measures. All are applicable to the organisational setting. It covers scales for response bias, well-being, self-esteem, social anxiety and shyness, depression and loneliness, alienation and anomie, interpersonal trust and attitudes towards human nature, locus of control, authoritarianism, sex roles, and values. It also gives a description of scale reliability and validity, references, scoring, administration, and a complete copy of each scale.

Appendix B: Standard, conventional item stems and their response categories

Below are some of the standard item stems and their response categories as used in management research.

Five-point response categories

Item stem
Please indicate your extent of agreement or disagreement with the following statements.

Scale categories/points

1. Strongly disagree
2. Disagree
3. Neither agree nor disagree
4. Agree
5. Strongly agree

Item stem
Overall, how good . . . ?

Scale categories/points

1. Very poor
2. Poor
3. Fair
4. Good
5. Very good

Item stem
How satisfied are you with . . . ?

Scale categories/points

1. Very dissatisfied
2. Dissatisfied
3. Neither satisfied nor dissatisfied
4. Satisfied
5. Very satisfied

Item stem
How often . . . ?

Scale categories/points

1. Far too little
2. Too little
3. About right
4. Too much
5. Far too much

OR

1. Never
2. Rarely
3. Sometimes
4. Frequently
5. All the time

OR

1. Never
2. Seldom
3. About as often as not
4. Very often
5. Always

OR

1. Practically never
2. Once in a great while
3. Sometimes
4. Fairly often
5. Very often

OR

1. Rarely
2. Less than half the time
3. About half the time
4. Most of the time
5. All the time

Item stem
How many of . . . ?

Scale categories/points

1. Almost none
2. Less than half
3. About half
4. More than half
5. Nearly all

Item stem
How true is . . . ?

Scale categories/points

1. Completely false
2. Mostly false
3. Partly false and partly true
4. Mostly true
5. Completely true

Item stem
How do you rate your chance . . . ?

Scale categories/points

1. No chance
2. Slight chance
3. Reasonable chance
4. Good chance
5. Very good chance

Item stem
To what extent . . . ?

Scale categories/points

1. Not at all
2. To a small extent
3. To some extent
4. To a large extent
5. To a very large extent

OR

1. To a very little extent
2. To a little extent
3. To some extent
4. To a great extent
5. To a very great extent

Seven-point response categories

These are seven-point versions of some of the stems above plus some others. These may give you more spread.

Item stem
Please indicate your extent of agreement or disagreement with the following statements.

Scale categories/points

1. Strongly disagree
2. Disagree
3. Slightly disagree
4. Neither agree nor disagree

5. Slightly agree
6. Agree
7. Strongly agree

OR

1. Strongly disagree
2. Moderately disagree
3. Slightly disagree
4. Neither agree nor disagree
5. Slightly agree
6. Moderately agree
7. Strongly agree

Item stem
How satisfied are you with each of these?

Scale categories/points

1. Very dissatisfied
2. Dissatisfied
3. Slightly dissatisfied
4. Neither satisfied nor dissatisfied
5. Slightly satisfied
6. Satisfied
7. Very satisfied

Item stem
How often do you get . . . ?

Scale categories/points

1. Not at all
2. Almost never
3. Seldom
4. Sometimes
5. Frequently
6. Almost always
7. Always

Item stem
How true is . . . ?

Scale categories/points

1. Never or almost never true

2. Usually not true
3. Sometimes but infrequently true
4. Occasionally true
5. Often true
6. Usually true
7. Always or almost always true

Item stem
How likely is it that each of these will happen . . . ?

Scale categories/points

1. Not at all likely
2. Bit likely
3. Somewhat likely
4. Quite likely
5. Moderately likely
6. Very likely
7. Extremely likely

OR

1. Extremely unlikely
2. Quite unlikely
3. Slightly unlikely
4. Neither likely nor unlikely
5. Slightly likely
6. Quite likely
7. Extremely unlikely

Item stem
How important is . . . ?

Scale categories/points

1. Not at all important
2. Bit important
3. Somewhat important
4. Quite important
5. Moderately important
6. Very important
7. Extremely important

Item stem
Please indicate how accurate each statement is in relation to . . .

Scale categories/points

1. Very inaccurate
2. Mostly inaccurate
3. Slightly inaccurate
4. Uncertain
5. Slightly accurate
6. Mostly accurate
7. Very accurate

Part 5

Methods of data analysis

10 Quantitative data: Data set-up and initial analysis

Objectives

At the end of this chapter you will be able to:

- *process raw data prior to computer entry;*
- *summarise the preliminary techniques of data analysis that need to be done prior to analysing data to test research questions and hypotheses;*
- *select what statistics have to be done to describe the sample;*
- *define a correlation matrix and list what information you need from it before running multivariate analyses; and*
- *explain which technique you need to use for handling missing data when running analyses.*

CONTENTS

Analysing data: Initial quantitative analyses	190
The main stages in data analysis	190
Basic concepts needed	191
Changes to the raw data prior to data entry	195
Preliminary/initial analyses of the data	198
Bivariate analysis	207
Conclusion	216
References	217
Chapter review questions	218

Analysing data: Initial quantitative analyses

Having collected his or her quantitative data, the researcher's next task is to analyse it. The data that are discussed in this chapter will be subject to quantitative analysis, although many of the principles are the same for data management (and some for analysis) of qualitative data. The aim of data analysis is to obtain results that test the study research questions or hypothesis as accurately and easily as possible. Researchers need to manage this process carefully, not only to get it right, but also to make it efficient and logical. The main assumption underlying our approach is that researchers have set up hypotheses and/or specific research questions and are applying techniques to test those hypotheses and research questions. Therefore, the approach is focused.

The main stages in data analysis

Data analysis occurs in three main stages:

1. data management prior to data entry;
2. initial data analysis to check the suitability of your data after data entry; and
3. the data analysis that tests your research questions and/or hypotheses.

Stage 1: Data management prior to data entry

After the data have been collected, they need to be managed to allow computerised data entry for statistical analysis. These processes should be carried out both prior to, and immediately following, data input to check its accuracy and quality.

Stage 2: Initial data analysis to check the suitability of your data after data entry

Initial data analyses are performed in order to test for assumptions underlying the data, to gain descriptive data, and to help determine the property of the measures. Thus, this stage of data analysis consists of initial, or preliminary, data analyses, to describe the sample, check for data errors, check the reliability of measures for this sample, construct scale scores, and check if the data have the properties that will allow the intended techniques of analysis to be used. These analyses precede the substantive tests.

Stage 3: The data analysis that tests your research questions and/or hypotheses

The data need to be analysed with a technique suited to testing the research questions/hypotheses. Thus, in this third stage of data analysis a set of analyses are applied specifically to test the research questions and/or assess if there is support for the hypotheses proposed for the study. The techniques need to be carefully chosen, based on the specific research questions and/or hypotheses made. The objective is to choose a minimally sufficient analysis (Wilkinson & TFSI, 1999). This chapter will describe elementary statistical techniques for summarising quantitative data. However, most studies will usually involve a multivariate statistical technique – that is, one where there are three or more variables analysed simultaneously. Multivariate analyses are employed in management research because control variables need to be taken into account, more than one independent variable is usually assessed, there may be more than one dependent variable, and the relationship between a particular independent variable and the dependent variable(s) needs to be calculated, taking into account the other independent variables. These multivariate techniques are discussed in the next chapter.

Basic concepts needed

Univariate, bivariate, and multivariate techniques of analysis

There are several ways of categorising techniques of data analysis in terms of their broad purposes and applicability. Most techniques for answering research questions and/or hypotheses in management research can be classified as 'univariate', 'bivariate', or 'multivariate'. Researchers need to understand these techniques in order to set up their initial research design, as well as to prepare the data for entry and to carry out the initial analyses.

Univariate analysis

Univariate analysis involves the analysis of one variable only. Univariate analyses are used to describe the sample on key variables or to answer simple research questions involving one variable (e.g., 'How many females are employed in the organisation?'). Univariate statistics include percentages and measures of central tendency (e.g., means) and dispersion (e.g., standard deviations). This is typically a preliminary method of analysis.

Bivariate analysis

Bivariate analysis assesses the relationship between two variables. The most common bivariate statistics are correlation coefficients.

Multivariate analysis

Multivariate analysis assesses the relationships among three or more variables simultaneously. There are several multivariate statistical techniques, the most notable being multiple regression analysis. Multiple regression analyses a single dependent variable and two or more independent variables. Some statisticians refer to statistical techniques involving only one dependent variable as univariate and restrict the term 'multivariate' to the more limiting case of multiple dependent variables. We will use the term in the more general sense, where three or more variables are analysed. Multivariate techniques are discussed in the next chapter.

The different types of data

Quantitative data consist of sets of observed or measured variables. The common way of classifying data is to distinguish between nominal, ordinal, interval, and ratio scales or levels of measurement.

Nominal scales of measurement

Nominal scales of measurement simply classify data into two or more discrete categories and attach a label to the classifications (e.g., your name as opposed to other people's names; male versus female; country of birth). Nominal data consist of unordered categories, but the categories must be mutually exclusive and exhaustive. To facilitate data analysis, numbers may be assigned to the categories of a nominal variable, but the numerical codes convey no indication of order or quantity. For example, calculating a mean does not make sense with nominal data, such as country of birth. Usually nominal data will be analysed using frequencies and percentages across categories. Multivariate techniques such as logistic regression can also be applied to nominal dependent variables (see Chapter 11).

Ordinal scales of measurement

Ordinal scales of measurement have categories arranged in order of magnitude (e.g., ranks) but the differences are not quantitative (Smithson, 2005). For example, if a researcher appraised subordinate performance, he or she could place subordinates in a rank order from 1 (best) to 20 (worst). The researcher could then correlate the appraisal scores, using Spearman's rank coefficient with, for example, rankings on selection interviews. Likert scale items are measured on an ordinal response scale (e.g., strongly disagree, disagree, neither agree nor disagree, agree, strongly agree). Strictly speaking, a mean does not make sense for ordinal data. Statistics such as medians and percentiles are used to summarise ordinal data.

Interval scales of measurement

Interval scales of measurement are quantitative and have equal intervals that reflect a linear relationship with the underlying construct measured (Smithson, 2005). For example, the difference between 10 degrees Celsius and 20 degrees Celsius is the same as the difference between 20 degrees Celsius and 40 degrees Celsius. However, 20 degrees is *not* twice 10 degrees, because they are not measured from an absolute zero. We can perform arithmetic on interval data. Therefore, statistics such as means and standard deviations make sense for interval data. As noted above, strictly speaking, Likert response categories are ordinal data. In other words, the distance between the response categories in Likert response scales (e.g., 1 strongly disagree, 2 disagree, 3 neither disagree nor agree, 4 agree, and 5 strongly agree) are not necessarily equal. However, these data are commonly analysed as if they are interval-type data; provided there are five or more response categories, the underlying construct is conceptualised as theoretically continuous (Tabachnick & Fidell, 2001).

Ratio scales of measurement

Ratio scales of measurement are quantitative and have an absolute zero. Examples of ratio data are height and age, which both start from a true zero point and have equal intervals. One hundred kilograms is twice 50 kilograms, because there is an absolute zero and the intervals between kilograms are equal. Similarly, a profit of $10 million is twice the profit of $5 million. Again, means and standard deviations (and related statistics) can be used with ratio data. The ratio scale is the most powerful, followed by interval, ordinal, and then nominal scales. It is best to aim for interval or ratio data in measuring variables where possible, as they allow a greater range of more powerful statistical techniques to be used for analysing data (see below).

Continuous versus categorical variables

Another common way to classify data is the distinction between categorical and continuous variables. Categorical variables classify the data into two or more discrete groups or categories (e.g., country of birth). These categories can be ordered (ordinal data) or unordered (nominal data). The simplest type of categorical variable is dichotomous (male/female, presence/absence). Continuous variables are those that can theoretically take on any quantitative value within their range and where the size of the number reflects the amount of the variable (Smithson, 2005; Tabachnick & Fidell, 2001). Continuous variables have interval or ratio scales. When measuring continuous variables, precision is limited by the nature of the intrument used to generate the scores. Examples of continuous variables are weight and time. Many psychological constructs such as happiness and intelligence are theoretically continuous in nature. Researchers will often measure their variables as continuous, but later group the data into discrete categories. For example, age as measured in years may be grouped into broader age groups for analysis. In general, this is not a good practice as it results in loss of information. It is also interesting to note that because they have only two possible values, dichotomous variables can be used in many statistical techniques that assume quantitative variables. (Indeed, many readers may not be aware that when a variable is coded as 0 or 1, the mean is equal to the proportion of cases coded 1 and is thus meaningful.)

Changes to the raw data prior to data entry

In management studies, data often come from questionnaires. Hence, questionnaires will be the example used here, but the same principles apply if a researcher were using any data source, including hard data he or she had obtained or calculated from public or organisational records (e.g., return on investment, absence frequency).

Data are usually entered into a computer program for statistical analysis. The most popular of these programs is SPSS for Windows. Before entering the raw data into these programs, researchers need to check it for accuracy, as this will save time later. The two key principles for checking data are:

- not to enter data until they have been checked for problems and corrected; and
- not to enter data for a case (a person, an organisation) where there is too much missing data.

Entering data

Researchers should apply the following steps before entering data into a computer data file.

1. Number all surveys with an identification number and, if available, their source code; the latter may be the organisation from which they were collected. (This information will not be available for anonymous surveys.)
2. Check all surveys for missing data. Individual surveys also need to be checked to see if there is so much missing data that it is not worthwhile proceeding with data entry for that individual.

3. Data are entered in a matrix consisting of columns (variables) and cases (e.g., respondents).
4. All data are coded numerically. Variables are assigned numerical codes to facilitate data analysis, even if they are categorical (nominal/ordinal) in nature.
5. All data must be entered with a particular variable always in the same column for each case (e.g., respondent). Each case has exactly the same number of columns of data entered. Each data cell contains only one coded value. Missing data for any variable are often handled by leaving a cell blank.

Check for errors

Researchers need to ensure that they assiduously check all surveys for errors. Sometimes it is possible to correct errors before the data are coded. There may be objective data where the researcher knows the correct answer, but the respondents have provided incorrect answers. For example, if a researcher asked respondents, even in a carefully worded question where each term was defined, whether they are employed in the public or private sector, they can become confused and mark the incorrect option. Respondents – for example, in banks – may think they are employed in the public sector (because banks can be publicly listed on the stock exchange), whereas they are actually employed in the private sector. In circumstances where researchers know the correct response, or have the source of the data (e.g., name of the organisation), they can re-code the answers for that question for each respondent, prior to data entry.

Errors may also arise because respondents confuse their hierarchical level – subordinate, supervisor, lower-level manager, middle-level manager, senior manager, executive, chief executive officer. There are several reasons why this can occur. Researchers should ensure that they have checked questions in a survey that allow them to verify responses. For example, a researcher may check if the managerial level given is consistent with the answers to other demographic questions, such as asking respondents to write in their job title and occupation, as well as questions about the number of subordinates, owner-manager status, salary, and promotions in the managerial hierarchy. A job title often provides the researcher with an indication of a participant's level in the organisation. The researcher may ask for the number of subordinates to whom the respondent directly delegates work and the number of subordinates accountable to him or her. If the respondent is a supervisor or above, he or she should have subordinates. If the respondent does not have subordinates, the researcher can conclude that the respondent is not a supervisor. Moreover, as people increase in level, they often have fewer people to whom they directly delegate work, but many whose work is accountable to them. In addition, researchers should check the responses of small business owners, who may class themselves as chief executive officers but in reality they are not. Respondents can also accidentally provide incorrect information in terms of their sex, age, or education. There are certain circumstances where demographic information can be checked incorrectly. For example, if the researcher had only mailed out the survey to women, an incorrect response to gender would easily be identified by checking that item. Alternatively, the researcher may have the participants' names and therefore an indication if they are male or female. In situations where researchers have longitudinal data, they can often check consistency across waves; for example, people cannot change sex, or go down in age or up by two age categories.

Check data entry
Checking the accuracy of data entry is an essential prerequisite to any quantitative data analysis. One way that researchers can verify the data on entry is by re-entering the data over the data already entered. The data are entered twice so that the researcher can identify if there are two different numbers being entered in the one column. (There can only be one correct number.) However, if researchers cannot afford to re-enter data, they still need to check that it is correctly entered. Another way to identify data entry errors is by obtaining frequencies on each variable. A frequency table provides percentages for each of the values (categories) of a variable. A researcher may have five response categories, from 1 strongly disagree, 2 disagree, 3 neither disagree nor agree, 4 agree, to 5 strongly agree. Examination of the frequencies will identify any out-of-range values. The response values for the above item can only be 1 to 5. If there are any response values outside of this

range, then the researcher has a data entry problem. Researchers are also advised to check the raw data score against the original survey.

Preliminary/initial analyses of the data

Before proceeding with any data analysis to test your hypothesis, several preliminary steps need to be taken. These tests are carried out to determine whether the researcher can actually use the data in the way he or she intended.

Describing the sample

In any research, investigators need to describe their sample. Univariate descriptive statistics are used for this purpose. These data are usually derived by frequencies/percentages for each demographic variable for individuals (e.g., gender, age, education level, marital status, managerial level, years of company tenure, years of full-time work experience, and occupation type) and organisations (e.g., industry type, employer sector, organisation size, ownership, and revenue). Researchers should also include the means and standard deviations of variables that are continuous and, ideally, the range of these values for their sample. Researchers often provide a table with a description of their sample (percentages, means, and standard deviations) with appropriate comments for the reader to understand who constitutes the sample and what their characteristics are (e.g., all managers in mid-career).

The researchers need to check the sample description to see if there is anything odd about the data. For example, by checking these descriptions, the researcher may note that there are part-time employees in the sample when only full-time employees should have been surveyed. In this example, the researcher may select out only the full-time employees in the sample for analysis and then attempt to uncover the reason for the anomaly.

The sample description is also needed to assess if any controls should be included in analyses (e.g., in multiple regression analyses). For example, men and women employees often differ on variables (e.g., tenure, organisation size, public/private sector, education level, work continuity, marital status, or number of children) that may affect the prediction of the dependent variables. Hence, such variable(s) need to be controlled in analyses to allow the effects of independent variables on dependent variable(s) to be assessed.

Testing if non-respondents are different from respondents

Another issue that researchers need to assess, prior to analysing data, is that of potential non-response bias. This is a particular concern with survey data. It may be possible to compare the frequency of the sample respondents with those of the non-respondents from the population from the original sample. For example, if people were mailed from *Who's Who*, the sample that returned the survey can be compared statistically, if the researcher knows who they are, to those who did not return the survey, based on the information on variables given in *Who's Who*. The variables need to be coded from *Who's Who* (e.g., organisation type, size, industry, profits, etc.) and compared statistically to the answers to those questions for those who replied. Statistical tests (e.g., chi-square tests) can be used for the comparison and the aim is to see if the respondents differ from the non-respondents and, if they differ, how they differ.

For example, Tharenou (1999) had a Time 1 sample returned from which she could not describe the characteristics of her non-respondents. However, the study she was conducting was longitudinal, and therefore she could do so for her later mail-outs. She re-mailed at Time 2, a year later, and found that 79% returned the sample. Using chi-square tests, she found that her non-respondents differed systematically from her respondents. Specifically, the non-respondents were younger, less educated, and had worked fewer years; worked more in the private than the public sector, and in larger rather than smaller organisations; were more likely single and childless; and were lower in managerial level and occupational type (fewer managers and administrators, professionals, and paraprofessionals; more clerks) than were the respondents. The study predicted advancement in management, and the variables differentiating respondents from non-respondents may have biased the results. The effect of the non-respondents on the results was not known. For example, non-respondents may have been less likely to have advanced than respondents because of some factors (lower education, occupation type) but more likely to have advanced because of others (younger, larger organisations), perhaps overall not affecting the results. Thus, determining the response rate and characteristics of the sample can help a researcher to determine not only how generalisable the results are to the larger population, but also if any bias arises when predicting the dependent variable.

Where it is not possible to directly compare respondents with non-respondents (perhaps because the survey was anonymous), a comparison can often be made in aggregate with relevant population-level statistics (e.g., comparing the industry profile of a business survey with official government statistics on industry, etc.).

Properties of the data and assumptions underlying the technique(s) of analysis

Most statistical tests used to test hypotheses and answer research questions make a number of assumptions about the data to be analysed. The techniques of data analysis need to conform to the assumptions that underlie them. Tabachnick and Fidell's (2001) text provides a comprehensive discussion of the statistical assumptions underlying the main analytical techniques used in the General Linear Model (GLM). Common assumptions of these statistical techniques are normality, linearity, and homoscedasticity. Not all statistical techniques make the assumptions. So, it is important to consult a statistics textbook for more information on specific tests.

Testing normality and dealing with non-normal data
The assumption of normality is important for the results of many statistical tests to be accurate. These tests are described in detail later. Univariate normality is the assumption that the scores on a continuous variable are normally distributed about the mean (i.e., the bell-shaped distribution). For example, if continuous data have unacceptable skewness (scores are asymmetrically distributed about the mean) and kurtosis (distribution is too peaked or too flat), they are not normal and techniques that rely on normality may not be accurate.

Multivariate normality is the assumption that all variables and all combinations of variables are normally distributed. Multivariate normality is required for many of the multivariate techniques. Multivariate normality is more difficult to test for, as it is not feasible to test every linear combination of variables and often the tests are oversensitive. However, if univariate normality is violated, then multivariate normality will certainly be violated to some extent also. Likewise, when variables are univariate normal, there is a greater likelihood (but no guarantee) that the data will be multivariate normal.

Simple tests for univariate normality on a continuous variable's scores are kurtosis and skewness. For example, absolute values of kurtosis should not be greater than 5 and absolute values of skewness should not approach 2 (Kendall & Stuart, 1958). Wilkinson and TFSI (1999) recommend graphical techniques for assessing normality. For example, the histogram of a variable needs to have a roughly symmetrical bell-shaped curve. If the variables are not approximately normal, then they can be transformed to see if it makes any difference to the results. Tabachnick and Fidell (2001) discuss appropriate transformations for non-normality. The usual transformations are a square root transformation for mild non-normality, a log transformation for moderate non-normality, and an inverse transformation for severe non-normality. It should also be noted that many statistical techniques are relatively robust to moderate violations of normality. However, unless there are compelling reasons to do so (e.g., severe non-normality), we believe that transformations should generally be avoided.

Testing linearity and dealing with non-linear data

Many statistical tests (but not all) assume linearity. Linearity is the assumption that there is a straight-line relationship between two variables. Linearity can be checked by inspecting the scatterplot between pairs of variables. Alternatively, violations of the assumption of linearity may be tested using residual plots, with the predicted values of the dependent variable plotted against the residuals. These plots are provided by programs such as SPSS for Windows upon request. Most techniques are relatively robust to moderate violations of this assumption, unless the relationship between two variables is clearly curvilinear (deviates markedly from a straight-line relationship). Violation of linearity does not invalidate the analysis but rather weakens the power of the statistical test to detect an effect (Tabachnick & Fidell, 2001). Special statistical procedures (e.g., polynomial regression) can be used to model non-linear relationships.

Homoscedasticity

Homoscedasticity is the assumption that the variability in scores for one variable is approximately the same at all values of another variable. The word 'homoscedasticity' is derived from the conjunction of the Greek words *homos,* which means 'the same', and *skedastikos,* which means 'able to spread or scatter'. In order to check for this assumption, researchers should generate bivariate scatterplots for each combination of variables and check to see that the scores do not disperse as they move up or down each scale. The shape of the scatterplot should roughly conform to an oval or cigar shape.

Many statistical techniques, including Pearson correlation coefficients and multiple regression, assume homoscedasticity. In statistical tests that compare the means of independent groups (e.g., *t*-tests, ANOVA), homoscedasticity is also an important assumption and is referred to as homogeneity of variance. Homogeneity of variance in *t*-tests/ANOVA can be tested through Levene's test of equality of variance.

Most techniques are relatively robust to moderate violations of homoscedasticity. If this assumption is seriously violated (known as heteroscedasticity), the researcher may consider transforming the dependent variable in different ways (square root or logarithm) to see if one of those transformations makes the relationship more homoscedastic. However, it should be noted that this approach may create difficulties as the researcher's interpretation is confounded by the fact that it is based on the transformed scores. There are also versions of *t*-tests and ANOVA that do not assume homogeneity of variance (see Kline, 2004; Tabachnick & Fidell, 2001). Another option when comparing groups is for the researcher to adopt a more conservative alpha criterion (.025 for moderate heteroscedasticy and .01 for severe heteroscedasticity) for tests of statistical significance (Tabachnick & Fidell, 2001).

Absence of multicollinearity

Multicollinearity occurs when two (or more) independent variables are highly correlated. Highly correlated independent variables cause computational and interpretational problems in techniques such as multiple regression. One method of checking for multicollinearity is to examine the bivariate correlations. Tabachnick and Fidell (2001) have suggested that if two independent variables are correlated .70 or higher, they may suffer from multicollinearity. If two variables are highly related, this suggests that they are so similar that one should be dropped (the theoretically least defensible) or they should be combined in some way (Tabachnick & Fidell, 2001). In multiple regression, you can also examine the tolerances and Variance Inflation Factors (VIF) for evidence of multicollinearity. These two statistics measure the degree to which the variance in one independent variable is explained by the other independent variables. A tolerance $< .10$ or VIF > 10 may indicate multicollinearity (Kline, 2005).

Outliers
Outliers are extreme data points that can have a disproportionate influence on the conclusions drawn from most statistical techniques. Univariate outliers (extreme scores on a single variable) can be detected by examining histograms and frequency tables. In many cases, outliers are simply data entry errors that can be easily corrected. Statistics that can identify multivariate outliers (extreme scores on a set of variables) include the studentised deleted residual and Mahalanobis distance. Cook's distance allows an examination of whether outliers are influential cases. These cases can be deleted from the analysis if they appear problematic. Assuming the data are accurate, we believe the best approach is to run the relevant statistics with and without the outliers to see if they make any difference to the results. Another option is to transform variables with univariate outliers. Outliers often tend to be associated with non-normal distributions. A transformation will tend to improve the shape of the distribution and 'pull in' the outliers (Tabachnick & Fidell, 2001). A final approach for univariate outliers is to change the scores on the variable so that they are less extreme. Orr, Sackett, and Dubois (1991) assessed how researchers dealt with outliers. Their findings indicated that:

- researchers disagree as to the appropriateness of deleting data points from a study;

- researchers report greater use of visual examination of data than numerical diagnostic techniques for detecting outliers; and
- while outlier removal influenced effect size measures in individual studies, outlying data points were not found to be a substantial source of variance in a large test validity data set.

Reliability of measures

The researcher should check the reliability of measures for their sample. At minimum, researchers should report Cronbach alpha coefficients for all multi-item measures. Researchers may also need to construct composite or total scale scores by summing/averaging items on multi-item measures, including the reversal of any negatively worded items prior to this. These tasks are easily done in statistical packages such as SPSS for Windows (see Pallant, 2005). New scales developed for the study will need to be factor analysed prior to use to establish unidimensionality and construct validity. Factor analysis is a multivariate technique and is discussed in the next chapter.

Missing data

Missing data need to be avoided because they reduce sample size and are a source of error. Roth (1994) has recommended that:

- data collection instruments (e.g., questionnaires) be used that are easy to follow;
- rigorous follow-up occur of interviews and questionnaires to reduce the amount of missing data; and
- re-sampling occur of the cases with missing data.

While the above steps will reduce the amount of missing data, they will not eliminate it. Once missing data is greater than 10% of the sample, substantial problems arise in determining the best way to handle it. Five main techniques are used in statistical analysis to deal with missing quantitative data: listwise deletion, pairwise deletion, mean substitution, maximum likelihood, and multiple imputation.

Listwise deletion

In listwise deletion, any case with missing data will be deleted from the analysis in question. Listwise deletion is commonly used in multivariate techniques such as multiple regression and factor analysis. With listwise deletion, a very small percentage of missing data can drop out a large number of cases from the sample. This is why it is important for researchers to deal with missing data problems before they start any analysis. For example, with listwise deletion of survey data, the researcher is likely to be left with very little of the sample to analyse, as respondents usually have missing data. As a general rule, listwise deletion should be avoided. Not only does it result in the loss of an inordinate number of respondents and reduced power, but it also means that missing data on just one item (e.g., salary) loses that entire respondent, thus potentially biasing the sample.

Researchers are advised to examine the pattern of missing data to assess whether they are missing at random. If the pattern appears random and there are few cases with missing data, then listwise deletion may be an acceptable approach (Tabachnick & Fidell, 2001). Note that listwise deletion is often the default option in many statistics packages such as SPSS for Windows.

Pairwise deletion

Pairwise deletion removes cases only where they are missing in a particular relationship to be calculated. In other words, all available non-missing pairs of values are used to calculate the statistics. Like listwise deletion, it is commonly used in multiple regression and factor analysis. Although some researchers have identified potential computational problems with pairwise deletion, the method has the advantage over listwise deletion of removing fewer cases while still acknowledging the missing data, thus biasing the sample less, and provides more accurate estimates than mean substitution, discussed below (Roth, 1994; Roth, Campion, & Jones, 1996; Switzer, Roth, & Switzer, 1998).

Mean substitution

With mean substitution, the mean of a variable for the entire sample is substituted for missing scores on that variable. The problem is, the mean for the sample may not necessarily reflect how the individual case would have responded to the item. This method, therefore, leaves everyone in the sample with no missing data, but it can be inaccurate, depending on which variable is substituted. For example, it might not be best to substitute the average of absenteeism for a particular employee's absenteeism. Mean substitution may also cause attenuate variance as well as distorted intercorrelations between variables (Schafer & Graham, 2002). We do not recommend mean substitution.

Recently, two new approaches – maximum likelihood and multiple imputation – have been developed for dealing with missing data; they have considerable advantages over the conventional methods discussed above. Presented below is a brief summary of these techniques. Researchers are advised to consult Allison (2002) and Schafer and Graham (2002) for a detailed discussion.

Full information maximum likelihood method
The full information maximum likelihood (FIML) technique for dealing with missing data utilises the observed data to generate the best possible first-order moment estimates to describe the mean, and second-order estimates to describe the covariances, assuming that the data are missing at random. (See Allison, 2002, and Little and Rubin, 1987, for discussions of the causes of missing data.) With FIML, all available information about the observed data is used, including the means and variances, based on the available data points for each variable. This approach estimates the relevant parameters without requiring the researcher to fill in (impute) the data set. The advantages of this technique for dealing with missing data are: (1) it is based on the commonly known statistical properties of maximum likelihood (Allison, 2002; Roth, 1994); and (2) it often reduces bias due to non-response even when the missing-at-random assumption has not strictly been met (Little & Rubin, 1990). The drawbacks of this approach are: (1) it requires quite complex computational methods; (2) estimates are specific to the model being applied (Sinharay, Stern, & Russell, 2001); and (3) it deals with the missing data step during data analysis.

Multiple imputation
Multiple imputation (MI) is a procedure by which missing data are imputed (estimated) through a number of iterations to produce several different complete-data estimates of the parameters. The parameter estimates produced from each imputation are then combined to

provide an overall estimate of the complete-data parameter (i.e., the average), in addition to estimates of the standard errors (Newman, 2003). The advantages of multiple imputation are: (1) it incorporates random variation (Allison, 2002); (2) the imputations reflect missing data uncertainty as well as sampling variation (Schafer & Graham, 2002; Sinharay et al., 2001); (3) it deals with the missing data step entirely separate from the data analysis step (Collins, Schafer, & Kam, 2001); and (4) it produces estimates to complete the data set (Little & Rubin, 1987). A disadvantage of this technique is that preparation of raw data is required prior to the procedure being undertaken (Graham & Hofer, 2000). While the maximum likelihood approach for dealing with missing data is more appropriate for normally distributed continuous variables, multiple imputation can be utilised with nearly all statistical techniques (Allison, 2002).

Bivariate analysis

Following initial analyses, researchers may apply bivariate analysis to assess the relationship between two variables. Usually one variable is designated as the dependent variable and the other as the independent variable. Bivariate analysis can be used to answer simple research questions/hypotheses concerning two variables. However, bivariate analysis does not provide researchers with a means to answer more complex hypotheses or research questions. Multivariate analyses are required for these purposes.

The following bivariate statistical techniques are commonly used in management research.

Pearson product moment correlation coefficient

The relationship between two variables can be calculated using a correlation coefficient. There are many types of correlation coefficients. The one most commonly known in organisational research is the Pearson correlation coefficient (r), which is used to calculate the strength and direction of the linear relationship between two continuous variables, but which can also be used if one or both of the variables are dichotomous (Kline, 2005). The Pearson correlation coefficient ranges from −1 to 1, where 0 is no association and 1 represents perfect association. The direction (or sign) of the correlation can be positive (as one variable increases, the other variable also increases) or negative (as one variable increases, the other variable decreases). The researcher can also square r to obtain the proportion of shared variance; that is, how much the two variables overlap and have in common.

Pearson's correlation coefficient is a measure of linear (straight-line) association. It is important to examine a bivariate scatterplot to check if the variables are related in a curvilinear manner before using Pearson's correlation coefficient. A scatterplot can also identify outliers, which can distort the correlation coefficient. It is possible that two variables may have a close to zero linear relationship as measured by r, but display a strong non-linear association. If there is evidence of marked non-linearity, special statistics can be applied to model curvilinear association. There are other correlation coefficients for categorical variables (nominal and ordinal data) (see Kline, 2005). For example, Spearman's rank order correlation is a special case of r where both variables are treated as ordinal.

It is conventional to test if the correlation coefficient is significantly different from zero. This is done with a test of statistical significance. This test tells us whether there is enough evidence to reject the null hypothesis that the observed relationship is zero in the population from which the sample came. The researcher should first check the probability values associated with the correlation coefficient to determine whether the relationship is statistically significant or not ($p < .05$ or better – e.g., $< .01$); if the latter, it is called non-significant. Another option is to report a confidence interval for the correlation coefficient (see Smithson, 2005). The confidence interval can be used as a test of statistical significance and also provides useful information on the plausible values of the correlation coefficient in the population. Statistical tests of Pearson's correlation coefficients make the assumption that the variables are bivariately normal, but these tests are fairly robust provided there are no extreme outliers.

If statistically significant, the researcher should check the direction and magnitude of the correlation coefficient to gauge how strong or weak it is and whether it is a positive or negative association. Cohen (1988, 1992) suggested that, as a rule of thumb, $r = .10$ is a small effect size, $r = .30$ is a medium effect size, and $r = .50$ is a large effect size. However, Cohen cautioned that any evaluation of effect size requires judgement regarding the practical importance of the study effects within a given context.

When interpreting a correlation coefficient, be careful of not assuming that a correlation necessarily means the two variables are causally related. Correlation is only one of the conditions for inferring causality. Inferring casuality is always more a matter of the type of research design (e.g., experimental vs. field study) than of the type of statistical technique used.

Correlations coefficients are commonly reported in a matrix format. A correlation matrix is all the correlations between all the variables in your study – the dependent variables, independent variables, and control variables. When researchers construct a correlation matrix, it is conventional to report the statistical significance levels of the correlations. If data are missing, we recommend using pairwise deletion when constructing correlation matrices. Correlation matrices are used in three main situations:

1. to check for multicollinearity; that is, two independent variables are correlated .70 or more, giving an indication that they are highly related;
2. to determine whether demographic variables or other background variables that are not independent variables are correlated with the dependent variable; the researcher might then want to control for them in later analyses; and
3. to obtain an indication of the initial (zero-order) relationship between the dependent variable and each independent variable.

Whenever a correlation matrix is constructed, it should always include the dependent variable. The researcher can then see how related each independent variable is to the dependent variable at the bivariate level. Additionally, as a rule, researchers should always calculate the means and standard deviations for each variable in the correlation matrix (together with information on the sample size). The researcher needs to know the mean and standard deviation for each variable so that he or she can tell what level it is at and how spread its scores are. For example, are they all young and restricted in age? Is the amount of support they get from supervisors modest at best (near the mid-point of the response scale) and not very spread? In addition, researchers can also include in a correlation matrix the range (the maximum and minimum scores) for all variables.

Cross-tabulations and chi-square tests

When comparing two categorical variables, it is common to report data in the form of cross-tabulations (also called contingency tables). These tables show the frequency with which cases occur across two variables. To facilitate interpretation, percentages are usually reported. Variables with many categories are not appropriate for cross-tabulations. The analysis is usually conducted on nominal variables (unordered categories); however, it can also be used on ordinal (ranked) or even interval or ratio data provided there are only a few scores.

A chi-square test of independence can also be used to establish the presence of an association between two categorical variables. In a chi-square test of independence, the groups must be independent, meaning an observation can fall into only one group such as gender or industry type, or employer sector. In general, the lowest expected frequency should be 5 or more for a chi-square test to be valid (Kline, 2005). An alternative rule used by some researchers is that at least 80% of cells in the table should have expected frequencies of 5 or more (Pallant, 2005). If these assumptions are violated, it may be possible to combine categories if this is theoretically meaningful. A chi-square test of independence then tests whether there is sufficient evidence to reject the (null) hypothesis that the two variables are not related. For example, a researcher may wish to know if women are more likely to be employed in clerical and secretarial occupations than men, and if men are more likely to be managers, tradespersons, and labourers, from, say, the eight Australian standard occupational categories. To answer these questions, the researcher requires two variables to calculate a chi-square and this involves looking at their frequency in categories and determining whether these are the same for the two groups (e.g., gender and occupational categories).

If the chi-square test is statistically significant, the researcher must then examine the percentages to interpret the nature of the relationship. There are also useful correlation coefficients that summarise the information in cross-tabulation tables, including Phi (a variant of r for 2×2 tables) and Camers V (for larger tables). Smithson (2005) provides useful information on calculating effect sizes and associated confidence intervals for interpreting strength of association in cross-tabulation tables and chi-square analysis.

t-tests and one-way analysis of variance (ANOVA)

Often researchers want to compare if two groups are different. When researchers have a continuous dependent variable, they can test for differences on that variable between two groups by using a t-test for independent samples. A t-test for independent samples tells us whether there is a statistically significant difference in the means of the two groups. In other words, is there enough evidence given the sample at hand to reject the null hypothesis that the means of the two groups are equal. There is also a t-test for paired samples which can be used to compare the means for a sample tested on two different occasions – for example, intervention studies with a before and after assessment of the effect of an intervention.

Often one wants to compare the means of three or more independent groups. One-way between-groups analysis of variance may be used to examine the effects of levels of one independent variable on a continuous dependent variable. The independent variable is called a factor (e.g., the occurrence of performance appraisal) and is represented by a categorical variable with three or more groups (with two groups it yields the same result as a t-test). So, this technique is an extension of the t-test.

For example, one group may have had their performance appraised with a conventional technique (the experimental or treatment group) and the other not had their performance appraised, and a third might have had a new form of performance appraisal. Thus, the occurrence of performance appraisal is a factor with three levels. The dependent variable might be employee performance on the job. The ANOVA would test if the factor (the independent variable) was related to performance and if that relationship is statistically significant, using an F-test and significance levels. The means given for the groups would indicate which group had the better job performance. Thus, if the F-test was statistically significant, the researcher would inspect the means to see which of the three groups had the highest mean for performance. Special tests (called post hoc comparisons – e.g., the Tukey HDS test) can be used, once the F-test is statistically significant, to see which of the group means differ significantly from each other where there are three or more levels of the independent variable.

Both the t-test for independent samples and one-way between-groups ANOVA assumes the groups come from independent, normally distributed populations with the same variance. However, the tests are robust to moderate departures from normality, provided there no out-liers. To test the assumption of equal variance, we can use Levene's equality of variance test. If there is evidence of unequal variances, there is a version of a t-test for unequal variances. Similar procedures are available for one-way ANOVA (Pallant, 2005).

There are also measures of strength of association (effect size) for t-tests and ANOVA. Eta-squared is the most commonly reported and tells us what proportion of the variance in the dependent variable is explained by the independent grouping variable. According to Cohen (1988), a small effect size is an eta-squared of .01, medium is .06, and large is .14. Smithson (2005) has also provided information on calculating confidence intervals for common effect sizes in t-test and ANOVA.

The debate over statistical significance

We have spoken a lot about tests of statistical significance. Tests of statistical significance are inferential statistics and tell us the probability of a given effect (or one more extreme) assuming the null hypothesis is true (Kirk, 2001; Kline, 2005). In plain English, tests of statistical significance tell us if an effect is due to chance.

The null hypothesis tested is usually that there is no effect or a zero relationship. The statistical significance criterion (called alpha) is the probability of a Type I error – that is, rejecting the null hypothesis when it is true (Cohen, 1992). By convention, results of statistical tests are reported as statistically significant if their corresponding probability (p) values are equal to or less than the .05 significance level. A significance level (alpha) of .05 or smaller means that the null hypothesis is rejected no more than 5% (1 in 20) of the time when it is true (Tabachnick & Fidell, 2001).

Alpha sets the Type I error for a single test (Kline, 2005). When multiple significance tests are conducted, more stringent alpha levels are commonly applied. For example, a Bonferroni adjustment can be conducted to correct for the inflated Type I error rate that occurs when multiple tests are conducted. To do this, you simply divide your original significance level (alpha) by the number of tests you intend to conduct (e.g., .05/5 tests = .01; .01 is the adjusted alpha level for each individual test). However, the lower your level of alpha, the lower the statistical power to detect an effect (Kline, 2005). This can lead to an increased risk of a Type II error – not rejecting the null hypothesis when it is false. Given the relatively low statistical power of much management research (see below), there is some debate about the value of corrections such as the Bonferroni adjustment.

There has been a rigorous debate (see Cohen, 1994; Kirk, 1996, 2001; Kline, 2005) about whether tests of statistical significance really mean anything. However, they are the conventional method used to detect if there is an effect. Statistical tests are heavily influenced by sample size. But researchers need to understand that statistical tests provide no information on the size of the effect. Indeed, it is well known that in very large samples, potentially trivial effects will be statistically significant. Nor do statistical tests imply that the observed effect is of substantive or practical importance. The significance test merely indicates that the observed effect is not likely to have arisen from random sampling error or chance. That is all that can be gleaned from a statistically significant result. It is also important to understand that a non-significant result does not necessarily mean there is no effect, but only that one could not be detected with sufficient confidence given the sample at hand.

Despite their limitations, we believe tests of statistical significance are important tools for testing hypotheses in the context of sampling error. Statistical tests are useful aids in pattern recognition or signal detection (Wilkinson & TFSI, 1999). However, we strongly encourage researchers to report effect sizes, as these statistics give the practical meaningfulness of the magnitude of the relationship (Thompson, 1999). Effect size measures can assist in evaluating how 'important' our results are in a substantive sense (Kirk, 2001). One word of caution: While a large effect is more likely to be of substantive significance, it is also important to understand that so-called 'small effects' can also be judged to be of importance (Prentice & Miller, 1992).

When the dependent variable is scaled in meaningful units (e.g., IQ, number of deaths), an unstandardised effect size (e.g., a difference between two means) provides a useful measure of the magnitude of effect. However, when the units of measurement of the dependent variable have no familiar metric, a standardised effect size (e.g., correlation or standardised regression coefficient) is commonly reported (Wilkinson & TFSI, 1999). Kline (2005) has provided an excellent discussion of available standardised effect sizes for researchers to use.

To improve statistical reporting we also believe that researchers should, wherever possible, report confidence intervals for their statistical estimates. For example, confidence intervals can be easily calculated for correlation or regression coefficients. Programs such as SPSS for Windows can generate confidence intervals for basic statistics. It should be noted that confidence intervals convey the same information as a conventional test of statistical significance, but also much more. Confidence intervals provide an estimate of the range of plausible values within a given level of confidence (Kline, 2005). For example, if a 95% confidence interval for a correlation or regression coefficient excludes zero, then the result is statistically significant at the .05 level. But the confidence interval also contains information on the precision of the effect. In sum, confidence intervals are very useful in helping to determine if an effect is practically significant (Kirk, 2001).

Power and effect size

When using tests of statistical significance, it is important that researchers establish whether their data have sufficient statistical power to test their hypotheses. Power is defined as the long-term probability of rejecting the null hypothesis (Cohen, 1992). If statistical power is low, we run the risk of not identifying an effect when it actually exists (a so-called Type II error). Ideally, power should be set to at least .80 (Cohen, 1992). Mone, Mueller, and Mauland (1996) found that power analyses were not typically conducted, researchers perceived little need for statistical power, and power in published research was low. Their study also indicated that ANOVA has lower power levels than other techniques, and that low power is usually due to small sample sizes (too small to detect an effect of that size).

So, sample sizes need to be large enough to detect the minimum size of hypothesised effects. In management research, small to medium effect sizes are usually the norm. For example, correlation effects sizes are often seen in the .1 to .3 range. The smallest effects need the largest sample size to have sufficient power for detection. Using correlations as an example, when $r = .10$, the sample size must be 783 to have .80 power at the .05 level of statistical significance. This example highlights the importance of obtaining large samples in management research where the effect size is predicted to be small. It also demonstrates how impractical it may be in achieving such large sample sizes. However, for a large effect ($r = .50$), a sample size of only 28 is required for power of .80 at the .05 level. The corresponding sample size for a medium effect ($r = .30$) is 85.

Following Cohen (1992), there are three main determinants of statistical power:

1. the significance criterion (alpha), which is the probability of a Type I error – that is, rejecting the null hypothesis when it is true (alpha is usually set at .05 but may be lower – e.g., .01);
2. the sample size; and
3. the effect size, which reflects the magnitude of a phenomenon in a population; for example, the impact of the independent variable on the dependent variable.

Maxwell (2004) has argued that an important factor contributing to the persistence of underpowered studies is that most involve testing multiple hypotheses. He has suggested that while the power of any individual test might be low, the probability of obtaining a statistically significant result for at least one test, when the study involves tests of multiple hypotheses, may be quite large.

According to Maxwell (2004), power can be increased by:

- increasing sample size (consider undertaking a collaborative multi-site study if it is not feasible for a single researcher to obtain a large sample);
- collecting data longitudinally;
- improving experimental design efficiency;
- improving experimental control; and
- conducting meta-analyses, either excluding underpowered studies or including all studies but adjusting for the effects of possible

publication bias (i.e., studies obtaining non-significant results tend not to get published) to avoid unbiased estimates.

So, increasing sample size is only one way of increasing statistical power. Ideally, power analysis should be conducted before the data are collected to determine the required sample size. The difficulty with power analysis is in identifying plausible values of the effect size in the population. These values need to be derived from past research and theory. However, it is probably safe to assume that small to moderate effects are the norm in management research. Cohen (1988, 1992) has developed power analyses tables and formulae to calculate statistical power for most analytical techniques (correlation, multiple regression, ANOVA, t-test, chi-square). Software such as SPSS also provides tools for conducting power analyses.

Conclusion

Data need to be managed in order to be suitable for data entry prior to analysis. This requires that researchers inspect their data for problems such as errors and missing data or for other changes prior to data entry. The data coded and entered into the raw data file need to be as correct as possible, with as little missing data as possible. The data entry needs to be verified and all cases (e.g., respondents) need to have identification codes. Once entered, the data will need some initial preliminary work before attempting the data analysis to test the research questions and/or hypotheses. Frequencies will have to be checked for out-of-range scores on the variables and other anomalies addressed. Also, tests can be used to see if there are group or other differences that may need controlling in later analyses. Measures need to be checked for reliability and validity. Checks are needed to assess if the assumptions needed for the particular kind of data analysis have been met. Issues of statistical power and effect size are important considerations in interpreting research findings, and we believe confidence intervals are an effective reporting strategy. Once the initial/preliminary data analyses have been done, then the main techniques of analysis need to be chosen to test the research questions or hypotheses of the study. Researchers may apply bivariate analysis to assess the relationship between two variables. These analyses are not sufficient for more complex research questions/hypotheses. Multivariate analyses are usually required and are the subject of the next chapter.

References

Allison, P. (2002). *Missing data*. Thousand Oaks, CA: Sage Publications.

Cohen, J. (1988). *Statistical power for the behavioral sciences*. New York: Academic Press.

Cohen, J. (1992). A power primer. *Psychological Bulletin, 112*, 155–159.

Cohen, J. (1994). The earth is round ($p < .05$). *American Psychologist, 49*, 997–1003.

Collins, L.M., Schafer, J.L., & Kam, C. (2001). A comparison of inclusive and restrictive strategies in modern missing data procedures. *Psychological Methods, 6*, 330–351.

Graham, J.W. & Hofer, S.M. (2000). Multiple imputation in multivariate research. In T.D. Little, K.U. Schnabel, & J. Baumert (eds.), *Modeling longitudinal and multiple group data: Practical issues, applied approaches and specific examples*. Hillsdale, NJ: Lawrence Erlbaum Associates.

Kendall, M.G. & Stuart, A. (1958). *The advanced theory of statistics*. New York: Hafner.

Kirk, R.E. (1996). Practical significance: A concept whose time has come. *Educational and Psychological Measurement, 56*, 746–759.

Kirk, R.E. (2001). Promoting good statistical practices: Some suggestions. *Educational and Psychological Measurement, 61*, 213–218.

Kline, R.B. (2005). *Principles and practice of structural equation modeling*. New York: The Guildford Press.

Little, R.J.A. & Rubin, D.A. (1987). *Statistical analysis with missing data*. New York: John Wiley & Sons.

Little, R.J.A. & Rubin, D.A. (1990). The analysis of social science data with missing values. In J. Fox & J.S. Long (eds.), *Modern methods of data analysis* (pp. 374–409). Thousand Oaks, CA: Sage Publications.

Maxwell, S.E. (2004). The persistence of underpowered studies in psychological research: Causes, consequences, and remedies. *Psychological Methods, 9*, 147–163.

Mone, M.A., Mueller, G.C., & Mauland, W. (1996). The perceptions and usage of statistical power in applied psychology and management research. *Personnel Psychology, 49*, 101–120.

Newman, D.A. (2003). Longitudinal modeling with randomly and systematically missing data: A simulation with ad hoc, maximum likelihood, and multiple imputation techniques. *Organizational Research Methods, 6*, 328–362.

Orr, J.M., Sackett, P.R., & Dubois, C.L.Z. (1991). Outlier detection and treatment in I/O psychology. *Personnel Psychology, 44*, 474–486.

Pallant, J. (2005). *SPSS survival manual: A step by step guide to data analysis using SPSS for Windows (Version 12)* (2nd ed.). Sydney: Allen & Unwin.

Prentice, D.A. & Miller, D.T. (1992). When small effects are impressive. *Psychological Bulletin, 112*, 160–164.

Roth, P.L. (1994). Missing data: A conceptual review for applied psychologists. *Personnel Psychology, 47*, 537–560.

Roth, P.L., Campion, J.E., & Jones, S.D. (1996). The impact of four missing data techniques on validity estimates in human resource management. *Journal of Business and Psychology, 11*, 101–112.

Schafer, J.L. & Graham, J.W. (2002). Missing data: Our view of the state of the art. *Psychological Methods, 7*, 147–177.

Sinharay, S., Stern, H.S., & Russell, D. (2001). The use of multiple imputation for the analysis of missing data. *Psychological Methods, 6*, 317–329.

Smithson, M. (2005). *Statistics with confidence*. Thousand Oaks, CA: Sage Publications.

Switzer, F.S., Roth, L.R., & Switzer, D.M. (1998). Systematic data loss in HRM settings: A Monte Carlo analysis. *Journal of Management, 24*, 763–784.

Tabachnick, B.G. & Fidell, L.S. (2001). *Using multivariate statistics* (4th ed.). New York: Allyn and Bacon.

Tharenou, P. (1999). Is there a link between family structures and women's and men's managerial career advancement? *Journal of Organizational Behavior, 20*, 837–863.

Thompson, B. (1999). Why encouraging effect size reporting is not working: The etiology of researcher resistance to changing practices. *The Journal of Psychology, 133*, 133–140.

Wilkinson, L. & The Task Force on Statistical Inference (TFSI) (1999). Statistical methods in psychology journals: Guidelines and explanation. *American Psychologist, 54*, 594–604.

Chapter review questions

1   What are the three main stages in data analysis?
2   What is the purpose of each stage?
3   What are univariate, bivariate, and multivariate techniques of analysis?
4   What is the difference in purpose between univariate, bivariate, and multivariate analyses?
5   What are the different types of data?
6   What steps need to be taken to check for errors in data?
7   How do you describe the sample?

8   How do you check statistically for the characteristics of non-respondents?
9   What are properties of the data and assumptions underlying the technique(s) of analysis?
10   What do you do about missing data?
11   What is the purpose of a chi-square test?
12   What is the purpose of a t-test?
13   What is a Pearson product moment correlation?
14   What are correlation matrices, and why do you have them?

11 Quantitative data: Multivariate data analysis for answering research questions and hypothesis testing

Objectives

At the end of this chapter you will be able to:

- *list the techniques of multivariate analysis most used in management research and describe their purposes;*
- *summarise the purpose of common techniques of multivariate analysis, including: multiple regression, moderated regression, mediated regression, multivariate analysis of variance, and structural equation modelling;*
- *explain why multivariate techniques of analysis are needed for management research;*
- *list the general steps in hierarchical regression, moderated regression, and mediated regression; and*
- *interpret a regression analysis.*

CONTENTS

Analysing data: Multivariate analyses	221
Techniques of multivariate analysis	221
Meta-analysis	240
Conclusion	245
References	246
Chapter review questions	248

Analysing data: Multivariate analyses

This chapter will discuss multivariate statistical techniques that can be used to test research questions and/or hypotheses as they were set up in the research design. For example, correlational field surveys are often analysed using multivariate statistical techniques. Alternatively, a researcher may have run a field experiment in which he or she had a treatment group and a control group (e.g., one trained group and one untrained group) and measured the dependent variables both before and after the intervention for both groups. He or she would use statistical techniques to compare the groups for evidence of an effect.

As a precursor to analysing data to test hypotheses or answer research questions, the researcher is strongly advised to examine studies similar to his or her own (on the topic or a closely related one) and determine how those data were analysed. This provides the opportunity to model the analysis on those that have been used in the research area and extend them if necessary.

Techniques of multivariate analysis

Multivariate analysis assesses the relationships among three or more variables. There are several multivariate techniques. Tabachnick and Fidell (2001) have described almost all of these techniques and their text is a useful resource when undertaking multivariate analyses. Grimm and Yarnold (1997) have provided a less technical explanation for most of the multivariate techniques. The main techniques, and references to articles or texts that explain each technique in detail, are listed below.

- multiple regression (Wampold & Freund, 1987), including mediator and moderator regressions (Baron & Kenny, 1986; Lindley & Walker, 1993);
- discriminant analysis (Betz, 1987);
- logistic regression (Wright, 1997);
- multivariate analysis of variance, including with covariance (MANOVA, MANCOVA; Haase & Ellis, 1987; Porter & Raudenbush, 1987);

- factor analysis – both exploratory and confirmatory (Fabrigar, Wegener, MacCallum, & Strahan, 1999; Ford, MacCallum, & Tait, 1986; Henson & Roberts, 2006; Hurley, Scandura, Schriesheim, Brannick, Seers, Vandenberg, & Williams, 1997; Tinsley & Tinsley, 1987);
- structural equation modelling (MacCallum & Austin, 2000; Fassinger, 1987; Harris & Schaubroeck, 1990; Kelloway, 1996);
- multi-level modelling (Raudenbush & Bryk, 2002); and
- meta-analysis (Durlak, 1997; Fried & Ager, 1998; Hunter & Schmidt, 2004; Rosenthal & DiMatteo, 2001).

It is important to note that none of the multivariate techniques of analysis listed above prove causation. They are all correlational in nature. Cause–effect interpretations have more to do with the research design than the analytical technique. Moreover, even the methods of analysis that imply directions of paths to effects, such as structural equation modelling, do not convey information about causal relations in the data. An experimental design is the strongest for making causal inferences. As stated previously, in correlational field (survey) studies, the minimum requirements needed to make any plausible inferences are a strong theoretical basis, longitudinal data to establish temporal precedence, and methods of analysis that help to control for other (potentially confounding) variables.

The following is a brief discussion of some of the most common multivariate techniques used in management research.

Multiple regression

Multiple regression is employed when researchers want to know the extent of the relationship of two or more independent variables with a dependent variable, usually taking into account other variables, especially controls. It is one of the most popular multivariate techniques used in management research.

Multiple regression uses several independent variables, called the predictor variables, to assess the extent of their relationship simultaneously with a single dependent variable, the criterion variable. The aim of this analysis is to determine how much of the variance in the dependent variable is predicted by the independent variables and which of the independent variables is most predictive.

Ordinary least squares regression, the most common form of multiple regression analysis, is a linear technique using a least squares estimation procedure. It requires a continuous dependent variable. Hence, it should not be used with a dichotomous dependent variable, such as turnover, when logistic regression should be used (see below). There are also regression techniques for ordinal dependent variables (e.g., ordered probit models) (Tabachnick & Fidell, 2001).

In multiple regression, independent variables can be continuous or dichotomous. Dichotomous independent variables are acceptable because, with only two values, they can only have a linear relationship with the dependent variable (Tabachnick & Fidell, 2001). Hence categorical independent variables with three or more categories (e.g., marital status) must be coded into a series of dichotomous variables. These dichotomous variables are usually coded as 0 or 1 and are called dummy variables. To avoid multicollinearity, the number of dummy variables used in the regression is one less than the number of groups for that variable. More detail on coding categorical variables can be found in Tabachnick and Fidell (2001).

The proportion of variance in the dependent variable, predicted or explained by the set of independent variables in the regression model, is indicated in a statistic called Multiple R^2. This statistic informs researchers about the predictive power of the regression model. In a small sample (say $N < 100$), the adjusted Multiple R^2 should also be reported as it gives a better estimate of the population effect size.

To interpret the direction and magnitude of the relationship of any independent variable with the dependent variable, researchers usually examine the standardised (i.e., data that have been converted to z scores with a mean of zero and a standard deviation of one) regression (beta) coefficient. The beta coefficients allow researchers to compare variables measured on different scales. Which independent variables are statistically significant is indicated by the probability levels of the associated beta coefficients, which are calculated from t-tests. Usually only statistically significant coefficients are interpreted (e.g., $p < .05$ or better). (Note that confidence intervals can also be calculated for regression coefficients – see Kelley & Maxwell, 2003). A statistically significant regression coefficient indicates that the relationship is significantly different from zero in the population from which the sample came. The direction (positive or negative) of the beta coefficient informs the researcher about the direction of the relationship. The magnitude of the relationship (effect size) is then inspected to assess how 'important' the variable is in predicting the dependent variable. It has a unique contribution, because the effect of the other independent variables on the dependent variable has been controlled in the equation. Therefore, the advantage of multiple regression is that when it calculates the regression coefficient for an independent variable, it is at the same time removing (called partialling or controlling) the effects of the other independent variables. Consequently, the researcher is able to assess the unique effect or relative contribution of that independent variable on the dependent variable, uncontaminated by the other predictor variables.

Several assumptions underlie multiple regression, which include:

1. *Normality of the dependent variable.* Regression is robust to moderate violations of normality, provided there are no outliers. If the dependent variable is seriously non-normal, an appropriate transformation is recommended.
2. *Linearity of relationship between the dependent variable and each independent variable.* Special regression procedures (e.g., polynomial regression) can be used to model non-linear relationships.
3. *Homoscedasticity (homogeneity of variance).* This means the dependent variable scores have the same dispersion/variability around the regression line through them, meaning they have equal spread. Regression is robust to moderate violations of homoscedasticity. A transformation of the variables is often recommended to address serious heteroscedasticity.
4. *Independence.* Each case should be independent of one another. This is a critical assumption for statistical tests to be accurate. If the data have a hierarchical structure (e.g., employees within work teams), multi-level regression techniques may be appropriate (see Tabachnick & Fidell, 2001).

The assumptions of regression can be partially checked by examining the distribution of the dependent variable and bivariate scatterplots, or through examination of the residuals (the difference between observed and predicted dependent variable scores) after running an initial regression. For example, if normality is present, the residuals will be normally distributed. See Tabachnick and Fidell (2001) for details on assessing assumptions for multiple regression.

Although not an assumption of regression as such, the independent variables must not be multicollinear. According to Tabachnick and Fidell (2001), the best option for addressing multicollinearity is to delete one or more redundant variables from the regression equation, or to combine them in some way (e.g., a composite score). See the previous chapter for more information on how to deal with multicollinearity.

Ideally, a researcher should conduct a power analysis before the data are collected to determine the required sample size for a multiple regression (Maxwell, 2000). The aim is to gather the smallest number of cases to have reasonable statistical power to detect an effect (Tabachnick & Fidell, 2001). Other researchers have recommended minimum sample size rules. Stevens (1996) recommends that at least 15 cases per independent variable are needed, although some researchers are prepared to have a minimum of five cases per independent variable. These rules of thumb must be treated with caution given the low statistical power of much management research to detect effects. To minimise sample loss in regression analysis, it is recommended to use either pairwise deletion for missing data or one of the more advanced techniques discussed in the previous chapter.

Types of multiple regression

There are a number of different types of multiple regression. The most common type is called standard (simultanenous) regression. In standard regression, all the variables are entered simultaneously. This is appropriate for testing many simple models. Each independent variable is examined in terms of its 'unique' predictability of the dependent variable after controlling for all the other independent variables in the equation. Two other types of multiple regression are stepwise and hierarchical regression.

Stepwise regression
In stepwise regression, the program will first enter the predictor variable that most explains the dependent variable. Then, after its effect is removed, the predictor variable that next most explains the criterion is

entered, followed by the variable that explains the third-largest amount of the variance (if there is any left to remove), and so on. Thus, only the variables that significantly explain the dependent variable will be entered. Some variables will therefore not be entered. Stepwise regression is essentially a 'fishing expedition', which capitalises too much on chance and therefore should not be used for hypothesis testing (Thompson, 1995).

Hierarchical regression analysis
In hierarchical (also called sequential) regression, the researcher chooses variables to be entered in blocks or steps, according to a theory or logic. For example, a researcher might want to test the effect of being motivated to attend training on participating in training and development, separate from all other effects. First, the researcher would enter demographic variables (e.g., age, sex, marital status, etc.) in a block to partial out their effects and equalise respondents on them. Then, simultaneously, in the next step he or she would enter job and industry variables (e.g., managerial level, occupational level, organisational size, employer category) to partial out the effects of job and organisation and neutralise respondents on them. Following this, in step 3, the researcher would simultaneously enter work environment variables (e.g., supervisor's support for training, barriers to training, and company training policies) to remove organisational effects. Then, finally, in step 4, the researcher would enter motivation to attend training to determine whether it has a unique effect, above and beyond all the previous variables. This is called an incremental effect. It is possible to test, at each step, the increment in variance explained by the addition of that step (R^2) and to obtain an F-test, calculated for the increment in variance, to see if the increases are statistically significant at each step. In order to examine whether motivation counts, the researcher would check whether the last increment in variance and the variance for the total equation are statistically significant, as well as the direction and magnitude of the beta coefficients at each step.

Moderated/interaction regression analysis: The 'when' test

Two special cases of multiple regression exist – moderated regression and mediated regression – and Lindley and Walker (1993) have provided a clear, short, and easy-to-read explanation of these two types of test. In moderated regression analysis (see Aguinis, 1995), the researcher is attempting to examine whether a third variable influences the strength and/or direction of the relationship between the independent and dependent variables. The relationship between two variables varies as a function of a third variable, labelled a moderator. Thus, moderated regression analysis tests *when* the relationship between two variables is strongest (Lindley & Walker, 1993). The moderator interacts with the independent variable to predict the dependent variable. Although most moderated regression models have only one variable acting as a moderator, it is possible to have more than one moderator. First, the researcher needs to be clear about what the dependent variable is. Then, he or she needs to decide what the independent variable is. Finally, the researcher is required to decide what the moderator variable is (the 'when' variable). These choices are made on theoretical grounds. Thus, moderated regression analysis is used when researchers want to know if another variable affects the relationship between the independent and dependent variables. For example, the relationship might be higher under one condition than another (men vs. women; the public sector vs. the private sector).

In terms of the steps in conducting moderated regression, first the interaction term between the independent variable and the moderator variable is calculated. To calculate the interaction, a researcher simply multiplies the two variables together. This is called a product term and represents the interaction effect. To avoid multicollinearity, researchers are advised to transform the independent and moderator variables by either subtracting individual scores from the mean for the variable – called centring – or converting them to standardised (z) scores (z-scores are by definition centred). By multiplying the two (centred or standardised) scores together, it is possible to determine whether their systematic variation is related to the change in the dependent variable (e.g., job dissatisfaction will predict absenteeism from work more for women than men). An interaction (moderator) effect is indicated if the product term is statistically significant, with the independent and moderator variables also included in the equation. An interaction effect can also be tested by entering the product (interaction) term as a separate step in a hierarchical regression. The addition of the interaction term should be statistically significant in terms of the increment in variance explained above and beyond a model without the product term

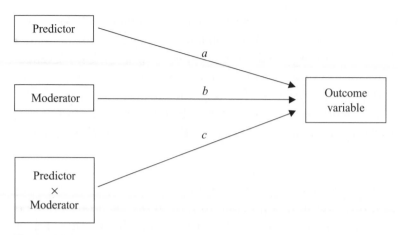

Figure 11.1 The moderation model

included. Tabachnick & Fidell (2001) recommend that if a standard-ised solution is desired for moderated regression, researchers should standardise (z score) all variables, including the dependent and inde-pendent variables, prior to forming the product term and interpret the resulting unstandardised coefficients as the betas. This procedure will generate correct standardised (beta) coefficients for the product term(s) in moderated regression models. The moderator model is pre-sented in Figure 11.1. Note that there are three paths that lead to the outcome variable: the impact of the predictor on the outcome variable (path *a*), the impact of the moderator variable (path *b*), and the inter-action (product) of the predictor variable and the moderator variable (path *c*).

Following identification of a statistically significant interaction, it is useful to plot the effect in order to interpret it. In the example above, the effect can be plotted for men and women on the same graph in order to identify the difference in the lines. The plots that are drawn show how the lines between job satisfaction and absenteeism arise when they are separately plotted for men and women. The Y-axis would be absenteeism (the dependent variable) and the X-axis could be split into high job satisfaction and low job satisfaction. The plots help to inter-pret the effect; however, in this example, with a dichotomous mod-erator variable, the researcher could also just interpret the effect by simply splitting the sample into men and women and re-running the regression analyses. The researcher would then inspect the strength of the regression coefficient for men and that for women in the two equations. Interaction plots can also be drawn where the independent and moderator variables are both continuous. See Tabachnick and Fidell (2001) for details on plotting interaction effects.

Mediation analysis: The 'how' test

The purpose of mediation analysis (Baron & Kenny, 1986) is to examine whether an independent variable leads to another variable (the mediator), which then transmits the effects of the independent variable to the dependent variable. Thus, the effect of the independent variable on the dependent variable is mediated/transmitted by another variable. Although mediation analyses can involve more than three variables, the present discussion focuses on models with only three variables. The most common way to test for mediation is to use multiple regression. An alternative for testing more complex mediation models is to use structural equation modelling, which is discussed below.

Baron and Kenny (1986) have stated that three steps need to be carried out in order to test for a mediator effect. These tests can be conducted using standard or hierarchical regression. The three steps for mediation are:

1. Regress the mediator variable on the independent variable (path a), because they need to be related (statistically significant) if the mediator really does mediate the independent variable.
2. Regress the dependent variable on the independent variable (path c) because in the Baron and Kenny model they need to be related (i.e., the regression coefficient needs to be statistically significant) if the independent variable could have its influence mediated by another variable.
3. Add the mediator variable to this last equation (path b). To test this, run a regression analysis with both the independent variable and the mediator predicting the dependent variable. What should happen, if the mediator completely transmits the effect of the independent variable on the dependent variable, is that now the regression coefficient for the independent variable is no longer statistically significant (path c), because all of its effect is removed by going

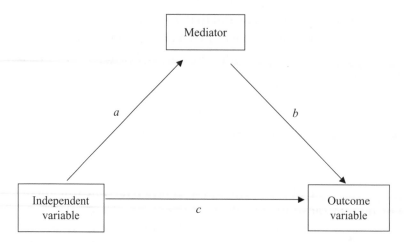

Figure 11.2 The mediation model

through the mediator variable. Note that the mediator must be statistically significant in this equation, after controlling for the independent variable. If the mediator is statistically significant and the independent variable is now no longer significantly different from zero (when it was in step 2), then there is a full or complete mediator effect. It is possible to have a partial mediator effect, where the regression coefficient for the independent variable goes down in magnitude, but is still statistically significant (James & Brett, 1984).

Logistic regression analysis

Logistic regression is a technique that is used when the dependent variable is a categorical variable with two or more categories. The most common form of logistic regression is used with a dichotomous variable (two categories). This is called binary logistic regression. In circumstances when the dependent variable has two categories (e.g., turnover, did not turnover), researchers should not use multiple linear regression as described previously, because a dichotomous dependent variable will not meet the assumptions of ordinary least squares regression. In logistic regression, the independent variables can be categorical or continuous. Logistic regression coefficients can be used to estimate odds ratios for each of the independent variables in the model.

A researcher can also conduct a hierarchical logistic regression analysis where variables are entered in steps/blocks and can calculate chi-square-based tests to indicate if those steps significantly add to the prediction of the dependent variable, over and above the variables already in the equation. Researchers can also enter interaction terms and test for moderator effects. Logistic regression does not provide an overall variance-explained figure as in R^2 for multiple regression, but there are 'pseudo' R^2 measures of the predictive power of the model available (Tabachnick & Fidell, 2001).

Finally, there is a form of logistic regression that can be used with a dependent variable with three or more categories. (This is called multinominal logistic regression and is discussed in advanced statistics books – for example, Tabachnick and Fidell, 2001.)

Discriminant analysis

Logistic regression analysis has essentially taken the place of discriminant analysis in management research. In situations where the dependent variable has two categories, researchers are advised to use logistic regression as it is more flexible and, unlike discriminant analysis, does not have any distributional assumptions (e.g., multivariate normality).

Discriminant analysis (see Betz, 1987, for a description) tests whether two or more groups (e.g., men and women; private sector vs. public sector) differ on a set of variables. The groups should be mutually exclusive. It is a multivariate technique because there are multiple variables on which the groups are simultaneously contrasted. When the comparison is occurring, the effect of any variable estimated has the effect of all other variables partialled from it. Discriminant analysis provides a test, overall, of whether the two groups are different (the squared canonical correlation which indicates how much variance is explained) and produces one or more discriminant functions that differentiate the groups.

Discriminant analysis is useful for building a predictive model of group membership based on observed characteristics of each case. The procedure generates a discriminant function (or, for more than two groups, a set of discriminant functions) based on linear combinations of the predictor variables that provide the best discrimination between the groups. The functions are generated from a sample of cases for which group membership is known; the functions can then be applied to new cases that have measurements for the predictor variables, but have unknown group membership.

The results of this analysis indicate which combination of interdependent variables can significantly differentiate the groups, as well as the relative strength of the variables for differentiation. The magnitude and significance level of the individual variables indicates whether each differentiates between the groups. These discriminant loadings are the structural loadings – the correlations between the predictors and the discriminant functions. They are a little complex to interpret, but basically there is also a group mean (the centroid), which indicates by its sign whether the structural coefficient is lower or higher for one of the groups, than for the other. There is also a test given of how well the two groups are predicted by a linear composite of variables, by providing the percentage accuracy of predicting membership in each group. In discriminant analysis, it is also possible to hold out a group where, after the weights for the initial group are calculated, they are applied to the hold-out group to see if they predict membership. Many of the statistical assumptions of multiple regression apply to discriminant analysis (see Tabachnick & Fidell, 2001).

Multivariate analysis of variance (MANOVA)

Another popular multivariate technique of analysis is MANOVA, which has factors (with two or more levels) and two or more dependent variables. As mentioned previously, the acronym 'ANOVA' stands for 'analysis of variance' and MANOVA stands for 'multivariate analysis of variance'. (See Haase and Ellis, 1987, for a description of MANOVA.) ANOVA and MANOVA are usually applied to test experimental or quasi-experimental designs. These techniques test for whether the levels of the independent variable, or variables, affect the dependent variables. The way the technique does this is by comparing the means for the dependent variables across levels. The factors are usually tested as main effects (their independent effects) and in interaction (how they vary together – the 'when' test). Thus, the main effects of the factors and interaction effects between them are tested on the dependent variables.

For example, a researcher may wish to test whether respondents perform better after the introduction of a performance appraisal program than before, as in Tharenou (1995). If there is one dependent variable (e.g., performance), he or she would use ANOVA. However, in cases where there is more than one dependent variable, MANOVA would be used to analyse the data if the dependent variables were correlated. After having conducted the MANOVA to determine whether the overall test was significant, the researcher would then undertake univariate ANOVAs, run on one dependent variable at a time.

MANOVA assumes the dependent variables are related (positively or negatively), but does not perform as well with very highly positive-correlated variables (Tabachnick & Fidell, 2001). In MANOVA, there is an overall F-test to see if the overall test is statistically significant for the main and interaction effects for the analysis. Then, if they are statistically significant, the researcher would inspect the ANOVA results for each separate dependent variable to see the nature of the effect, as described in the previous paragraph.

The researcher can also partial out the effects of controls, such as demographic variables, in ANOVA and MANOVA. This technique is called ANCOVA and MANCOVA, with the 'C' meaning that the effects of the covariates are partialled from the dependent variables. (See Porter and Raudenbush, 1987, for a detailed explanation of analysis of covariance [ANCOVA].) Thus, in MANCOVA, the reseacher can control for other variables as covariates (they have to co-vary or be related to the dependent variables, otherwise this would be redundant) and then determine whether the effects of the factors are significant, once these have been taken into account. The researcher could also conduct a stepdown analysis, in which the variables are entered sequentially, to test whether those entered last still explain the dependent variable.

Factor analysis

Factor analysis is a multivariate technique that reduces several measured variables to a smaller number of dimensions composed of those measures that are most related to each other. These smaller sets of dimensions are called factors (not to be confused with the term 'factor' as used in ANOVA). For example, having developed a new multi-item measure for a study, a researcher needs to subject the scale items to factor analysis to determine if they are unidimensional. The aim of factor analysis in scale construction is to examine the stability of the factor structure and provide information that will facilitate the refinement of a new measure (Hinkin, 1995).

The best brief description of factor analysis with advice for organisational research is by Ford, MacCallum, and Tait (1986), with another good description by Tinsley and Tinsley (1987). There are two main types of factor analysis: exploratory analysis and confirmatory analysis. Kelloway (1996) comments that researchers appear to be using these techniques appropriately, using exploratory analysis (e.g., principal components) in the initial stages of research and moving towards confirmatory analyses as the state of knowledge on particular topics increases.

Exploratory factor analysis
An exploratory factor analysis is undertaken for the purpose of analysing scores from a sample on several variables to see if they can be reduced to underlying dimensions. Those variables that are highly related to each other will load on one factor. The most common method of exploratory factor analysis in organisational research is *principal components analysis (PCA)* with orthogonal rotation (Hinkin, 1995). Although, according to some methodologists, it is not strictly a method of factor analysis, the goal of principal components analysis is to arrive at a relatively small number of factors (technically called components) that will extract most of the total variance from a relatively large set of variables. Many analysts recommend *principal axis factor analysis*, which extracts as few factors as possible that can explain common (shared) variance; the variance shared by the variables. In any method of factor analysis, the first factor extracted explains the most variance, the second factor the second most variance, and so on. A researcher may not be interested in deriving scales from the smaller factors if they do not explain much variance.

Rotation is used to arrive at a clearer picture of the factor structure. There are two types of rotation usually used. The first, *orthogonal rotation* (e.g., varimax), assumes the factors resulting are not correlated to each other. The second type, *oblique rotation* (e.g., oblimin, promax), assumes the factors may be related in some way, and allows the factors that emerge to be correlated (a more realistic assumption for many constructs). Although orthogonal rotations are easier to interpret, oblique rotations are now becoming more commonly reported in the literature (Henson & Roberts, 2006; Tabachnick & Fidell, 2001).

To find the number of factors to rotate, two methods are commonly used. The default method used by the software program is to rotate *eigenvalues greater than one*, the Kaiser criterion (Cattell, 1958; see Kim & Mueller, 1978). It is the most commonly used method for determining the number of factors for rotation (Hinkin, 1995). An eigenvalue represents the amount of variance explained by a factor. However, extracting eigenvalues greater than 1 may give a researcher a lot of factors (overestimation). Hence, the other technique, called Cattell's *scree test*, is used to determine the number of factors to rotate. Pallant (2005) provides more information on methods for finding the optimal number of factors to rotate.

A researcher needs to interpret each final factor and give it a name or label. A factor is interpreted by determining what its highest loading variables are, and from those variables getting an idea of what the factor represents. A researcher should interpret factor loadings greater than at least .40 (Ford, MacCallum, & Tait, 1986), although some people interpret factors by loadings greater than .30. If there are variables with negative signs (loadings), they are still very important in understanding what a factor represents. What does not load is also important for interpreting and labelling the factor. For oblique rotation, a researcher usually interprets the pattern matrix, but the structure matrix provides additional information on the factor structure. A researcher also needs to report the intercorrelations between the obliquely rotated factors. Variables that load on more than one factor do not clearly represent one factor or another. A way to deal with these is to drop them and repeat the analysis without them.Exploratory factor analysis is generally applied to a matrix of Pearson correlations derived from the raw data. It is, therefore, assumed that the relationships among the variables are linear. When scales are being factor analysed, the variables are usually the individual items (e.g., Likert items) treated as continuous measures.

A score can be derived for a multi-item scale from a factor analysis in one of two ways. A researcher can take those items on the factor whose loadings are greater than the chosen cutoff (e.g., .40) and sum or average the scores for those items. That gives the items a unit weighting (weight of 1). It is important for a researcher to remember to reverse any negative signs when these items are summed/averaged. Also, if the items are measured on different scales, the data can be standardised (z scored) prior to constructing the scale score. The other way is to use the factor analysis program to derive a weighted score for each factor. Either way is suitable for deriving the multi-item scale, although Cattell (1958) states that the unit weightings for the items that 'loaded' are just as good.

To conduct an exploratory factor analysis, between five and ten cases (e.g., respondents) per item are recommended in order to get a stable solution (Guadagnoli & Velicer, 1988). Thus, if a researcher has a 20-item scale, he or she requires between 100 and 200 cases. Hinkin has advocated as a minimum a sample size of 150 observations for scale development procedures. Tabachnick and Fidell (2001) suggest that it is ideal to have at least 300 cases for factor analysis; however, in practice, 150 cases are probably sufficient for many applications. When conducting a factor analysis, it is best to use pairwise deletion for missing data in order to avoid loss of data. It is always best to obtain the mean, standard deviations, and number of cases for each variable. This tells the researcher if there is anything wrong or to note. It is possible that the researcher had a large sample, but that the factor analysis was only on a third of it because of missing data. The researcher may therefore have a very small sample-to-variable ratio, meaning the results are not likely to be very stable.

Confirmatory factor analysis

Confirmatory factor analysis is conducted to assess if the factor the researcher hypothesised a priori is supported by the data. So, assume that a researcher has measured employees' aspirations for management. There is a desired aspirations measure composed of 13 items, and an enacted aspirations measure composed of six items (Tharenou & Terry, 1998). If this were an exploratory analysis, the researcher would put all 19 into a principal components factor analysis and hope that the 13 items loaded on one factor and the six items loaded on the other.

However, in confirmatory factor analysis the researcher allows the 13 supposedly desired aspirations items to load on one factor and gives them a weight of zero to load on the second factor. On the second factor the researcher loads the six items on that factor and zero to each load on the first factor. This is the two-factor model (e.g., Tharenou & Terry, 1998). The researcher can also test a one-factor model in which all items load on only one factor (e.g., Tharenou & Terry, 1998) to see if that model fits better or worse than the two-factor model. If the two-factor model fits better than the one-factor model (e.g., .90 versus .86 with less error; Tharenou & Terry, 1998), then the two constructs are supported. More information on confirmatory factor analysis can be found below in the section on structural equation modelling.

Structural equation modelling
Structural equation modelling (SEM) is used to test complex models in which there are one or more independent variables and one or more dependent variables (Tabachnick & Fidell, 2001). In simple terms, SEM is a combination of multiple regression and factor analysis. At the same time as the structural regression model is estimated, a measurement (factor) model is usually estimated. Harris and Schaubroeck (1990), Fassinger (1987), and MacCallum & Austin (2000) have provided very good general explanations of this technique, while Kelloway (1996) has presented an excellent description of its use in management research. Kline (2005) provides a comprehensive introduction to structural equation modelling.

Essentially, structural equation modelling tests an interactive path model of several independent variables to one or more dependent variables. The independent variables are connected to each other via paths, often including mediator (intervening) variables. In other words, the independent variables can directly affect the dependent variable, or indirectly do so through influencing mediator variables that then impinge on the dependent variables.

The conceptual model being tested is theoretically based to explain the dependent variable. Several indicators, called the observed variables (e.g., scale items or other scores), measure each construct in the model. The observed variables are usually assumed to be continuous, but dichotomous independent variables may be used. The underlying constructs that they are each supposed to measure are called the latent variables or factors. Structural equation modelling tests the fit of the model to the data, while at the same time modelling measurement error (unreliability) in the observed variables. Unlike other statistical techniques in the General Linear Model, a strength of SEM is that measurement error is taken into account by factor models for each latent variable being estimated at the same time as the model is fitted to the data. Hence, structural equation modelling estimates the size of the paths (similar to standardised regression coefficients) in the model and the general fit of the model to the data, while correcting for measurement error.

It is best if the measurement model can be conducted when the substantive relationships (the theoretical model) are being tested. However, many researchers, as reported by Kelloway (1996), use a two-stage approach in which a measurement model, obtained by conducting confirmatory factor analysis, is fitted separately and prior to estimating a full latent variable structural model. In these situations the confirmatory factor analysis is used to obtain a good factor structure that fits well. This factor structure (the observed variables mapping on to the latent factors) is then used to test the structural path model.

With respect to confirmatory factor analysis, at least three indicators per latent variable is perhaps the most commonly cited rule and researchers simultaneously estimating measurement and structural models tend to apply this criterion (Kelloway, 1996). Harris and Schaubroeck (1990) have recommended that researchers include no more than 20 observed variables or measured indicators in total. The implication of having too many observed variables for underlying factors (i.e., latent variables) is that often a fit cannot be obtained. However, structural equation modelling is also carried out with single observed variables (e.g., a single item measure, or an averaged multi-item score) whose measurement error can be corrected by an estimate of reliability (e.g., an alpha coefficient or estimate of test–retest reliability). This latter approach is useful in smaller samples. (See below for rules on sample size.) Note, however, that some researchers do not advocate the use of structural equation modelling with total scale scores unless they are used as multiple indicators of latent variables.

Often, researchers test competing SEM models to assess which fits the data best. This is usually a model with full paths, according to the theoretical basis of the study and models under that main model (i.e., nested models), with fewer paths, based on theoretical propositions (e.g., Tharenou, 1993). Then, the fit of the models is compared to determine which model fits the data best. Kelloway (1996) found that approximately two-thirds of the studies in management tested competing models to determine which obtained the best fit to the data. Harris and Schaubroeck (1990) have recommended applying structural equation modelling in the following circumstances:

- when there is substantial past empirical research and theory on the relationships in the model;
- when there are 20 or fewer measured indicators (of the latent constructs); and
- when multiple models can be compared from the same data set to estimate the best model.

As with multiple regression, moderator effects can also be tested in structural equation modelling, although the procedures are somewhat more complex (see Kline, 2005). When the moderator is a categorical variable, a multi-group analysis can be performed. First, the total model is tested. Then a moderator test may be undertaken by splitting the sample into the two groups (Kelloway, 1996) that represent the high and low effects of the moderator (e.g., above the median on motivation, or below the median on motivation; or by two groups such as men and women). For example, a model may have been tested on the total sample to explain managerial advancement from a number of individual and situational variables (Tharenou, Latimer, & Conroy, 1994). It may have been, though, that the explanations differed for men and women. Thus, the sample would then be split into two and the model would be re-run on both samples. Then, the fit of the total model would be compared to the fit of the subgroup models to determine whether the total model had a worse fit than the subgroup models (see Tharenou et al., 1994). If this were the case, a moderator effect would exist.

Structural equation modelling is a large sample technique and shares the distributional and related assumptions of multiple regression (Kline, 2005). With respect to sample size, although it is possible to conduct structural equation modelling with as few as 150–200 cases, researchers are advised to obtain larger samples. According to Kline (2005), a sample size of 200 could be considered large and a sample under 100 cases is generally not suitable. Kelloway (1996) reported that the mean size of samples, in management studies generally, was over 600 respondents, but that for the latent variable models the mean sample size was smaller ($M = 278$).

Meta-analysis

Meta-analysis is a technique that summarises the empirical results from many studies of the same phenomenon to arrive at the 'true' empirical relationship between the variables. It is the statistical procedure that has led to the capacity to accurately summarise the results of many studies, of the same relationship, meaningfully. There are usually corrections to the individual statistics from separate studies that need to be made before combining them. These corrections are:

- sampling error, because the sample sizes were too small;
- range restriction on the variables, especially the criterion or dependent variable, because the scores for applicants on the selection devices were too restricted; and
- lack of reliability of the measures.

The technique is applied where many studies have examined the same relationship; for example, that organisational commitment is negatively related to intent to leave. The statistic used to measure the relationship is the Pearson correlation coefficient. Meta-analysis basically involves the averaging of the correlation coefficient, for all the studies, to arrive at an average r. This technique can also be used to summarise the empirical evidence from studies that have examined group differences on the same phenomenon; for example, that groups that have specific difficult goals perform better than groups that have vague, easy goals. It is a d-test in which the differences between means for experimental and control groups are averaged after correction.

As an example, the evidence for the predictive validity of selection devices for selecting successful future performers will be considered (Tharenou, 1994).

Earlier summaries of the evidence reviewing the efficacy of selection devices, such as ability and other tests to predict job performance, had concluded that selection devices were not generally applicable. For example, the prediction of job performance by intelligence may be represented by a validity coefficient, a Pearson correlation coefficient, which can range from −1.00 to +1.00. These appeared to be erratic; for example, being .00 in one study (i.e., no relationship), .21 in another (i.e., a very weak, meaningless relationship), .43 in a third (i.e., a positive useful relationship), −.24 in a fourth (i.e., a weak relationship but in the wrong direction), and .56 in a fifth (a positive, useful relationship). These predictions were thought to have varied because of the type of job, the organisation, or other local circumstances. Hence, it was concluded that the validity of selection devices varied according to job type or organisation. In other words, the effectiveness of selection devices was considered situationally specific.

However, more recent summaries, of many hundreds of selection studies using hundreds of thousands of employees and most of the common selection devices, revealed a substantially different view. It has been shown that inadequacies in the research designs of the earlier studies had resulted in these fluctuating validity coefficients (Tharenou, 1994). When these inadequacies were corrected, it was shown confidently that selection devices were generally applicable. The main flaws in the earlier research designs, which led to incorrect conclusions being drawn, were that sampling error occurred because the sample sizes were too small (less than 400), the scores for applicants on the selection devices were too restricted, and the devices were unreliable (Tharenou, 1999). The effect of such problems was previously not known, and so faith was placed in individual validity coefficients. Due to the limitations of the procedures for summarising results across studies, erroneous conclusions had been drawn by those earlier reviews and the few studies that had been done in many areas.

It has now been shown conclusively that the validity of a selection device cannot be estimated from one validity coefficient, from a single study (Guion, 1987). Rather, the average of validity coefficients from many studies is required (Guion, 1987, 1990; Guion & Gibson, 1988). As previously stated, inadequacies in the research designs of the earlier studies had resulted in these fluctuating validity coefficients. The main flaws that led to incorrect conclusions were as follows:

- Sampling error occurred because the sample sizes were too small.
- The scores for applicants selected by the selection devices were too restricted.
- The devices were less than perfectly reliable.

Steps for meta-analysis

Meta-analysis is conducted in a series of steps, and these steps shall be demonstrated by reference to the prediction of job performance by applicant interview scores. The approach described here is based on the method by Glass, McGaw, and Smith (1981); however, there is substantial variation in the way that meta-analyses are conducted (see Hunter & Schmidt, 2004; Rosenthal & DiMatteo, 2001). Due to the fact that many organisational studies assess the extent of the relationship between the study variable by calculating correlation coefficients, that will be the technique explained here. This procedure involves the seven steps described below.

1. The researcher decides the exact relationship for which he or she wants to determine the real magnitude of the coefficient. The example here is that organisational commitment is negatively related to intent to leave. This is calculated in studies by Pearson's r. First, all of the published or unpublished studies are found which have examined the relationship. The researcher should find every study that has been done using that statistic of that relationship.
2. The studies are inspected to see if they have used a common statistic in assessing the relationship between organisational commitment and intentions to leave. It is the simple Pearson correlation coefficient, the most commonly used statistic for assessing the extent of the relationship between any two variables.
3. Determine the correction factors that have to be used with each correlation coefficient. The three corrections are for: the size of the sample; the reliability of the criterion (turnover intentions) and the predictors (organisational commitment); and the restriction in range of scores on turnover intentions and organisational commitment. Single-validity coefficients have been conclusively shown to be subject to sampling error, unreliability, and range restriction.

Therefore, very large differences result in individual correlation coefficients that occur only because of statistical artefacts. The average of the distribution of validity coefficients is thus required (Guion, 1987). The figures used to provide the statistical corrections are obtained from the already existing data. They are most accurate when there are many previous studies with large samples on which to base the estimates.

4. The correction factors are applied to each correlation coefficient, from each study. Each validity coefficient, of each study, is corrected for its statistical limitations. When 75% or more of the variability in coefficients is found to be caused by these errors, situational specificity is rejected and validity generalisation is upheld (Guion, 1990; Guion & Gibson, 1988).

5. The average is then taken of the corrected *r*s. That is, the corrected extent of the true relationship between the two variables. It might be .32. Hence, after each study correlation coefficient has been corrected, an average is taken of all of the coefficients.

6. It is also possible to assess the confidence that can be placed in the average by calculating a 90% confidence interval (Guion, 1990).

7. The studies are then considered for any moderator variables. There may be ways the studies could be split so that the corrected *r*s can be averaged for subsamples. The studies may be split by any group variables (e.g., sex, industry, organisation size), or any other way, as long as there are sufficient studies to do this. For example, the studies on commitment were separated into those that measured attitudinal commitment and those that measured calculative commitment. Hence, any other variables that might affect the relationship are considered. By splitting the corrected correlation coefficients into two groups, average validity coefficients can be calculated for the studies in each group. If the averages differ for the two groups, then the relationship is moderated by the moderator variable. Many moderator variables can be examined by dividing up the studies in this way. Greater confidence can be placed in the results when a large number of studies are included in each separate subgrouping. The *r*s for the subsamples are then calculated to determine whether there is a moderator effect. It has been found that the *r* for attitudinal commitment and intent to leave is approximately .5, whereas the *r* for calculative commitment and intent to

leave is about .2. Thus, there is a contingency effect operating here. This same calculation is usually conducted for every type of demographic variable in the studies, in order to determine whether the correlations vary for different groups. If they do, the relationship is said to be moderated.

Confidence in results from meta-analyses

Certain criteria need to be satisfied in order for a meta-analysis to be considered robust (Guion, 1987, 1990; Guion & Gibson, 1988; Hunter & Hunter, 1984). These criteria are outlined below.

1. The number of studies averaged must be large – ideally in the order of hundreds of studies, particularly if subgrouping is to occur in order to test moderator effects. Otherwise, the meta-analysis can overcorrect.
2. The corrections should be based on large sample sizes. Otherwise, the estimates for corrections are not accurate and the corrected coefficients are dramatically different from the uncorrected coefficients and are hence suspect.
3. The relationship between the predictor (e.g., the interview) and criterion (e.g., performance) must be linear or Pearson's correlation coefficient cannot be correctly used.
4. If the corrected coefficients are very different from the uncorrected coefficients, after multiple corrections to overcome the three errors, the researcher needs to investigate how this occurred. It may be that, in practice, this same low reliability would occur, causing a practical problem.
5. Moderator effects should be tested so that it is known whether the validity is greater for certain groups or circumstances. Important moderator variables have been found in many relationships.
6. If different meta-analyses of the same relationship produce different results, then the meta-analyses will need inspection to assess the reasons. According to Tharenou (1994), this has occurred in the following circumstances:
   • The meta-analyses have not included the same studies.
   • The meta-analyses are actually using different constructs, although they may seem the same.

- One meta-analysis included a single, very large study with many validity coefficients. When excluded from the study pool, the conclusions drawn can be different.
- One meta-analysis used only published studies and the other included unpublished studies. Unpublished studies often have non-significant results and may therefore provide a more conservative estimate. However, unpublished results, from very large studies, can also provide a less conservative estimate. Meta-analyses should include as many unpublished studies as possible.
- One meta-analysis used multiple coefficients, from within each study, and the other chose to use only a single coefficient from each study. Often studies assess the same relationship by many correlation coefficients. Some meta-analyses average, or count, all of these for a study. Other meta-analyses may only choose one of the coefficients, usually at random, to include in the meta-analysis. It is best to use only one coefficient from each study (Guion, 1990) to avoid capitalising on chance.

Conclusion

This chapter has introduced multivariate techniques of analysis to test research questions and/or hypotheses of a study. Multivariate techniques include multiple regression, as well as its speciality types such as moderated or mediated regression, logistic regression, discriminant analysis, MANOVA, factor analysis, and structural equation modelling. Techniques such as multiple regression consider several independent variables at a time and allow the unique effect of a particular independent variable, as well as its relative importance compared to the other independent variables, to be examined. Before carrying out any multivariate analysis, researchers should ensure that there is a theoretical basis for their research question, as the results can only be meaningful in terms of a theoretical approach. This chapter has also provided a brief introduction to meta-analysis, which is a technique that summarises the empirical results from many studies of the same phenomenon to arrive at the 'true' empirical relationship between the variables.

References

Aguinis, H. (1995). Statistical power problems with moderated multiple regression in management research. *Journal of Management, 21,* 1141–1158.

Baron, R.M. & Kenny, D.A. (1986). The moderator–mediator distinction in social psychological research. *Journal of Personality and Social Psychology, 53,* 237–248.

Betz, N.E. (1987). Use of discriminant analysis in counseling research. *Journal of Counseling Psychology, 34,* 393–403.

Cattell, R.B. (1958). Extracting the correct number of factors in factor analysis. *Educational and Psychological Measurement, 18,* 791–838.

Durlak, J.A. (1997). Understanding meta-analysis. In G. Grimm & P.R. Yarnold (eds.), *Reading and understanding multivariate statistics.* Washington, DC: American Psychological Association.

Fabrigar, L.R., Wegener, D.T., MacCallum, R.C., & Strahan, E.J. (1999). Evaluating the use of exploratory factor analysis in psychological research. *Psychological Methods, 4,* 272–299.

Fassinger, R.E. (1987). Use of structural equation modeling in counseling psychology research. *Journal of Counseling Psychology, 34,* 425–436.

Ford, J.K., MacCallum, R.C., & Tait, M. (1986). The application of exploratory factor analysis in applied psychology: A critical review and analysis. *Personnel Psychology, 39,* 291–314.

Fried, Y. & Ager, J. (1998). Meta-analysis. In C.L. Cooper & I.T. Robertson (eds.), *International Review of Industrial and Organizational Psychology* (pp. 123–158). New York: John Wiley & Sons.

Glass, G.V., McGaw, B. & Smith, M.L. (1981). *Meta-analysis in social science research.* Beverly Hills, CA: Sage Publications.

Grimm, G. & Yarnold, P.R. (1997). *Reading and understanding multivariate statistics.* Washington, DC: American Psychological Association.

Guadagnoli, E. & Velicer, W.F. (1988). Relation of sample size to the stability of component patterns. *Psychological Bulletin, 103,* 265–275.

Guion, R.M. (1987). Changing views for personnel selection research. *Personnel Psychology, 40,* 199–213.

Guion, R.M. (1990). Personnel assessment, selection and placement. In M.D. Dunnette & L.M. Hough (eds.), *Handbook of industrial and organizational psychology* (pp. 327–398). Palo Alto, CA: Consulting Psychologists Press.

Guion, R.M. & Gibson, W.M. (1988). Personnel selection and placement. *Annual Review of Psychology, 39,* 349–374.

Haase, R.F. & Ellis, M.V. (1987). Multivariate analysis of variance. *Journal of Counseling Psychology, 34,* 404–413.

Harris, M.M. & Schaubroeck, J. (1990). Confirmatory modeling in organizational behavior/human resource management: Issues and applications. *Journal of Management, 16,* 337–360.

Henson, R.K. & Roberts, J.K. (2006). Use of exploratory factor analysis in published research. *Educational and Psychological Measurement, 66*, 393–416.

Hinkin, T.R. (1995). A review of scale development practices in the study of organizations. *Journal of Management, 21*, 967–988.

Hunter, J.E. & Hunter, R.F. (1984). Validity and utility of alternative predictors of job performance. *Psychological Bulletin, 96*, 72–98.

Hunter, J.E. & Hunter, R.F. (2004). *Methods of meta-analysis*. Thousand Oaks, CA: Sage Publications.

Hunter, J.E. & Schmidt, F.L. (2004). *Methods of meta-analysis: Correcting error and bias in research findings* (2nd ed.). Thousand Oaks, CA: Sage Publications.

Hurley, A.E., Scandura, T.A., Schriesheim, C.A., Brannick, M.T., Seers, A., Vandenberg, R.J., & Williams, L.J. (1997). Exploratory and confirmatory analysis: Guidelines, issues, and alternatives. *Journal of Organizational Behavior, 18*, 667–683.

James, L.R. & Brett, J.M. (1984). Mediators, moderators, and tests for mediation. *Journal of Applied Psychology, 69*, 307–321.

Kelley, K. & Maxwell, S.E. (2003). Sample size for multiple regression: Obtaining coefficients that are accurate, not simply significant. *Psychological Methods, 8*, 305–321.

Kelloway, E.K. (1996). Common practices in structural equation modeling. In C.L. Cooper & I.T. Robertson (eds.), *International Review of Industrial and Organizational Psychology* (pp. 141–180). New York: John Wiley & Sons.

Kim, J.O. & Mueller, C.W. (1978). *Introduction to factor analysis*. Beverly Hills, CA: Sage Publications.

Kline, R.B. (2005). *Principles and practice of structural equation modeling*. New York: The Guilford Press.

Lindley, P. & Walker, S.N. (1993). Theoretical and methodological differentiation of moderation and mediation. *Nursing Research, 42*, 276–279.

MacCallum, R.C. & Austin, J.T. (2000). Applications of structural equation modeling in psychological research. *Annual Review of Psychology, 51*, 201–226.

Maxwell, S.E. (2000). Sample size for multiple regression. *Psychological Methods, 4*, 434–458.

Pallant, J. (2005). *SPSS survival manual: A step by step guide to data analysis using SPSS for Windows (Version 12)* (2nd ed.). Sydney: Allen & Unwin.

Porter, A.C. & Raudenbush, S.W. (1987). Analysis of covariance: Its model and use in psychological research. *Journal of Counseling Psychology, 34*, 383–392.

Raudenbush, S.W. & Bryk, A.S. (2002). *Hierarchical linear models*. Thousand Oaks, CA: Sage Publications.

Rosenthal, R. & DiMatteo, M.R. (2001). Meta-analysis: Recent developments in quantitative methods for literature. *Annual Review of Psychology, 52*, 59–82.

Stevens, J. (1996). *Applied multivariate statistics for the social sciences* (3rd ed.). Mahway, NJ: Lawrence Erlbaum.

Tabachnick, B.G. & Fidell, L.S. (2001). *Using multivariate statistics* (4th ed.). New York: HarperCollins.

Tharenou, P. (1993). A test of reciprocal causality for absenteeism. *Journal of Organizational Behavior, 14*, 269–290.

Tharenou, P. (1994). Selecting the right people for the right jobs: The utility of personnel selection. In K.M. McConkey, H.J. Wilton, A.J. Barnier, & A.F. Bennett (eds.), *Australian psychology: Selected applications and initiatives* (pp. 69–80). Melbourne: Australian Psychological Society.

Tharenou, P. (1995). The impact of a developmental performance appraisal program on employee perceptions in an Australian federal agency. *Group and Organization Management, 20*, 245–271.

Tharenou, P. (1999). Is there a link between family structures and women's and men's managerial career advancement? *Journal of Organizational Behavior, 20*, 837–863.

Tharenou, P., Latimer, S., & Conroy, D.K. (1994). How do you make it to the top? An examination of influences on women's and men's managerial advancement. *Academy of Management Journal, 37*, 899–931.

Tharenou, P. & Terry, D.J. (1998). Reliability and validity of scores on scales to measure managerial aspirations. *Educational and Psychological Measurement, 58*(3), 475–493.

Thompson, B. (1995). Stepwise regression and stepwise discriminant analysis need not apply here: A guidelines editorial. *Educational and Psychological Measurement, 55*, 525–534.

Tinsley, H.E.A. & Tinsley, D.J. (1987). Use of factor analysis in counseling research. *Journal of Counseling Psychology, 34*, 414–424.

Wampold, B.E. & Freund, R.D. (1987). Use of multiple regression analysis in counseling research: A flexible data analytic strategy. *Journal of Counseling Psychology, 34*, 372–382.

Wright, R.E. (1997). Logistic regression. In G. Grimm & P.R. Yarnold (eds.), *Reading and understanding multivariate statistics*. Washington, DC: American Psychological Association.

Chapter review questions

1   What are multivariate techniques of analysis? What is the difference in purpose between bivariate and multivariate analyses?
2   What is multiple regression?
3   What is moderated/interaction regression analysis: the 'when' test?
4   What is mediated regression analysis: the 'how' test?
5   What is logistic regression, and when is it used?
6   What is discriminant analysis, and when is it used?

7   What is multivariate analysis of variance (MANOVA)?

8   Under what conditions is MANOVA used?

9   How does MANOVA differ from ANOVA?

10   What is factor analysis, and when is it used?

11   What is structural equation modelling, and when is it used?

12   'Structural equation modelling combines some of the features of multiple regression and factor analysis.' Discuss this statement. How does SEM go beyond the combination of multiple regression and factor analysis?

13   What is meta-analysis?

14   Why is meta-analysis called a 'quantitative' literature review?

15   What does meta-analysis end up providing?

12 Content analysis

Objectives

At the end of this chapter you will be able to:

- *define content analysis and describe the broad approaches taken;*
- *identify the research designs where content analysis is used;*
- *outline the basic steps in content analysis;*
- *clarify how content analysis helps to answer research questions;*
- *differentiate between different types of content analysis;*
- *explain what grounded theory is;*
- *explain what pattern matching is;*
- *explain in general how computer-assisted software can assist in content analysis; and*
- *recommend how to increase reliability and validity in content analysis.*

CONTENTS

Analysing qualitative data: Content analysis	251
Content analysis	252
Specialist data analytic techniques	259
Other issues	262
Computer methods of content analysis	263

Reliability and validity in content analysis   267
Conclusion   269
References   269
Chapter review questions   271

Analysing qualitative data: Content analysis

Having collected his or her qualitative data, the researcher must analyse them to arrive at an answer to the research questions (or hypotheses). Qualitative data may take several forms, including, but not restricted to, material from interview transcripts, company/organisational and public documents, responses to open-ended survey questions, print media, observational notes, and archival/historical material. It can also include non-textual materials such as pictures and sound. The methods are not the same for each type, but content analysis, also called textual data analysis, will be described here as a basic technique for analysing qualitative data.

The types of research design where content analysis is used

Several types of research designs use qualitative data that need content analysis (e.g., Mossholder, Settoon, Harris, & Armenakis, 1995; Sommer & Sommer, 1991). As stated previously, some of the research designs use qualitative data alone, while others use it as part of a design, primarily employing quantitative data. The various research designs where qualitative data are used on their own, as well as those where qualitative data are used in conjunction with quantitative data, are outlined below.

Qualitative data may form the main method for answering research questions in the following types of situations:

- Qualitative data alone (e.g., data from in-depth interviews, company documents, observation field notes) may be content-coded *to answer research questions*. The outcome is *a narrative or a story*. The narrative presented, or story, can be from a realistic perspective – a direct matter-of-fact portrait – or in an impressionist way – choosing dramatic material to tell the story (see Creswell, 2003). There are also many other ways of presenting the narrative.

- Qualitative data may be used *to build theory* that explains a particular phenomenon.
- Qualitative data may be gathered in such a way that the research design *allows comparison* – for example, between a treatment group and a control group, but also across treatments (e.g., organisations, countries).
- Qualitative data may be used *to compare trends across time* (e.g., company documents, historical accounts) and then related to other constructs.

Alternatively, qualitative data may be used in a mixed-methods design. Here are some examples:

- Qualitative data (e.g., open-ended survey questions, interview illustrations) may serve as *alternative measures of focal constructs* – for example, to validate quantitative measures (e.g., questionnaire measures).
- Qualitative data may be analysed *to obtain scores that are then related to other data* (e.g., to scores from standard questionnaire scales, objective data from companies, etc.). The statistical relationships (e.g., correlations) are calculated to test relationships or differences (e.g., between organisations with different types of business strategies and the effect on managers' perceptions of the types of human resource management practices).
- Qualitative data may be used to *illustrate quantitative findings*. Creswell (2003) has provided information on how qualitative data may be used to illustrate other relationships, such as those found from quantitative data.

Content analysis

Content analysis has been defined as a technique for systematically describing the form and content of written or spoken material (Sommer & Sommer, 1991). Holsti's (1969, p. 14) definition of content analysis is sufficiently broad to cover the field: 'any technique for making inferences by objectively and systematically identifying specified characteristics of messages.'

The analysis can be of content, in terms of the specific topics/themes, or structure, in terms of the location in the text analysed. Some content analytic methods have formal quantification as their aim (e.g., content analysis may reduce qualitative data to numbers and subject them to statistical analysis), while other methods of content analysis are more interpretive (qualitative) in nature. Some methods of content analysis are inductive, deriving explanation/theory and future hypotheses from themes identified. Others are more deductive, assessing the data against prior theory and formal hypotheses. Some researchers restrict the term 'content analysis' to quantitative analyses of textual materials. The term is used here in the more generic sense for any technique that extracts thematic information from qualitative materials. The choice of analysis is contingent on the research question and on what is already known about the topic. If the goal is subjective understanding, exploration and/or generation of new insights/hypotheses, and there is little knowledge, the more interpretive styles are recommended.

Content analysis can be conducted manually or by computer. Until recently, the majority of content analysis undertaken in management research was conducted manually. Computer software is now available to assist in content analysis. These programs are discussed below. To conduct content analysis using computer software, the researcher still needs to determine the themes and categories and the words, phrases, and so on that represent them. Thus, the process outlined is often used irrespective of the technique that may follow.

Basic steps in content analysis

Creswell (2003) has provided a detailed method for content analysis. Specifically, he has outlined eight steps for coding qualitative material (adapted from Tesch, 1990). Researchers can also undertake the steps using computer software (see below). Creswell's eight steps for categorising data are presented below.

1. Get a sense of the whole. Read through all transcriptions carefully. Jot down ideas as they come to mind.
2. Pick one document. Go through the document and ask: 'What is this about?' Think about the underlying meaning, rather than the substance.
3. Do this for several documents and make a list of topics. Cluster together similar topics. Form these topics into columns that might be arranged as major topics, unique topics, and leftovers.
4. Now take this list and go back to your data. Abbreviate the topics as codes and write the codes next to the appropriate segments of the text. Try out this preliminary organising scheme to see whether new categories and codes emerge.
5. Find the most descriptive wording for your topics and turn them into categories. Look at reducing your total list of categories by grouping topics that relate to each other (e.g., you could draw lines between your categories to show interrelationships).
6. Make a final decision on the abbreviation (i.e., code) for each category and alphabetise these codes.
7. Assemble the data material belonging to each category in one place and perform a preliminary analysis.
8. If necessary, re-code your existing data.

(*Source*: J.W. Creswell, *Research design – qualitative, quantitative and mixed method approaches* (2nd ed.). Copyright 2003 by Sage Publications, Inc. Reprinted by permission of Sage Publications, Inc.)

As can be seen from the above eight steps, coding is one of the central processes in content analysis. Coding is the process by which categories are established. Put simply, coding involves assigning labels to segments or chunks of text (Miles & Huberman, 1994). The easiest way for the researcher to do this is to read all the material first to identify the main topics/themes and list them as they are found. Themes are then formed into larger categories. A category is simply a 'group of words with similar meaning or connotations' (Weber, 1990, p. 37). Categories that repeat themselves are best; however, less frequent categories still need to be used. Categories that overlap, or duplicate, one another can be combined. The list of categories must be comprehensive, covering all the categories, in order to be analysed.

Template approaches to content analysis

Both King (1994) and Miller and Crabtree (1992) have summarised different approaches to content analysis that can be used in analyses of qualitative data. One of the most popular approaches to categorising data referred to by these authors is template analysis (Crabtree & Miller, 1992). With the template approach, text is analysed through the use of an analysis guide or template, consisting of a number of themes or categories relevant to the research question(s). The template or codebook is open-ended and undergoes revision after encountering the text. The generation of the themes, patterns, and interrelationships is usually an interpretive, rather than statistical, process.

Template approaches vary in the extent to which the codebook is built upon existing knowledge (a priori) or is developed from the initial analysis of the data (a posteriori). The former allows for the testing of theory, whereas the latter allows for a more inductive analysis. In practice, template approaches are most commonly used where there is prior knowledge/literature to guide the process of coding data. Irrespective of the template, it is applied to the text to identify the meaningful units or parts. The units are behaviour or language units such as words or phrases. If the text reveals inadequacies in the template, modifications and revisions are made and the text is re-examined. The analysis then proceeds to an interpretive phase in which the units are connected into an explanatory framework consistent with the text. To facilitate the generation of the connections, matrices and tables may be used. These final connections form the reported outcomes.

King (1994) has suggested a six-step structure for developing a template for analysing interview data. The steps are as follows:

1. Two researchers code four full interview transcripts. The coding is compared and disagreements are discussed.
2. The same four transcripts are given to an expert panel who are asked to devise their own codes. The factors identified by the expert panel and the researchers are compared.
3. Researchers then code all the transcripts. New codes are discussed and added if necessary.
4. The codes are then clustered into a smaller number of higher-order codes.

5. Inter-rater comparisons are done on higher-order coding on a sample of respondents. Researchers' codings are compared and the statistical coefficient of agreement is calculated.
6. Modification is made to the higher-order codes and re-coding is done of all transcripts.

With this approach, the researcher applies a template over the text, which identifies units that result in the categories being revised. (The categories are then checked back with the text.) The categories are then interpreted to determine connections, which are then verified against the text (Miller & Crabtree, 1992).

In summary, the steps involved in template analysis are

Template → Apply to text → Identify units → Revise categories (also return to text to reapply categories) → Interpretively determine connections → Verify → Report

Editing approaches to content analysis

Miller and Crabtree (1992) have outlined an approach to content analysis called editing analysis. Editing analysis involves an 'interpreter' rearranging the text in order to identify meaningful segments that stand on their own and relate to the purpose of the study. Researchers using editing analysis enter the text much like an editor searching for meaningful segments, cutting, pasting, and rearranging until the reduced summary reveals the interpretive truth. Due to its strong interpretive and inductive focus, editing analysis is more appropriate than template analysis if the goal is subjective understanding, exploration, and/or generation of new insights/hypotheses, and where there is little knowledge.

The editing techniques have a cyclical quality as subjective interpretations emerge from analysis of a particular theme or category and then are repeatedly compared with the original data. Similar to template analysis, in editing analysis the report comes from the text. However, the text is engaged without a template and meaningful units or segments that are relevant to the study are sought. These units are then organised into categories. The interpreter then explores the categories and determines the patterns and themes that connect them. From this point on, the process of editing analysis unfolds in a similar way to template analysis (Miller & Crabtree, 1992). The steps involved in editing analysis are:

Interpreter or editor → Apply to text → Identify units → Develop categories (return to apply to text) → Interpretively determine connections → Verify (return to text) → Report

Interpretation of the results of content analysis

The end product of content analysis is a set of categories summarising the data at hand. These categories must be interpreted in order to answer the research question(s). This can be done by *relating the categories to each other in some way to tell a story in relation to the research question(s)*. This story should not be just a description or simple summary of the data. Rather, it could involve a central construct to be explained and other variables that appear to explain or influence it. The researcher attempts to identify and describe patterns and then attempts to understand and explain them.

Creswell (2003) has suggested the following strategies in presenting the results of content analysis: that *long, short, and text-embedded quotes* should be varied; conversation can be scripted; text information can be presented in tabular form; category names can be used for informants; quotations can be intertwined with the researcher's interpretations; and indents can be used to signify quotes. The interested reader is referred to the book by Miles and Huberman (1994) in which an extensive range of strategies for displaying the results of qualitative analyses is outlined.

Lee (1999) has argued that three processes are commonly applied to determine theme content. These processes are:

1. Check on the agreement of the theme's content among *two or more researchers*. Multiple opinions on the same data by different people are obtained.
2. Check on the agreement by triangulation, which attempts to show agreement among *different sources or types of data*. For example, the themes agreed may be submitted back to participants to check on their coding judgements.
3. Check on *salient events or themes* (milestones, precipitating events) that dominate, stand out, or are crucial from individuals' stories or interviews.

The results of content analysis can sometimes be effectively communicated in numerical form. For example, researchers may count the frequency of categories to get a sense of their prevalence. The use of formal quantification is common in so-called quasi-statistical methods of content analysis. According to King (1994), a quasi-statistical approach seeks to turn textual data into quantitative data that can be manipulated statistically. In this approach, the content analyst selects a suitable unit of measurement – single words, phrases, or themes – and then categorises each unit found. Statistical analyses can then be carried out comparing individuals or groups on the distribution of units across categories. In this technique, the content analyst searches the text for words or semantic units or themes based on a codebook. The words and themes are then sorted into categories and manipulated statistically. This approach to content analysis has three distinguishing features: objectivity, systematisation, and quantification. As a result of these features, content analysis can be used for hypothesis testing, generalisation, and the separation of the data from the researcher for the sake of objectivity.

Examples of content analysis

Chang and Tharenou (2000) used content analysis and found 29 themes/topics that arose in data asking managers of multicultural work groups about the skills and behaviours needed to manage such groups. The 29 topics could be collapsed into five broad categories (called competencies) of cultural empathy, learning on the job, communication skills, general management skills, and personal style. The category of cultural empathy, for example, had the six themes/topics of cultural awareness, cultural understanding, respecting other values, treating people as individuals, using different perspectives, and experience in other cultures. The category of communication skills comprised listening, open door policy/being open, clear expression, non-verbal nuances, and knowing other languages.

Taber (1991) has provided an example of how to content analyse open-ended questions in a survey regarding job satisfaction. The four steps in the example by Taber – *analysis, induction, interpretation,* and *verification* – are discussed below.

1. **Analysis step**

   Each written passage was analysed into *unitary themes* and a verbatim transcript of each theme was written on a card. Each card contained only one theme, although the theme could run to more than one sentence or expression.

2. **Inductive step**

The researcher and one other analyst separately sorted and re-sorted the theme cards to develop *categories* inductively, in such a way that all the cards in one category had some commonality and were different from those in other categories. The passages were content analysed separately for the satisfaction and dissatis-faction responses. (These had been the two open-ended questions asked.)

3. **Interpretive step**

Categories were redefined and combined as a function of discus-sions between the two analysts until there was agreement on a *final set of categories*. By following that process, a number of categories were produced. (The same categories were useful for classifying the satisfying and dissatisfying themes.) The categories exhausted the types of themes present in the transcripts and were of sufficient level of abstraction *to classify uniquely all themes using a manageable number of categories*.

4. **Verification step**

To verify the clarity of the category definitions and their distinc-tiveness from one another, the theme cards were *again sorted sep-arately* by the analysts into the re-drafted interpretive categories. Where there was disagreement between the analysts, the card was discussed and then placed uniquely in one category or another.

Specialist data analytic techniques

Grounded theory

The technique of grounded theory, developed originally by Glaser and Strauss (1967), is often applied in the analysis of qualitative data – for example, in-depth interviews. Applications of grounded theory must result in the *generation or elaboration of explicit theory* (Lee, 1999, p. 173). The phrase 'grounded theory' often refers loosely to theory that is developed from a set of data. Grounded theory is defined here as a systematic approach to generating substantive theory that relates to a particular phenomenon of interest (Creswell, 2003). This theory typically consists of a series of hypotheses or propositions that emerge from the analysis. Strictly speaking, grounded theory is not a technique of analysis, but an entire approach to gathering and analysing data. A detailed description of grounded theory can be found in Strauss and Corbin (1998).

Grounded theory is largely an inductive technique, but in practice it combines both deductive and inductive logic in an iterative process of gathering and analysing data, to build substantive theory. Creswell (2003) has argued that the two primary elements of grounded theory are the constant comparison of data with emerging categories of information, and theoretical sampling to address similarities and differences in the data.

The defining characteristics of the general method of grounded theory are briefly set out in Lee (1999, p. 173) and in detail in Strauss and Corbin (1998). In summary, grounded theory:

- results in the creation of clear, explicit, and testable theory;
- verifies its resulting hypotheses throughout the course of the research project using an iterative methodology;
- uses open, axial, and selective coding methods to categorise the data; and
- systematically checks the conceptual development and relationships with the data. This involves the constant making of comparisons, systematic asking of generative and concept-related questions, theoretical sampling, systematic coding of procedures, suggested guidelines for attaining conceptual density, variation, and conceptual integration.

Lee (1999) has provided an example of how grounded theory is conducted. First, general themes are identified from several qualitative data sources. Hunches are developed; that is, data-based hypotheses. Verification of these hypotheses is attempted in subsequent data collection and inspection. Ideas are then modified (revised hypotheses) based on the new data. Finally, verification occurs of the revised hypotheses on still new data (i.e., the method of constant comparisons). In summary, themes are induced about the processes involved within and between their theorised constructs.

Pattern matching

Pattern matching is a technique of analysis often used in case study research (McCutcheon & Meredith, 1993; Yin, 2003). Pattern matching is a useful technique for improving the validity of the causal conclusions reached by case study researchers. With pattern matching, the theoretical configuration of independent and dependent variables is compared, for each case, against the pattern of observed characteristics to determine if they correspond for each new case.

Pattern matching is more of a deductive approach to qualitative analysis. This approach allows the anticipation of a particular pattern of variables, phenomena, or outcomes, prior to data collection. The expected pattern derives from existing theory or a set of conceptual propositions. These anticipated data can occur within one case or across multiple cases. The pattern may be static or dynamic. With less formal models, the anticipated pattern can serve as a benchmark with which to interpret case data. With more formal hypotheses and theories, the anticipated pattern can serve to falsify or corroborate these a priori ideas.

According to Lee (1999, p. 78), the two steps involved in pattern matching are as follows:

1. An expected pattern must be specified among variables, events, or acts, or some other phenomenon of interest, before case data are collected. The expected pattern derives from a formal theory or set of less formal conceptual propositions.
2. The expected pattern is compared with subsequently collected empirical case data for its degree of fit.

Yin (2003) recommends the following steps in pattern matching:

- Search for patterns by comparing results with patterns predicted from theory or the literature.
- Conduct explanation building, looking for causal links and/or to explore plausible or rival explanations and attempt to build an explanation about the case.
- Conduct time-series analysis in which a change in a pattern is traced over time.

Other issues

The advantages of content analysis of existing documents

In content analysis, often use is made of material already available, such as public or other documents (e.g., company annual reports). Sommer and Sommer (1991) have stated that there are several advantages associated with conducting content analysis on existing documents, which are outlined below.

- When material is already available (e.g., company reports, mission statements, human resource management policies), content analysis is unobtrusive, with the researcher having no effect upon the material collected.
- The technique is suited to comparisons – for example, of trends over time or organisations.
- The technique allows for simultaneous application of quantitative and qualitative techniques.

Kabanoff and Holt (1996) and Kabanoff, Waldesee, and Cohen (1995) also explained the advantages of using content analysis. Their studies assessed organisational values through content analyses of annual reports, internal magazines, and mission statements. In relation to values, these authors have identified the following advantages of content analysis:

- It describes organisational values unobtrusively.
- It allows a systematic and quantitative approach to dealing with qualitative data.
- It combines qualitative and quantitative elements by quantifying data that are normally considered qualitative in nature.
- It measures organisational values over extended periods and for relatively large organisational samples. The analysis of documents is suitable for longitudinal research, which stems from the availability of different kinds of text over long periods of time.
- It uses naturally evoked verbal behaviour as the source of data on values.

Kabanoff and Holt (1996) pointed out that content analysis assumes that language reflects the phenomena that people and organisations perceive as being important, and that the relative frequency with which particular words are used is an indication of their cognitive centrality or importance. Kabanoff et al. (1995) stated that the assumption underlying the use of content analysis for measuring organisational values in company documents is that organisations leave traces of their distinctive value patterns in their documents, and that these traces can be observed and measured. Measurement is accomplished by counting the frequency with which different values are referred to in the text being analysed. Frequent references are interpreted as an indication of the importance or centrality of those values.

Computer methods of content analysis

Manual and computer methods of analysis are both used in management research to analyse qualitative data. Content analysis by computer software has certain basic approaches and principles. Wolfe, Gephart, and Johnson (1993) have discussed computer-facilitated qualitative data analysis in terms of text retrieval, text analysis, and database management. Computer-aided analysis of qualitative data should be used when the processing strengths of computer software coincide with the purpose for which the analysis is being conducted (Mossholder et al., 1995). The volume of material is important; for example, if there are 30 interviews, a researcher would likely use computer analysis. If there are ten, he or she may decide to conduct the analysis manually. The purposes of the research also determine how a computer-facilitated analysis is used.

Reid (1992) and Tesch (1990) have constructed practical guides to using computer-aided analyses of qualitative data. Often the data will be analysed by a computer program such as NVivo (QSR NVivo) or The Ethnograph. The data are qualitative in the sense that text is usually being analysed, although non-textual materials such as photographs may be used. For example, a researcher may ask respondents about selection and promotion processes in their organisation and ask open-ended questions regarding discrimination. In this example, software such as NVivo can be used to assist the researcher in coding and retrieving text around themes and categories related to discrimination. A useful feature of these programs is that overlapping and nesting of codes are allowed. This makes the process of coding materials faster and more efficient. It is important to understand that computer programs such as NVivo do not automatically code the data. The researcher must still do the work of reading and interpreting the text and determining the themes/categories in the data. The software, however, takes over the physical organisation of storing and retrieving data. Programs such as NVivo can also be used to search the text for selected words and inform the researchers of the frequency of their presence. To use these text searches, researchers still need to specify what it is they are looking for. Once all the codes are entered, the researcher can then search for selected codes, or retrieve combinations of codes, across all or a selected subset of interviews, for example. In NVivo, it is also possible to organise the results of coding into 'trees' or catalogues to facilitate retrieval of material and subsequent theoretical interpretation. An excellent introduction to NVivo can be found in Gibbs (2002).

Kabanoff and Holt (1996) carried out computer-assisted content analysis of company documentation for organisational values over two time periods (three years and two years). Sections were used of annual reports, company-wide internal magazines, mission statements or corporate-values statements, or any other organisation-wide documents, produced by organisations for distribution to employees, that referred to organisational goals and values. However, sections that were purely financial, technical, or descriptive were not used. The sections that were used included human resource management policies, statements of corporate philosophy, management overviews, CEOs' annual reports or letters to shareholders, and any human-interest stories. The steps in the content analysis, which was computer-aided, were as follows (Kabanoff & Holt, 1996, p. 208):

- The words in the text were analysed against words specified in a content dictionary. The dictionary consists of different meaning-categories with each category containing words that are held to refer to the value being measured. The dictionary can be a standard one available that assigns words to particular meaning-categories, with additions to the dictionary made up for the study, whereby categories are created for the specific purpose, using software. This presumably involved identifying sentences with the target values and deciding what words went with those values.

- The text analysis program scored each sentence according to whether it contained one or more of the dictionary categories. The sentence was the unit of analysis.
- The raw score frequencies for each organisational value were divided by the number of sentences analysed for each organisation, in each time period, to allow for differences in the amount of text. The scores were standardised within document type to cater for the fact that not all organisations had every type of document. The total value score across all document types was divided by the number of document types analysed for each organisation. The standardised value scores were calculated for each organisation that reflected the frequency with which it referred to each value in each time period.
- The values were then used to cluster organisations into different value types. The changes in values over time for each type were then determined statistically.

Essentially, Kabanoff et al. (1995) used the software program to check words in the text under analysis against the words specified in a content dictionary, which consisted in their case of meaning categories, each of which contained words that were held to refer to the value theme being measured. The text program rated each sentence according to whether it contained one, or more, of the dictionary categories.

Advantages and disadvantages of computer-aided text analysis

There are a number of clear advantages that are associated with the use of computer-aided text analysis (e.g., Kabanoff et al., 1995). These advantages include:

- an *objective count* of words/phrases/terms. This objective approach may be an important advantage where quantification of categories is desired. When researchers judge text, they may overestimate controversial issues or see what they want to see;

- *reliability* in terms of classification/measurement by the computer program, because the coding rules are always applied in the same way;
- *efficient coding*, as well as *flexibility* because of the ability to refine the dictionary as knowledge about the text increases and reapply it to the same or new text;
- *standardisation and comparability* across forms of data; and
- the fact that standard dictionaries can be used to enhance the *validity* of the analyses.

The following are the attendant disadvantages of using computer-aided qualitative analysis (Mossholder et al., 1995):

- Computer-aided analysis cannot reveal all of the complexities embedded within data. Some aspects of the data may be lost with key word counts and compilations, because they deal with the explicit aspects of data. Data may be forced into a framework that is computer manageable and that process reflected in interpretations of the data.
- The context stated may not be taken into account (although software such as NVivo can do this). Computer-aided analysis often decontextualises data. However, there is some dispute about whether human coders can better judge a word's meaning in context (see Kabanoff et al., 1995).
- There may be so much human intervention needed that it offsets the efficiencies of computer-aided qualitative analysis. For example, the text needs to be read by the researcher and the themes/categories decided by the researcher, along with the words for each theme/category. The researcher needs to decide what the program is searching for, and he or she may need to have an inter-rater reliability check, to assess if another researcher agrees with those themes and illustrative words.
- The process could just become 'word crunching' instead of 'number crunching', unless theoretical rationales provide a basis for the analysis.
- The researcher may become distanced from the data.

How to increase reliability in content analysis

Weber (1990) notes: 'To make valid inferences from the text, it is important that the classification procedure be reliable in the sense of being consistent: Different people should code the same text in the same way' (p. 12). Reliability is particularly important where quantification of text is desired. In content analysis, reliability may be established for the two phases outlined below.

1. *Deriving the categories.* If two (or more) people do not agree or see the same themes/categories in the data, they may not be reliable.
2. *Counting the categories.* If two people do not count the same number of categories, then reliability is lacking.

The categories used to code text must be reliable. This requires that two researchers who undertake content analysis of the same material arrive at similar results (Sommer & Sommer, 1991), whether by content analysing the material manually or deriving categories by computer software. Reliability is greatest when the coding categories are clearly stated and do not overlap (Sommer & Sommer, 1991). In order to develop the original categories for coding, more than one rater should be used so that inter-rater comparisons can be carried out. Statistical coefficients of agreement are calculated and, if low, the reasons for inter-rater agreement need to be decided and fixed. Co-researchers code blind without consultation with each other and calculate their agreement statistically (King, 1994). Following on from this, the co-researchers explore reasons for disagreements, decide on an adjusted coding, and then code new transcripts to assess their agreement (and adjust if necessary). Independent raters, not associated with the study, can also be used. Once the categories have been derived in a reliable way, then the material needs to be content analysed reliably. To increase reliability of the content analyst, analysts must be trained by providing them with a detailed explanation of the scoring system, and with practice in scoring material (with correct answers given to provide them with feedback).

Goodwin and Goodwin (1985) have developed a simple formula to determine inter-rater reliability between two content analysts. The formula is:

$$\frac{1}{a + b}$$

where a is the number of items agreed on by the two analysts and b the number of items on which they disagree. A satisfactory level of agreement is considered to be .90 or greater. In addition, the researcher can code the text data twice, two weeks apart. On the second occasion the researcher codes without reference to the earlier coding and then re-codes the data. Following this, Goodwin and Goodwin's (1985) coefficient can be recalculated to determine if there is reliability over time. Armstrong, Gosling, Weinman, and Marteau (1997) have provided useful information on inter-rater agreement in coding qualitative data. Interestingly, they found that close agreement arose between raters on the basic themes, but that each analyst packaged the themes differently.

There are other statistics to calculate inter-rater reliability. A problem with a percentage agreement approach, however, is that it does not account for the fact that raters are expected to agree with each other a certain percentage of the time simply based on chance (Cohen, 1960). In order to combat this shortfall, reliability may be calculated by using Cohen's Kappa, which approaches 1 as coding is perfectly reliable and goes to 0 when there is no agreement, other than what would be expected by chance. Kappa is the most commonly used measure of inter-rater reliability. A detailed discussion of reliability indices used in content analysis can be found in Krippendorff (2004).

How to increase validity in content analysis

Reliability is a necessary (although not sufficient) criterion for validity. In content analysis, the concern in this context is with the validity of interpretations – whether a researcher's conclusion that 'x' is the main theme to emerge from the qualitative data is valid. There are a number of procedures that researchers can undertake to improve the validity of their qualitative data. They may, for example, make use of expert panels in order to compare their interpretations. Feedback loops can also be used where the researcher's interpretations are provided to the informants for verification and theory development. Additionally, researchers can actively seek disconfirming evidence in the data to try to 'embarrass' their interpretations. Finally, convergent validation can be attained through triangulation of different methods of comparison with findings of similar studies; triangulation through the use of multiple data sources (e.g., multiple respondents), multiple sources (e.g., participant observation, interviews, records, etc.), and comparison with the findings of other studies (Gilchrist, 1992).

Conclusion

Content analysis is a technique for systematically describing and analysing written, spoken, or visual material. The method is suitable for analysing qualitative data, conducting comparisons, and examining trends over time. Content analysis may be undertaken manually, or be computer-assisted, depending on the amount of data to be coded and the type of research question asked. It involves data reduction (derivation of themes and then broader categories) and then interpretation of thematic content. Reliability, to obtain consistent data, and validity, to measure the actual construct that is thought to be measured, require substantial effort to achieve rigour.

References

Armstrong, D., Gosling, A., Weinman, J., & Marteau, T. (1997). The place of inter-rater reliability in qualitative research: An empirical study. *Sociology, 31*, 597–606.

Chang, S. & Tharenou, P. (2000). *Competencies for managing a multicultural workforce.* Melbourne: Monash University.

Cohen, J. (1960). A coefficient of agreement for nominal scales. *Educational and Psychological Measurement, 20*, 37–46.

Crabtree, B.F. & Miller, W.L. (1992). A template approach to text analysis: Developing and using codebooks. In B.F. Crabtree and W.L. Miller (eds.), *Doing qualitative research* (pp. 93–109). Newbury Park, CA: Sage Publications.

Creswell, J.W. (2003). *Research design – qualitative, quantitative and mixed method approaches* (2nd ed.). Thousand Oaks, CA: Sage Publications.

Gibbs, G.R. (2002). *Qualitative data analysis: Explorations with NVivo*. London: Open University Press.

Gilchrist, V.J. (1992). Key informant interviews. In B.F. Crabtree & W.L. Miller (eds.), *Doing qualitative research* (pp. 70–89). Newbury Park, CA: Sage Publications.

Glaser, B.G. & Strauss, A.L. (1967). *The discovery of grounded theory: Strategies for qualitative research*. Chicago: Aldine.

Goodwin, L.D. & Goodwin, W.L. (1985). Statistical techniques in AREJ articles, 1979–1983: The preparation of graduate students to read the educational research literature. *Educational Researcher, 2*, 5–11.

Holsti, O.R. (1969). *Content analysis for the social sciences and humanities*. Reading, MA: Addison-Wesley.

Kabanoff, B. & Holt, J. (1996). Changes in the espoused values of Australian organisations, 1986–1990. *Journal of Organizational Behavior, 17*, 201–219.

Kabanoff, B., Waldesee, R., & Cohen, M. (1995). Espoused values and organisational change themes. *Academy of Management Journal, 38*, 1075–1104.

King, N. (1994). The qualitative research interview. In C. Cassell & G. Symon (eds.), *Qualitative methods in organizational research* (pp. 14–36). London: Sage Publications.

Krippendorff, K. (2004). *Content analysis: An introduction to its methodology*. London: Sage Publications.

Lee, T.W. (1999). *Using qualitative methods in organizational research*. Thousand Oaks, CA: Sage Publications.

Lee, T.W., Mitchell, T.R., & Sablynski, C.J. (1999). Qualitative research in organizational and vocational psychology, 1979–1999. *Journal of Vocational Behavior, 55*, 161–187.

McCutcheon, D.M. & Meredith, J.R. (1993). Conducting case study research in operations management. *Journal of Operations Management, 11*, 239–256.

Miles, M.B. & Huberman, M.A (1994). *Qualitative data analysis: An expanded sourcebook* (2nd ed.). Newbury Park, CA: Sage Publications.

Miller, W.L. & Crabtree, B.F. (1992). Primary care research: A multimethod typology and qualitative road map. In B.F. Crabtree & W.L. Miller (eds.), *Doing qualitative research* (pp. 3–30). Newbury Park, CA: Sage Publications.

Mossholder, K.W., Settoon, R.P., Harris, S.G., & Armenakis, A.A. (1995). Measuring emotion in open-ended survey responses: An application of textual data analysis. *Journal of Management, 21*, 335–355.

Reid, A.O. (1992). Computer management strategies for text data. In B.F. Crabtree & W.L. Miller (eds.), *Doing qualitative research* (pp. 125–145). Newbury Park, CA: Sage Publications.

Sommer, B. & Sommer, R. (1991). *A practical guide to behavioral research: Tools and techniques*. New York: Oxford University Press.

Strauss, A. & Corbin, J. (1998). *Basics of qualitative research: Grounded theory procedures and techniques* (2nd ed.). Newbury Park, CA: Sage Publications.

Taber, T.T. (1991). Triangulating job attitudes with interpretive and positivist measurement methods. *Personnel Psychology*, *44*, 577–600.

Tesch, R. (1990). *Qualitative research: Analysis types and software tools*. New York: Falmer.

Weber, Robert P. (1990). *Basic content analysis* (2nd ed.). Newbury Park, CA: Sage Publications.

Wolfe, R.A., Gephart, R.P., & Johnson, T.E. (1993). Computer facilitated data analysis: Potential contributions to management research. *Journal of Management*, *19*, 637–660.

Yin, R.K. (2003). *Case study research: Design and methods* (3rd ed.). Thousand Oaks, CA: Sage Publications.

Chapter review questions

1   What is content analysis?
2   What are broad approaches taken to content analysis?
3   What are the types of research design where content analysis is used?
4   How is content analysis carried out manually?
5   What are the basic steps of content analysis?
6   What is a template approach to content analysis?
7   What is the data analytic technique of grounded theory?
8   Why is it used?
9   What does it result in?
10   What is the data analytic technique of pattern matching?
11   Why is it used?
12   What are computer methods of content analysis?
13   What are the advantages and disadvantages of computer-aided text analysis?
14   How can reliability be increased in content analysis?
15   How can validity be increased in content analysis?

Part 6

Reporting research findings and ethical considerations

13 Writing up a quantitative or qualitative project

Objectives

At the end of this chapter you will be able to:

- *outline the general sequence of sections for writing a journal article or thesis/dissertation;*
- *compare the general sequence of sections for writing a journal article or thesis/dissertation for quantitative and qualitative research;*
- *identify what goes in an introduction/literature review;*
- *identify what goes in the method section;*
- *identify what goes in the results section;*
- *identify what goes in the discussion section; and*
- *explain the general principles of formatting the manuscript or thesis.*

CONTENTS

Writing up	276
General principles	277
How to write up a quantitative research report	283
How to write up a qualitative research report	296
Conclusion	308
References	309
Chapter review questions	310
Appendix A: Format checklist	310
Appendix B: The qualitative research report	312
Appendix C: Examples of research articles writing up qualitative data	314

Writing up

This section describes how to write an empirical research project for submission to a journal, and a thesis/research report. Most journal articles are shorter than research reports, usually between 30 and 40 double-spaced pages using 12 point font. The information applies only to an empirical study in which data – qualitative or quantitative – were gathered and analysed. The format may be longer for a thesis, where the researcher needs to show clearly – and to justify – everything he or she has done. Two types of write-up are described: quantitative and qualitative. 'Quantitative' is used to denote studies whose methods of analysis are primarily quantitative, while 'qualitative' is used to describe those whose analyses are primarily qualitative.

Before you start writing up, find a journal or two that has research on your topic and look for models to follow in the write-up. The first part of this chapter is written with respect to traditional empirical research. For that kind of research, the *Academy of Management Journal, Strategic Management Journal, Journal of Applied Psychology, Journal of International Business Studies, Administrative Science Quarterly*, and *Journal of Management* provide useful models. A research project may best suit other journals, so other models may need to be explored. Evaluations have been made of high-quality journals that a researcher may inspect to assess what a model journal should be (Caligiuri, 1999; Institute for Scientific Information, 1997; Tahai & Meyer, 1999).

The write-up should follow a publication manual or style guide – for example, the American Psychological Association's comprehensive *Publication Manual* (APA, 2002) or the US Academy of Management's style guidelines – Information for Contributors, published at the front of each issue of the *Academy of Management Journal*, and the Style Guide for Authors on the web at http://aom.pace. edu/amjnew/style_guide.html. The preferred styles of these two sources of guidelines on writing for publication are very similar, with the exception of the formatting of tables and reference lists.

To assist during the writing up stage, it may be worthwhile for the researcher to consult various resources. Bem (1995) shows how to write a literature review. Some other good references illustrating different styles for write-up are the University of Chicago Press (1993) and Brown

(1991). Journals also give information on how to write for publication, and a particularly useful checklist for writing up quantitative and qualitative data is from *Personnel Psychology* (Campion, 1993). The journal also includes an informative article on what reviewers look for in an article (Gilliland & Cortina, 1997).

General principles

Some principles and aspects of writing are common to quantitative and qualitative research articles (or ones that combine both qualitative and quantitative work) and, therefore, shall be discussed first.

Communication of rationale throughout

The main tip for writing a research report is to tell the reader (reviewer or examiner) *why* you are doing what you are doing and *why* you did what you did. A well-written research report (article or thesis) signposts everything throughout. If it does not, it is not intelligible to the reader. How do you do this? In all sections of the research report, say why you are doing what you are doing. It will be obvious to you, and you may think it is obvious to others what you are doing and why; however, it is not.

In the literature review (i.e., introduction), say why in this section or paragraph you are discussing that particular topic or variable or theory; that is, what it has to do with your research report and research question/hypotheses. Therefore, you need to apply what you are saying to your research question. In the method section, say why you chose that sample; for example, why did you include public- and private-sector employees? Why did you choose employees below middle manager level and in early to mid career? Say why you chose those measures, why you are using this method of analysis, or why you gathered the data this way. It is important to make the explanation clear and specific. 'Why?' is the big question to which you need to provide the answer for the reviewer or marker all the way through. Remember that the reader is your customer. Make it easy for the reader throughout the text. When you start a section, tell them *why you are writing this section.* Tell the reader at the start of a paragraph what you are doing in that paragraph and why. In your first couple of drafts you may not know just what you want to say. So, those introductory sentences in paragraphs may be missing from those early drafts. As you become clearer, you will be able to insert a sentence that tells the reader what you are talking about in this paragraph and what it has to do with your research question.

Make sure that *terms are all clearly defined,* that there are no abbreviations, and that tables and figures are clearly set out and in a standard format. Look on the marker as someone to please. Make sure the presentation is faultless. Don't leave things out that you would need if you were to understand the thesis.

Phrasing of the title

It is best for you to decide on your title early in the research process, as you will need direction in your project. In addition, the title often helps you to work out what your variables are; for example, the dependent variable – what you are trying to explain, and perhaps even the major independent variable – the influence or presumed cause. The first page is usually the title page. Work out a title that is a variation on your research question and write it first in the article, not last, to give you direction and help you work out what your research is really about. Then refine the title as you go along so that when the reader first meets it, they know the purpose of your study.

Presentation issues

Appendix A gives some common principles for presentation and typing of research articles/reports/theses.

Perfect presentation
A research article and a thesis need to have perfect presentation – no spelling mistakes, errors of punctuation, grammatical errors, errors in tense, or other problems. If the presentation is not perfect, why should the reviewer of the article or marker of the thesis think you ran

your multiple regression correctly? If you cannot get your spelling and punctuation and form of citation correct, why would the reviewer or marker think you correctly typed the numbers in your results tables? Some common errors arise in the following ways:

- The subject and verb are not consistently singular or plural.
- Adverbial clauses are used instead of sentences with verbs.
- The word 'its' is written with an apostrophe when it is not possessive. Do not use the word 'its' with an apostrophe unless you want to say 'it is'.
- The passive tense is used instead of the active tense. For example, rewrite 'Managerial level was predicted by aspirations (Gere, 2006)' (passive) as active: 'Gere (2006) found that aspirations predicted managerial level.' If you are citing one author who completed the study or made the statement, put their name at the front of the sentence to make it active voice, as in the example just given. If *you* did something, you may say, for example: 'I repeated the data collection a year later.'
- The pronoun 'we' is used when the 'we' is not the authors but in general. 'We', if used, should mean the authors of the article or report.

Setting out

The type size required for submission to academic journals is 12 point font. Reports are usually double-spaced (although in theses it is sometimes 1.5, but never single line spaced), including between paragraphs. Generally the typing is continuous, without excessive use of white space. White space is limited to one-inch margins (2.54 cm) around all four margins. Use first-, second-, and third-order headings (and a fourth if necessary). Have a look at a research article, or at the levels of headings given in APA (2002), to see how this is done. Check a proper guide (e.g., the APA manual) for punctuation, typing of statistical symbols, and so on. APA is useful for much other information, such as which tense to use. Indent each paragraph except the abstract with a tab.

Paragraphs

Use paragraphs when writing a research article or a thesis, not point form or lists. Point form or lists cannot construct an argument, integrate literature, offer explanation or analysis by theory, or critique previous work, but can only report non-integrated information. Paragraphs are not single sentences, because a single sentence cannot present a major thought. Paragraphs also have introductory/opening sentences and may have closing/concluding sentences. You often need to write the introductory/opening sentence last and in the second or third drafts, as you may not be clear about what the paragraph says until you have written it and re-read it. Paragraphs also have flow between them. They are linked to the one that comes before.

Flow of writing

Each section of the thesis needs to have an overall structure and argument. You need links from one section to the next. The paragraphs need to be appropriately written, as just described. The sequence of topics within a section needs to facilitate a logical argument. You do not use a numbered point system to write up, as is done in business and technical reports (e.g., do not use sections 1.1 and 1.2 and their subsections 1.1.1, 1.1.2, then 1.1.1.1, 1.1.1.2, etc.). The point system was developed for reports, and this is a research article or a thesis/dissertation. The point system was not developed for presenting critical arguments where paragraphs are needed and where the flow between paragraphs needs to be developed. The basis of a research article or a thesis/dissertation is critical argument, and that cannot be achieved in point form but needs continuous, free-flowing prose. Where the reader needs to have a signal that there is a change of tack, make a statement or use headings to achieve the same thing as major points (e.g., 1.1) and to allow prose to flow more freely. Bem (1995) and APA (2002) give good ideas on how to achieve flow.

Conciseness

You need to have a concise writing style. Leave out unnecessary material; your writing should not be long-winded or repetitive.

Plagiarism

Write your research report in your own words and do not include sentences or paragraphs taken from others, or a compilation of the written material of others (i.e., sentences, paragraphs). Include others' phrases or sentences as direct quotations.

Citations
Be sure to type citations correctly in the text. You need to:

* give the date in brackets after the authors' names, each time they appear;
* spell out all the names when there are three or more authors the first time they are given;
* use 'et al.' only from the second mention of three or more authors;
* give citation(s) at the start of or throughout a paragraph, not at the end of it;
* include a year every time you cite someone;
* include a citation for every statement you make that is a factual statement;
* back up and justify everything that you say;
* separate out different types of citations – for example, do not mix together citations of individual empirical studies, citations of reviews, and citations that are opinions or theories; and
* include all citations in the reference list, even if you just mentioned someone's name.

Some specific sections

The abstract
After you have written your research report, you need to write your abstract. It says specifically:

* what the study's research questions were;
* how the data were collected, including the sample;
* what results were found, their support/lack of support for the hypotheses, or the answers they provided to the research questions; and
* conclusions drawn from the results to explain the phenomenon.

In a thesis, the abstract performs the same function as a very brief introductory chapter in a book (i.e., it spells out why the study is being done, why it is important, its definitions, and its objectives – aims, significance, implications, etc.). Put material at the front of the critical literature review to lead into the research; do not have it as a separate chapter.

Reference list

The reference list contains all the references cited in the text. It does not include any that were read but not cited. (That is a bibliography.) The format used needs to be a completely accepted one for academic writing. The American Psychological Association's *Publication Manual* (2002) is useful – and unique – because it shows how to set out every possible type of reference material. Footnotes are not used for citations. Citations in the text are the name(s) of the author(s) followed by the date. For three or more authors, spell out all the authors' names in the first instance. For second and subsequent citations, use 'et al.' after the first author's surname.

Follow the correct format for setting out the reference list. In the reference list:

- include only references cited in the text;
- use a standard method, not one you made up yourself;
- include the beginning and end page numbers for an article in a journal;
- include the beginning and end page numbers for a chapter in a book;
- include all authors' names for all references, not just the first author;
- use initials instead of the authors' first names; and
- use the correct form of capitalisation for the particular method chosen.

The American Psychological Association (APA, 2002) method gives clear guidelines, as does each issue of the *Academy of Management Journal*.

Tables

Tables have only horizontal lines. The horizontal lines are not in the table proper, but only at the top in the boxhead and at the bottom. Don't use vertical lines or shading.

Appendix

The reference list is followed by the tables, figures, and appendices, in that order. Material tangential to a thesis (e.g., descriptive material, factor analyses of measures, some results, etc.) should be included as an appendix. Each appendix needs a title page, with 'Appendix A' and its title, 'Appendix B' and its title, and so on.

How to write up a quantitative research report

Here the sections for a quantitative research report (article, thesis) are explained. Quantitative reports usually have specific hypotheses or research questions, standard data collection processes including measures, results sections written in terms of whether they support specific hypotheses or not, and so on. A qualitative study may (or may not) have these same sections. Much of the following explanation of the critical literature review/introduction and the discussion applies both to quantitative and qualitative studies and their write-ups.

Writing the critical literature review/introduction

The critical literature review is an argument for your hypotheses and/or research questions. The critical literature review that leads to the hypotheses is also called the introduction. Check journal articles in a similar area to see the various ways to write arguments and research questions and hypotheses. A high-quality literature review:

- provides a logical, persuasive argument throughout the introduction to form your research questions and hypotheses;
- gives descriptions of the results, critiques of individual empirical studies categorised into sections for your argument, and summaries of common findings from several studies;
- cites highly relevant articles that are focused directly on your hypotheses or research question(s);
- selects high-quality refereed journals as sources of articles (Caligiuri, 1999; journal citation reports in the Institute for Scientific Information, 1997; Tahai & Meyer, 1999);
- includes contemporary references, such as a majority of references from the previous ten years and especially from the current or just prior year;
- is concise/brief and focused;

- demonstrates an in-depth understanding and comprehensive knowledge of the research area; and
- includes conclusions about previous literature reviews done on the topic or its parts.

The literature review needs to be a critique, through:

- offering a thorough analysis of the concepts/conceptual arguments/theories;
- showing critical insight;
- including criticisms offered by previous reviewers of the empirical evidence on the topic and critical opinions of noted scholars on the topic; and
- providing a comprehensive analysis of *empirical studies* on the topic, including their content (theory/framework, findings) and, if necessary, their methodology (research designs, samples, sites, measures, methods of analysis). An empirical study is one where data are analysed to provide tests of hypotheses and/or research questions. It usually includes the independent variable(s) and the dependent variable, and data are analysed by multivariate techniques. An empirical study is not descriptive, but analytical with respect to the antecedents of the dependent variable. Do not focus on criticising only the methodology. Your main criticism should be substantive – why we still do not understand the particular phenomenon or know the answer to a particular question from the *results* of the studies.

All material in the literature review should be specific to the topic. Include only material that is directly relevant to the research questions and hypotheses. Empirical literature and theories should be specifically applied to the research problem and lead to the research questions/hypotheses drawn. The literature review needs to flow and argue for the hypotheses, through:

- providing an overall structure with an ordered sequence of sections for your argument (e.g., significance of the topic) facilitating logical argument rationales for the hypotheses;
- providing links (flow) from one section to the next; and
- having appropriate paragraphs comprising several sentences (not one sentence or a full page), including introductory/introducing

sentences (the most important part of the paragraph) and closing/ conclusive last sentences.

The critical literature review/introduction may consist of a sequence including an opening paragraph, definitions, theoretical background, and so on. It is best, therefore, to include some headings in the literature review/introduction.

The opening paragraph

The opening paragraph should discuss the *importance* and *significance* of the study, and include a statement of its specific objectives/research question(s). Why are you doing this study? Why is it important? The importance of the topic is why it is of *practical importance*; for example, in terms of its implications for practice. The significance of the topic is its *theoretical importance*; that is, what it will add to our understanding of this phenomenon and how previous theory/explanation is weak in this regard. The objectives of your study are the research question(s) that you are asking. You need to be clear about your objectives before you proceed, so that you can state what you are about to say in your study.

Definitions

Next come definitions of the constructs you are explaining (dependent variable) and the explaining/explanatory variables (independent variables). The variables – for example, the dependent and independent variables – need to be clearly defined before you proceed any further. The definitions should come from well-known scholars in the field and be cited appropriately. The definitions should be able to be turned into measurement. They should be given when the variable is first mentioned, so they will usually be included early (e.g., in the second paragraph).

Conceptual framework

The underlying theory/conceptual framework follows, with its specific relevance to the research questions of your study. Others will have tried to explain this phenomenon and will have developed an explanation or theory. Alternatively, there will be theories developed for other phenomena that are applicable to explaining your topic. The theory needs to be presented, including why it is relevant and how it is applicable to what you are trying to do. Therefore, the theory needs to be applied to your specific research question. You may be testing the theory (a deductive approach), or it may form a backdrop for the information you will gather on your topic (a more inductive approach). The theory helps to provide a rationale/justification for your research questions and/or hypotheses. You may add your own logic, explanation, or theory. The logic or argument you provide leads to your research questions and/or hypotheses.

Research summary and critique
It is also important to include a categorised summary and a critique of the empirical research evidence in order to justify and argue the hypotheses. This section provides a summary of past research and points out its limitations in relation to answering your specific questions. Empirical studies – that is, those that have gathered primary data to analyse and provide evidence in relation to this topic – need to be summarised and critiqued. Hence, they need to be grouped or classified so that they are presented in some logical fashion and sequence from which to draw conclusions. Accordingly, the studies' findings are summarised, and are critiqued in terms of answering the research question. When you present their evidence and examine their flaws, what conclusions can you draw about the relationship? What hypotheses arise from those summaries of the research? Those conclusions can then be used to phrase the research questions or specific hypotheses.

Hypotheses
The hypotheses (testable, directional propositions) are usually inserted along the way in the introduction, just after the section that led to each being drawn. That means before each hypothesis is the argument for it, rather than their being presented in a long list. The critical review of the empirical literature may be able to be done in sections/categories; therefore, the research questions or hypotheses can usually be drawn at the end of each section. Some research questions or hypotheses need to be drawn at the end of the literature review, as they are integrative and come from the total, not its parts. You should write highly specific hypotheses, specifying the variables and the direction of relationships. You might include an overall critique of the past evidence and theory

on the topic in relation to how it answers the research questions (and thus leading to future hypotheses). You may want to sum up or to draw new conceptual criticisms (what we do not know yet, what we have not done yet, what theory would say/predict), and highlight common methodological problems from past studies (what is wrong with past studies – samples, measures, research design, methods of analysis, validity, reliability, etc.).

Methodology

A section on your study's methodology, and how you are going to do it, may be appropriate, especially if there is any special need to test the question or any special problems. This means the end of the literature review leads neatly into the method section. You might want to state here any relevant methodological issues, usually about your research design, and how you will test the research questions and/or hypotheses. It could be justification for the way you are conducting the study; for example, the site and sample you have selected.

Summary

You may wish to include an overall summary of the purpose of your study; that is, the overall rationale for the research questions and/or hypotheses. You may need to sum up briefly your overall arguments for your research questions and propositions. You usually do not need to list your hypotheses here if you have inserted them throughout the introduction.

Rationale

You need to be clear in the literature review/introduction why this study is being done. Ask yourself the following questions about your rationale for the study, and write down your answers. You need to ensure that this material is included in your literature review/introduction – either throughout it, or in a separate section that consists of your answers to the questions.

- The most important question is: What does this study do in relation to your research question that is *new*? (It usually can't just be methodological, in terms of the research design or sample, or measures.)
- Why is the study being done?

- After the study is done, what will we know that we do not know now?
- What difference will the study make?
- What contribution will the study make? How will it add to the literature?
- What is wrong with past studies in relation to answering the research question?
- In what way will the findings from the study add to the findings already known from past studies on the topic?
- Which hypotheses of the study have not been previously empirically tested?
- How will the study add to the theory that is relevant to explanation of the dependent variable?
- Which parts of theories, yet untested, will it test?

Writing the method section

The method section is written following the format from a major journal. If you are writing a thesis, you need to include more evidence about the reliability and validity of your measures and more justification of everything, because you are being assessed on your learning. The method section is composed of subsections including 'Respondents and Sample', 'Measures', and 'Procedure', and ends with a 'Method of Analysis' subsection, but these may vary from the American Psychological Association (2002). Some theses have an introductory section justifying their overall research design.

Overall research design is an optional section and is usually only included in a thesis. You may find yourself in a position where you need to explain the type of research design you are using and provide a rationale for it. As management is multidisciplinary, it includes many types of research designs that may span the different disciplines. There needs to be adequacy of the research design in terms of the overall design itself, so you may need to justify this type of design for answering the questions and hypotheses. The justification/argument links back to the research questions and literature critique to show how it answers your research questions and hypotheses. The methods of data collection must be clarified, as well as the advantages and disadvantages of the design for this particular research question. Many possible approaches to research design could suit your research question and might follow on from previous studies. (However, some of them might be cross-sectional, when you need a longitudinal design to test your question.) You may start with an explanation of where your design fits into, for example, the broad categories of quantitative and qualitative techniques. Then you might describe your specific research design so that it is clear as to how it will be done.

Possible research designs include both experimental and quasi-experimental designs, case studies, and correlational field studies (surveys). Often, types of designs are combined to help answer the research question. You need to provide a justification for the general approach (quantitative or qualitative) you use, as well as the specific research design within that approach in relation to the research question and/or hypotheses. You may wish to include in that justification for the research questions and/or hypotheses information in relation to the measures, samples, and so on. The design may combine approaches to enable the research question to be answered. In this case, you will need to provide an explanation of how the combination helps to answer your research questions better than an individual approach alone.

Sample

At the outset you need to justify the type of sampling you have used. Is it a probability sample (e.g., simple random sample or stratified random sample), stratified sampling, or convenience sampling? If you have completed calculations to determine the sample size (e.g., power analysis), you should provide them. The size of the sample should be clearly specified.

Description of respondents

When describing the sample, include a table if possible so that who they are (or what they do) is clear on relevant characteristics. If the sample is people, they may include personal characteristics of sex, age, education, work experience, marital status, occupation, managerial level, and other demographic information, as well as the characteristics of their organisations, such as organisational size, industry type, employer sector, and so on. You may also have a different type of sample; for example, organisations. Their characteristics will need to be given in percentages (categorical variables) or means (continuous variables); for example, organisational size, industry type, employer sector, profitability, location, geographical dispersion, etc.

Measures
It is particularly important to check how an article that covers a similar topic to yours presents the measures section. It will usually have a paragraph on each variable (e.g., job satisfaction) and on how it is measured. All information about the measurement of a particular variable is given in one section that is preceded by a third-order heading. Within this section, you need to do the following:

- Define the variable. You may have defined it in the literature review, but the reader needs to be absolutely clear about what it is.
- Explain exactly how the measure is derived. For example, is it the average of ten, five-point items? Is it a five-point scale ranging from *1* (fewer than 100 people) to *5* (500 or greater)? You may say that managerial aspirations was the average of 13, five-point items ranging from *1* (not at all true) to *5* (completely true), of which five were reverse scored. Is it a return on investment figure taken from annual reports? If so, how was it calculated?
- Provide examples of items if the items are not well known, or provide the whole multi-item scale (e.g., the 13 items measuring managerial aspirations) as an appendix. If a measure is a multi-item scale, give one or two examples of the items so that the reader understands what the measure is.
- Provide *reliability* evidence for substantive variables. The measure should have evidence for its reliability (alpha coefficients, stability) from scores on previous samples that need to be given. You must also calculate the reliability of the measure in your sample. Those figures can be included in the measures section or provided in the form of a table in the results section. Reliability is usually measured by Cronbach's alpha and/or by test–retest reliabilities (i.e., correlation coefficients).
- Give *validity evidence for substantive variables.* For example, evidence for construct validity arises through factor analysis, convergent validity through correlations with similar constructs, discriminant validity through correlations with different or dissimilar constructs, and so on. It is important to justify that the measure measures what it

says it measures. Even objective measures such as the various measures of an organisation's profitability have various arguments put forward as to what they really measure and critiques of them as measures of profitability. You may undertake factor analyses of your own measures if they are developed for the study, or you have extended other measures, or you feel it is needed. Those results, including their tables, may be placed here or in the results section. In a thesis, you need to give the tables of results for factor analyses. These may go in an appendix and be referred to in the measures section. In an article, you may not need to provide them although you refer to them. You may also need to complete confirmatory factor analysis for established measures, not just exploratory analysis.

Some variables (e.g., the dependent variable, or a major independent variable) are so important that their validity needs to be strongly established. For example, if you have split your sample by managerial level and it is self-reported, you may need to prove it is an accurate measure by:

- obtaining outside validation (company records), by careful definition of each level; and
- conducting analyses showing that the levels are linked to variables they should be linked to (e.g., salary, number of subordinates, number of promotions – convergent validity) and not linked to variables that might be spuriously related to managerial level (e.g., size of the organisation, number of levels in the organisation, age of respondent – divergent validity).

Procedure

You may have a brief procedure section explaining exactly how you gathered the data. What did you do? What did you tell the respondents the study was about?

Method of analysis section

You may need a justification for your methods of analysis that may include purpose, applicability, assumptions, etc. It is usually placed at the end of the method section. You need to cite from the major statistics books or articles. This is particularly important for methods that are not the typical ones, but it may also be necessary to justify the use of traditional methods such as MANOVA. The section describes the methods of analysis (e.g., moderated regression, mediated regression) and its assumptions, and backs these up with well-known statistics books and authors. In addition, the section includes a description of the methods of analysis you are using, how you used them (the steps, for example, in a hierarchical regression), why you used them (in terms of your research questions), and, in a thesis, any underlying assumptions and problems with the techniques. By the time the reader gets to the results section, they will then understand the purpose, method, assumptions, and limitations of the techniques generally and for these data (e.g., multicollinearity, missing data). In a thesis you may need to do quite a lot of work on this, whereas in an article you just need to make the major points.

Writing the results section

The results section needs to have subsections with headings. There are usually two broad areas of the results: the preliminary analyses, and the testing of the research questions and hypotheses; there may also be sections within these broad categories. It is also important to write the results in the past tense. Quantitative data (e.g., surveys) or qualitative data (e.g., in-depth interviews), or both, may be analysed and you may like to keep separate the sections reporting these two types of data.

If you are undertaking a traditional quantitative study, your results are written only in relation to your hypotheses, whether using quantitative or qualitative data, except for the first part of the results. In the first part of the results, you include a section outlining your preliminary analyses. Before you start reporting on the hypotheses, you will need to do three things:

1. discuss any required issues with respect to diagnostics, such as outliers;
2. present a correlation matrix, including demographic/background data, and point out any relevant issues concerning relationships (i.e., multicollinearity); and
3. point out anything else relevant about the data that the reader needs to know in order to read the hypotheses sections. For example, you

would do a MANOVA if you had correlated dependent variables, and you will need to tell the reader if they are correlated.

Support for hypotheses

You then need to sectionalise the results into paragraphs on each hypothesis and state whether it was supported or not. You need only report the results in terms of whether or not they supported your hypotheses, or how they answered your very specific research questions. In a thesis, you may have headings for each of your hypotheses or research questions, so that you have sectionalised the results into specific hypotheses, or groups of hypotheses. Remind the reader of what the particular hypothesis was, and then present the results that showed whether or not it was supported. You may need to complete several drafts. In the first draft, for example, you may just write out the results; then go back and amend that and continue the draft writing process.

Tables

It is best to prepare the tables before completing the results section, as this will save time in writing up the results. Seeing your results in tables (e.g., regression results: beta coefficients and their statistical significance, variance explained) is often the only way to determine if what you found supports your hypotheses or not. The tables need to be set out correctly. You will save time if you follow a model table from a high-quality journal such as the *Academy of Management Journal*, which provides good models for various statistical techniques. Before doing the tables, find articles that report research similar to yours and the same method of analysis; for example, correlation matrices, tables of means and standard deviations and alpha coefficients, MANOVA results, ANOVAs, multiple regression, moderated regression analysis, factor analysis (even if these are placed in the appendices or the method section), logistic regression, structural equation modelling, canonical correlation, log linear analysis, etc. Then follow the format used for the tables in these studies when constructing your tables.

Ideally, tables should not contain abbreviations; however, if they are necessary, then they must be explained in the notes to the table. A table needs to be self-explanatory and should not repeat information found in the text. It is also important to examine models of how to type statistics symbols and information for your particular technique. When setting out the tables, keep these models in front of you and follow them closely. Watch out for capitalisation, underlining, indentation, punctuation, the exact setting out of notes, significance levels in notes, headings, and so on.

Qualitative data

You may be including qualitative data, such as quotes from interviews, statements from company reports, or information from open-ended survey questions, as well as quantitative data to flesh out and help explain the numbers. You may also be analysing qualitative data alone to answer your hypotheses. Often qualitative data use examples of what people have said, and these are placed in the text as indented quotes in italics. You may also present tables representing analysis of qualitative data. You may have a separate section presenting your qualitative data with respect to how they answer the hypotheses. Often when qualitative data are used only as quotes to give examples, they may be placed in the discussion.

Writing the discussion

Any discussion should be a similar size in page numbers to its literature review/introduction and should discuss whether or not the hypotheses were confirmed, and why and how the findings relate to the theory (i.e., to explain the findings). In a thesis, especially, headings may be needed to mirror areas; for example, 'Theory', 'Evidence', 'Limitations', 'Future Research', 'Practical Application', 'Conclusion'. It is important to discuss the results in the present tense.

The discussion finishes off the story you started when you wrote your critical literature review. It is the mirror-image of it. You said there what you were going to do and why, and what you thought would happen. In the discussion, you are saying what happened and what it means for the research question you asked. So, in a sense, you have come full circle and so you would usually start off by reminding the reader what you were doing and why. An important issue is that you now write in an integrative way to answer your research questions. You will no longer write in terms of the hypotheses or specific variables, and you will no longer use the word 'hypothesis'. That is writing as separate chunks; you are now writing the discussion as a whole, not as small sections.

To write the discussion, you might like to consider a sequence such as this.

1. *What did you find overall?* Include an introductory paragraph reminding the reader of what you were investigating (reminding them of your introduction/critical literature review and summarising your specific results). This section repeats the research objectives and summarises the major findings. It is best then to revert to normal, user-friendly language (e.g., don't use terms such as 'hypothesis 1, 2' etc.) and to use plain English.

2. *What does your study add to knowledge?* Include a paragraph saying what your thesis adds to knowledge. You may also do this throughout the discussion if you think it should be said in that way. It is a good idea to say what your thesis adds to the previous literature on this topic. You undertook the study because there were things about the topic that were not known. What is known now that was not known before? How is your study different from previous studies? What have you contributed here? How has your study helped to resolve the original problem?

3. *What do your results mean?* Include an explanation of what your results mean in relation to that theory and for this sample. What do your results suggest is the explanation for the phenomenon you were explaining? This is the place where you keep referring to your sample and their situation or environment(s), as you are explaining your findings for this sample and situation/context. They may have been different for other samples and situations. Why did you obtain the specific results with respect to each hypothesis?

4. *How do your results fit with theories underlying or relevant to them?* Do they fit the theories, modify them, disagree with them, and if so, how and why? What theoretical implications can you draw from your study? This is now written in an integrated way, not in terms of individual hypotheses or individual variables. Explain specifically whether your results are similar or dissimilar to the theory, including for this sample, and their theoretical implications.

5. *Do your results fit with or not fit with past evidence, and why?* State whether your results are similar to past evidence, and provide

reasons for this similarity/dissimilarity, especially explaining why dissimilar results occur, particularly for this sample. Do your results fit with previous evidence? If they do not, why not? What is the reason for this sample and situation? Make sure to point out consistencies with previous results.

6. *What are the limitations of your study?* You need to outline the substantive/conceptual/theoretical limitations of your study, as well as the methodological (e.g., sample, measures, research design, methods of analysis) limitations. 'Substantive/conceptual limitations' refers to what we still do not know or cannot explain, and what these results still do not explain. The limitations lead to future research.

7. *What future research should now be done?* This section explains where we go from here. It can reverse the substantive/theoretical and methodological limitations and present future research in terms of solving these problems. It may also include other issues for future research on this research question arising from your results and the theory.

8. *What are the practical implications from your specific results?* The section outlines what should be done differently now in practice from what we know from these specific results. It should not go beyond the results found. It may advise organisations or managers or human resource managers or employees what they should do now. It may also advise governments and the public sector.

9. *What is your conclusion?* In a thesis, especially, you will have a final paragraph that sums up everything: what you were trying to accomplish, what you found, what it means, how the phenomenon is best explained, and what should be done now.

How to write up a qualitative research report

A qualitative research report is usually based on interpretive analysis of qualitative data. The data usually comprise some form of primary data, collected specifically for the purposes of the research (e.g., interviews, participant observation, case studies) and may also include secondary data – data that have not been collected for the purpose of the study (e.g., company documentation, archives). Quantitative data may also be included in qualitative theses (e.g., surveys). Historical analyses are also considered to be qualitative. Lee (1999) provides a good checklist for how to write up qualitative research, provided in Appendix B.

Examples of qualitative research

Thesis writing is often expedited by having some good models to follow. Appendix C provides a limited number of examples of recent journal articles (from high-quality journals) that are qualitative. There are many more, and a number of journals provide sound examples. Lee (1999) and Lee, Mitchell, and Sablynski (1999) also provide good examples of qualitative research.

General principles in writing up qualitative research

The write-up of a qualitative research study:

1. often has the same type of sections as a quantitative thesis: litera-ture review, method, results, and discussion;
2. is usually written up as a critical argument, not in a descriptive way;
3. is integrated from the beginning to the end in terms of logic and consistency and the question being answered;
4. has a research question or questions that frame the research;
5. usually does not have hypotheses, but some have specific propo-sitions and/or conceptual frameworks arrived at from a critical analysis of the literature, which are then addressed through anal-ysis of data;
6. usually starts the method section justifying why a qualitative research design was used with respect to that type of approach in general, and this specific question in particular;
7. carefully describes the context/sites and the background to the analysis;
8. does not necessarily describe how reliability or validity were gained, but emphasises how rigour was achieved;
9. shows how the process (data collection, analysis, etc.) was system-atically done and gives detailed information on each aspect;

10. describes several sources of data and contrasts the similarities and discrepancies in their findings to help answer the research question(s);

11. often in the results/findings section, analyses the data with respect to the propositions or research question(s), doing so across the methods (e.g., interviews, observation, company documents) so that their results are integrated and not within a method;

12. uses content coding as the method of analysis (drawing themes from the text across different data sources and methods), sometimes followed by pattern matching;

13. in the discussion, draws together the results from several different data sources (managers, employees, case 1, case 2);

14. in the discussion, compares the findings of this study with prior research;

15. in the discussion, often derives a future conceptual model and future research questions or hypotheses to be tested; and

16. in the discussion, usually provides implications for practice.

Different models for writing up qualitative research

In this section, some models are presented that may be useful for writing up theses that are based on qualitative data. Unlike a quantitative thesis, there is no best way to write up a qualitative thesis. Therefore, several models are presented here.

A quantitative write-up approach

Apart from the models that follow, there are also write-ups of qualitative research that completely follow the format of a quantitative write-up. The only difference is that the data are qualitative (e.g., interviews, focus groups).

Model A: Traditional qualitative write-up

This model is written up in four sections: literature review, method, results, and discussion. In this approach, the literature review critiques the literature and results in research questions and propositions, rather than hypotheses. The basis of the review is a critical approach.

The method section follows the principles of having subsections titled 'Sample', 'Design and Procedure', and 'Measures'. Yin (1994) is a useful reference. The important characteristics of the sample are described. For example, if one company is used, there should be a table giving interviewees' characteristics. Due to confidentiality, they are identified by position/title, or in other ways (e.g., Mr X). The section on design and procedures describes how organisational access was obtained and how data were gathered; for example, how interviews were structured and how they proceeded (i.e., timing, tape-recordings). How organisations were approached, including letters (these should be included in an appendix to the thesis), is also described. There is a section justifying the use of a qualitative approach with respect to this research question and in general. This may include the notion of deriving emerging theory when little is known about an area (or for other reasons). Usually, there will be data triangulation and that is described (i.e., how this was done to help validity and rigour).

A qualitative thesis describes the several different kinds of data that are gathered. The interview (e.g., its content) is described and justified. The appendix gives a full copy. How the interviews were piloted is described, as is how the questions were altered, based on data obtained from the pilot.

The method of analysis section describes how the data were analysed. Included is basic information on transcription (e.g., done within 24 hours). Also included is how the information was actually analysed – what was done. How the data analysis is integrated from the different sources is described (e.g., from interviews, documentation, observation). There may be some simple statistics undertaken, which are also reported. Eisenhardt (1989) gives a useful description of how to build theory from the case study approach. The way in which results are written will vary according to whether there is information from one organisation or several. If one organisation is used, background data are given to set the context, and then the information is analysed with respect to each research question. The data are not described, but are analysed and presented with respect to how they answer each research question or proposition. In the results, there should be analysis of the information to say what it means with respect to the question, rather than a tendency to quote. If there are several organisations, the research questions are answered with respect to each organisation. Results are not written, for example, as reports of each interview, but are only given in terms of how they answer the research questions. When information comes from different types of data, the analysis is still in terms of the research questions. Therefore, the analysis should integrate the different data sources. Appendices may include transcribed interviews.

In the discussion section, if there were several organisations analysed in the results section, this is where their results are integrated and brought together to draw conclusions. The aim is to say what the results mean and to refer back to the literature review in terms of the theories/models/approaches and prior studies it reviewed. The kinds of questions answered are:

- What have we learned?
- What are the implications for other research and for future practice?

The discussion may be inductive where theory is derived from the results of this study. A model may then be developed based on the data, representing how things fit. More specific hypotheses for testing in the future could be presented. A critical approach is also taken in the discussion section. The discussion tells a story based on the results. It can describe what is proposed by theory or models, describe what happens in reality, and make recommendations from the discrepancy. Alternatively, different types of data gathered for the results (e.g., company records, interviews of managers) may have come up with conflicting answers to the question. In these cases the discrepancy is explained in the discussion to show how the phenomenon can be understood. Therefore, any discrepancies from results from the different types of data are explained. For example, interviews may give different answers and be more explanatory than quantitative information gathered.

Model B: An elaboration and modification of Model A

The write-up presents a coherent analysis of a research question or questions by providing an integrated development of ideas with respect to the research question(s) through unfolding of relevant literature. A way forward is ultimately presented through the identification of key variables in a particular situation, the development of a particular framework, or by presentation of testable hypotheses. The write-up also demonstrates a solid understanding of the purpose of the research with respect to the choice of design. There is an explanation of why the phenomenon is best suited to explanation by a qualitative design. There can be an answer to a 'How' question; for example, explaining how a particular intervention works, when there has been no previous theory in the area. There can also be an answer to a 'Why' question: why this might be a concern for researchers. Accordingly, there is recognition that it is not always possible to isolate cause and effect when the phenomenon is embedded in a broad organisational context.

The literature review is dependent on the nature of the field, but shows that the writer has a sound understanding of the basic underlying conceptual framework for the area. Hence, there can be a conceptual framework or an acknowledgement of related theories. Two types of write-up may arise, based on Yin's (1994) protocol; these types initially affect the write-up of the literature review.

- An exploratory case design in which there are no preconceived notions but there are broad research questions from which to start. This type is inductive, where the data are allowed to emerge and the literature unfolds. It may arrive at emergent theory. The literature review results in broad research questions.
- An explanatory design in which there are broad research questions and a specific set of propositions (with respect to those questions) starting from a literature base. In this case the literature review also has drawn from it (apart from the broad research questions) a set of propositions that suggest relationships.

Yin (1994) and Eisenhardt's (1989) references can inform the write-up of the method and research design section. Covered under the heading 'Method and Research Design' is the justification for the research design and the sample or site collection. The write-up refers back to the research questions and the established rationale for the type of research design appropriate to these questions. There is an introductory section explaining why this design best suited the question(s), and there is a demonstrated understanding of the different outcomes from quantitative and qualitative research. Also included is the rationale for the selection of sites for the study.

Following Yin (1994), a systematic process is shown to be conducted that assists rigour. The objective is analytical generalisability, not statistical generalisability (e.g., not random sampling logic, but other forms). The write-up shows data saturation in which the author continues to gather data until a consistent set of themes or patterns emerges. Reliability is attained in this way, although there can be more traditional forms included, such as inter-rater reliability. Usually, there is description of how qualitative data have been triangulated in terms of methods (e.g., interviews, brief survey, secondary data), or other ways (e.g., interviewing people at different levels to find out the impact of a phenomenon on them, such as interviewing employees and managers). The write-up shows the capacity to integrate various sources of data and perspectives – relevant theory/literature, primary data (interviews, open-ended survey questions), secondary data (company documentation, annual reports, media), or participant observation where it is set up beforehand as part of the design.

How to organise and manage the data analysis is also described (i.e., how the data were collected and analysed). You need to describe how the data were managed as they were collected to facilitate analyses (e.g., taped, field notes). Miles and Huberman (1994) provide several options for analysis and for presentation of qualitative data. Whether the data are analysed using computer-assisted methods (e.g., NVivo) depends on the amount of data (e.g., if 15 or more interviews). The write-up shows that a systematic working through of the data occurred to pick out the emerging themes. Computer-assisted methods such as NVivo can facilitate this analysis. The method is particularly suited to an exploratory design in which theory emerges, rather than to an explanatory design.

In case study research, the write-up of the results can proceed as the presentation of the results of analyses of a series of single cases, if there is more than one case. Hence, there is an analysis of a series of sites. Usually, each section starts with a description of the case site. Then the data are examined with respect to the literature. The research question is applied to the context of the specific case while simultaneously folding in the relevant literature. The data and themes from each case site are analysed with respect to the specific research questions, and the results show if the themes support/link with/reflect previous research. The analysis may result in an overall pattern in the data that related to the research question. There is usually triangulation between data sources: the primary data (e.g., interviews) and secondary data (e.g., participant observation, documents). The researcher is looking for patterns and conflicts or disagreements. The literature is folded in at the same time for each site. Overall, there is a strong analytical approach taken to the presentation of the qualitative context, not just a descriptive one.

The discussion/integratory chapter addresses the research questions across the cases. The chapter starts with a summary of the sites (e.g., nature of organisations, type of industries) to provide a broad contextual comparison. A systematic approach is then taken in comparing the outcomes with respect to the research questions across the cases, including their similarities and differences. Unanticipated emerging themes from the data are acknowledged. Some kind of framework, emerging from the site(s) and from the research question, is built to suggest how this phenomenon can be considered in the future. Accordingly, a conceptual framework is inductively derived. Generalisability is constrained to the sites. Hence, a rationale or explanation is developed for why similarities or differences might have been manifested across the cases. The literature is integrated with data from the cases. The end may be a set of themes that can be carried forward to subsequent development of a conceptual framework, or identification of critical variables for future research. That is then built on in terms of implications for research and practice. The write-up does not over-interpret the data. The researcher's own perceptions do not drive the development of the argument, and the researcher needs to be careful of how much or how little can be made of the data. This is helped by triangulation.

Model C: A problem-based approach
This type of thesis looks at a social problem and adds to social knowledge about organisations. The thesis is written in an integrated way with all parts connected. Each section/chapter has an introduction and conclusion that helps to structure the section and connect it to the remainder of the thesis. The methodology is not discussed in detail in the thesis but is provided in an appendix. So, if a semi-structured interview is used, it is placed in an appendix and referred to when it becomes relevant. The methodology could be a case study using company documentation (e.g., written policies) and interviews exploring the perceptions of those implementing the policies and those receiving them, or even those outside the organisation. The question might be what factors in the organisation make this practice successful or not

successful. Some sort of gap in organisational practice will be examined. The aim is to complete a mosaic, to be exhaustive and provide information on what is really happening.

The first chapter – the introduction – basically outlines what the problem is and why it is worth studying (i.e., the real reasons, the significance). It is written in plain English and is a communication about a social problem. A brief overview is then given of the overall pattern of the thesis. Following this is a description of how the problem will be studied – the method – and the justification for the choice of method used (e.g., two case studies, or an already gathered survey database). Usually, the first chapter ends with a simple research argument that has been arrived at by a critical argument.

The next chapter is the literature review. The relevant literature is found and reviewed, and may combine two literatures previously not combined. The thesis needs to show a good grasp of the existing literature. There needs to be an argument about how this will add to knowledge.

The first chapter of results (e.g., of survey data) follows. The chapter may present quantitative data, for example, from a survey. There is justification of why these data are being used. Any statistical analyses (e.g., factor analyses) are usually placed in an appendix. The data and models are analysed, and there is an explanation of why the researcher cannot get far enough with only numbers. The chapters that follow are usually qualitative, such as case studies. They each start with description of the background detail (e.g., the organisation, the product). The different case settings/sites are then described. The findings are given, for example, from participant observation of production processes and from a small number of interviews of employees and managers.

The next section is the discussion, where there is an expansion of the results. There is a comparison between the cases, of the conclusions from the data, and an explanation of why the case study was a useful method. The information obtained from people is used to provide richness and to bring the data to life. Motives are explored, judgements of effectiveness are made, direct quotes are usually used, and then recommendations are made for improvement. When particular practices are being considered, questions such as 'What were the obstacles in the way?' are answered. The discussion is written in an integrated way and refers back to the literature. The results are contrasted with published findings. The discussion will usually arrive at information that forms the basis for research questions for future study.

Model D: An expanded problem-based approach

This model has sections called 'Introduction', 'Literature Review', 'Hypotheses and Research Method', 'Case Study' chapters, and 'Conclusions'. The introduction briefly states what the problem is and why it should be addressed – justifying the question being asked, clearly giving the aim of the thesis and identifing the research question, and giving a brief overview of the thesis. The literature review is next. The type of question determines the amount of literature to be reviewed. The literature review first provides a historical review, followed by a review of the contemporary literature that includes both Australian and overseas literature. Some literature reviews end up with broad questions, others with specific, directional propositions. The latter may be derived from prior empirical studies or from others' conclusions.

The next section covers the hypotheses and research method. The section describes exactly how the thesis was done; how organisational access was gained, who the contacts were and how the process was carried out (e.g., initially through the managing director, then subsequently worked with the human resources manager), and how interviews were carried out, including all detail (e.g., taped, notes, how many interviewed, how a cross-section was achieved if done and the levels interviewed and why, the interview questions, how long the interviews were, whether focus groups were used, etc.). This allows an assessment of how judgements were made by the researcher. The information is very detailed. How triangulation is achieved is spelled out; for example, information is checked with different people until there are decreasing returns.

Next are the case study chapters. When there is more than one case study, they are written as separate chapters. The beginning of each provides the background, both external and internal to the company. First the industry is described, then the company (i.e., financial status, ownership, product, who are its competitors, market position). This information is obtained from written documentation such as annual reports, the media, etc. Hence, a profile of the company is given. The second part of the chapter analyses the qualitative data gathered in relation to the specific questions. If there were three research questions, there are three main headings. Each question is addressed in turn and the different types of data are gathered (e.g., interviews, company documentation). These data are brought to bear simultaneously, and in an integrated way, on that question. Therefore, there is analysis, not description, and the data gathered are analysed with respect to questions and only given and used for that purpose. In these analyses, the literature from the literature review is referred to in order to state if the analyses of the data provide support or non-support to past work. If past work and views are not supported, an explanation is given.

The conclusion is a brief chapter that starts off with reminding the reader what the thesis set out to do and stating how the thesis tested that question(s). It then outlines what conclusions can be drawn from the analyses done. Additionally, it states where literature is supported or not; where there is a variation, it explains why. This chapter concludes by addressing the research questions across the case studies and drawing together the arguments. Literature could be brought in, but no new material is presented and the chapter is kept short.

Addressing reliability and validity in a qualitative research report

Reliability and validity are usually thought of in terms of rigour in qualitative research. Most of the models given above place great emphasis on the way in which data are gathered and analysed in terms of being systematic and consistent, and described to enable conclusions to be drawn as to whether they are valid. In addition, different sources and methods of data collection allow discrepancies to be found in order to increase valid findings.

Some authors have also specifically considered the issues of validity and reliability in qualitative research. In qualitative research, a study is valid if it examines the topic that it claims it examines (King, 1994). The concern is with the validity of interpretations – whether a researcher's conclusion that 'x' is the main theme to emerge from the interviews is valid. Expert panels may be used with which to compare interpretations. Feedback loops can be used to return to participants with interpretations and to develop theory. Researchers can actively seek contradictions in the data. Convergent validation can be used through triangulation of different methods of comparison with findings of similar studies. Gilchrist (1992) also discusses validity and espouses that this may be checked by recycling analysis back to key informants and participants, searching for disconfirming evidence through sampling and prolonged engagement, and triangulation through use of multiple data sources such as multiple respondents and multiple sources such as participation observation, interviews, records, and so on.

Creswell (2003) discusses how to obtain internal and external validity. Internal validity here is the accuracy of the information and whether it matches reality. Creswell's suggestions are:

- Find ways to triangulate the data, or to find convergence among sources of information (e.g., interviews, observations, document analysis), different investigators, or different methods of data collection. Triangulation also strengthens reliability (i.e., reduces measurement error).
- Get feedback from informants (member checking). Take the categories or themes back to the informants and ask whether your conclusions are accurate.
- Conduct repeated observations at the same research site.
- Identify how informants and participants will be involved in all phases of the research (i.e., participatory research). Key informants might be identified for interviews or observation, and participants might gather data or review the findings as they emerge.
- Clarify researcher bias.

Although unusual in qualitative research, at times, reliability may need to be calculated. This can be done for interviews or other textual data where quantification is the goal. Inter-rater comparisons can be used when coding themes or categories. Co-researchers code blind without consultation with each other, calculate their agreement statistically, then explore reasons for disagreements, decide on an adjusted coding, and then code new transcripts to assess their agreement (and adjust if necessary). Independent raters not associated with the study can be used. Inter-rater comparisons can be calculated when developing the themes or categories to code in qualitative data. Statistical coefficients of agreement are calculated; if low, the reasons for inter-rater agreement need to be decided and fixed. Independent raters not associated with the study can be used. To increase reliability of the content analyst, they are usually trained by providing a detailed explanation of the scoring system and then given practice in scoring material with correct answers given to give them feedback. Goodwin and Goodwin (1985) have developed a formula to determine inter-rater reliability between two content analysts. Creswell (2003) suggests that in case study research, where multi-site cases are explored, the same patterns or events can be examined to see if they replicate from case to case. See Chapter 8 for details on reliability in qualitative analysis.

Reliability and validity have also been considered for company documentation. Other researchers can be trained in the method in order to verify the findings. The other researchers can check the general rigour of the study and the representativeness of the documents. Different researchers may also arrive at differences in interpretations of the same text, providing validity problems. Company documents must not be used on their own, in order to provide reliability and validity checks. Various sources give good advice on how to write research articles. Campion's (1993) editorial from *Personnel Psychology* provides a checklist for quantitative research, qualitative research, and reviews. Lee (1999) provides a checklist (Appendix A) to follow for qualitative studies.

Conclusion

Writing up a qualitative research thesis has no set format as in a quantitative thesis. However, the structure will in effect determine if the thesis answers the question. It is very important in a qualitative thesis to have a strong conceptual, critical argument, so that the logic is clear all the way through, and to write the thesis in an integrated way. Part of its quality is the persistence with which it makes the argument or logic for its approach, and combines the data collection, analyses, interpretation, and discussion with the original question presented and the prior literature. If the thesis is to demonstrate rigour, then the way it has been carried out needs to be carefully described, showing that the approach has been systematic and carefully done and documented. The results must not be over-interpreted, and usually a conceptual framework is derived that leads to future research.

References

American Psychological Association (2002). *Publication manual of the American Psychological Association* (5th ed.). Washington, DC: American Psychological Association.

Bem, D.J. (1995). Writing a review article for *Psychological Bulletin*. *Psychological Bulletin, 118,* 172–177.

Brown, M. (1991). Put it in writing. In D. Kelly (ed.), *Researching industrial relations* (pp. 72–80). Sydney: Australian Centre for Industrial Relations Research and Teaching.

Caligiuri, P.M. (1999). The ranking of scholarly journals in international human resource management. *The International Journal of Human Resource Management, 10,* 515–519.

Campion, M.A. (1993). Article review checklist. *Personnel Psychology, 46,* 705–718.

Creswell, J.W. (2003). *Research design – qualitative, quantitative and mixed method approaches* (2nd ed.). Thousand Oaks, CA: Sage Publications.

Eisenhardt, K.M. (1989). Building theories from case study research. *Academy of Management Review, 14,* 532–550.

Gilchrist, V.J. (1992). Key informant interviews. In B.F. Crabtree & W.L. Miller (eds.), *Doing qualitative research* (pp. 70–89). Newbury Park, CA: Sage Publications.

Gilliland, S.W. & Cortina, J.M. (1997). Reviewer and editor decision-making in the journal review process. *Personnel Psychology, 50,* 427–452.

Goodwin, L.D. & Goodwin, W.L. (1985). Statistical techniques in AREJ articles, 1979–1983: The preparation of graduate students to read the educational research literature. *Educational Researcher, 2,* 5–11.

Institute for Scientific Information (1997). *1997 Social Sciences Citation Index JCR Journal Citation Reports.* Philadelphia, PA: Institute for Scientific Information.

King, N. (1994). The qualitative research interview. In C. Cassell & G. Symon (eds.), *Qualitative methods in organizational research* (pp. 14–36). London: Sage Publications.

Lee, T.W. (1999). *Using qualitative methods in organizational research.* Thousand Oaks, CA: Sage Publications.

Lee, T.W., Mitchell, T.R., & Sablynski, C.J. (1999). Qualitative research in organizational and vocational psychology, 1979–1999. *Journal of Vocational Behavior, 55,* 161–187.

Miles, M.B. & Huberman, A.M. (1994). *Qualitative data analysis: An expanded sourcebook* (2nd ed.). Thousand Oaks, CA: Sage Publications.

Tahai, A. & Meyer, M.J. (1999). A revealed preference study of management journals' direct influences. *Strategic Management Journal, 20,* 279–296.

University of Chicago Press (1993). *The Chicago manual of style* (14th ed.). Chicago.

Yin, R.K. (1994). *Case study research: Design and methods* (2nd ed.) (pp. 1–17, 127–153). Thousand Oaks, CA: Sage Publications.

Chapter review questions

1 How does a researcher communicate to the reader the rationale for choices and literature throughout a research report?
2 How should a title be phrased?
3 What needs to be included in the abstract?
4 How do you write a quantitative research report?
5 How do you write the critical literature review/introduction?
6 How do you write the methodology/method section?
7 How do you write the results section?
8 How do you write the discussion?
9 How do you set out your reference list?
10 What are issues for presentation in writing up a research report?
11 What are general principles that should be followed in writing up a qualitative thesis?
12 What are different models for writing up qualitative research?
13 How do you address reliability and validity in a qualitative thesis?

Appendix A: Format checklist

Format

☐ Is the entire document – including quotations, references, figure captions, and all parts of tables – double-spaced? Is the assignment neatly prepared and clean?
☐ Are the margins 1 inch (2.54 cm) on all sides?
☐ Are the title page, abstract, document text, references, appendices, tables, and figures on separate pages (with only one table or figure per page)? Are they ordered in the stated sequence with the text pages between the title and the references?
☐ Are all pages numbered in sequence, starting with the title page?

Title page

☐ Is the title between 12 and 15 words in length?

Paragraphs and headings

☐ Is each paragraph longer than a single sentence but no longer than one typed page?

☐ Do the levels of headings accurately reflect the organisation of the paper?

☐ Are all headings of the same level typed in the same format?

Abbreviations

☐ Are any unnecessary abbreviations eliminated and any necessary ones explained?

☐ Are abbreviations in tables and figures explained in the table notes and figure captions?

References

☐ Are references cited both in the text and in the reference list?

☐ Do the text citations and reference list entries agree both in spelling and in the date?

☐ Are journal titles in the reference list spelled out fully?

☐ Are the references (both in the parenthetical text citations and in the reference list) ordered alphabetically by the authors' surnames?

☐ Are inclusive page numbers for all articles or chapters in books provided in the reference list?

Tables and figures

☐ Does every table column have a heading?

☐ Are tables horizontally ruled?

☐ Have all vertical table rules been omitted?

☐ Are the elements in the figures large enough to be legible?

☐ Is the placement of each table and figure indicated in the text?

☐ Are all figures and tables mentioned/applied in the text?

Quotations

☐ Are page numbers provided in the text for all quotations?

Appendix B: The qualitative research report

Theoretical or conceptual basis

1. Was the study derived from a:
   a) formal theory;
   b) semi-developed conceptual structure; or
   c) generated topic?
2. Did the study serve to:
   a) generate new theory;
   b) extend or elaborate existing theory; or
   c) not generate new theory?
3. Is the study's theory or general topic sufficiently interesting to merit journal pages?
   Because the organisational sciences have a strong applied tradition, a practical application – instead of a theoretical basis – can also justify a study.
4. Did the researcher intend to solve a distinct managerial problem or concern?
5. Is the study's problem or concern sufficiently important to merit journal pages?

Literature review

1. Are key references cited?
2. Are critical references cited?
3. Are too many references cited, such that they distract more than they clarify?
4. Are the references accurate?

Conceptual development

The following questions presume theory testing and the appropriateness of hypothesis testing. If these presumptions are incorrect, these questions should be ignored.

1. Are hypotheses presented at the appropriate level of analysis?
2. Are the hypotheses falsifiable?
3. Are the hypotheses central to their theoretical, conceptual, or applied basis?
4. Do the hypotheses involve theorised processes or outcomes?
5. Are the hypotheses adequately operationalised?
6. Do the hypotheses derive from key or central constructs (e.g., persons, events, places)?

Sample and context

1. Was subject selection based on:

   a) random sampling;
   b) accessibility; or
   c) theoretical sampling?
2. Alternatively stated, was it a probabilistic, convenience, or theoretical sample?
3. What information was given to subjects before, during, and after the study?
4. What were the subjects' social and emotional states before, during, and after the study?
5. What was the nature of the researcher's rapport with the subjects before, during, and after the study?

Data

1. What kinds of data and how much data were collected?
2. How were the data recorded?
3. What specific steps were followed in data collection?
4. What specific questions were asked?
5. Was there an interview agenda?
6. Were data transcribed, and if so, how?
7. Do the collected data fit with the researcher's general topic, theory, or applied issue?
8. Do the data adequately describe the study's focal concern or research issue?

Analysis

1. What techniques were applied, and were they adequately applied?
2. Did the analysis involve more global interpretations or more formalised analysis?
3. Is the analysis sufficiently described, such that it could be replicated based on the description?
4. If categories were developed, how were the categories defined?
5. If categories were defined, how were they imposed on the data?
6. Does the researcher's interpretation fit with what is already known about the research issue or applied problems?

Verification

1. What checks were implemented to allow the researcher to argue for reliability?
2. What controls were implemented to allow the researcher to discount bias and selective interpretations?

3. What arguments allow the researcher to imply *validity*?
4. What arguments allow the researcher to imply *generalisability*?

Discussion

1. Are the results clearly and concisely summarised and explained?
2. Do the study's implications follow closely or distantly from the data?
3. Are the study's limitations concisely stated?
4. Are the study's overall and specific contributions to the larger body of knowledge clearly and convincingly stated?
5. Are alternative explanations adequately considered?

(*Source:* T.W. Lee, *Using qualitative methods in organizational research*, pp. 174–176. Copyright 1999 by Sage Publications, Inc. Reprinted by permission of Sage Publications, Inc.)

Appendix C: Examples of research articles writing up qualitative data

Adler, N. & Docherty, P. (1998). Bringing business into sociotechnical theory and practice. *Human Relations*, *51*(3), 319–345.

Ashcraft, K.L. (1999). Managing maternity leave: A qualitative analysis of temporary executive succession. *Administrative Science Quarterly*, *44*, 240–281.

Biereama, L.L. (1996). How executive women learn corporate culture. *Human Resource Development Quarterly*, *7*, 145–164.

Bradley, I.M. & Ashkanasy, N.M. (1997). Using theory to structure qualitative research: An investigation of gender and identity in performance appraisal. In L.N. Dosier & J. Bernard Keys (eds.), *Academy of Management Best Paper Proceedings*, 386–390.

Butterfield, K.D., Trevino, L.K., & Ball, G.A. (1996). Punishment from the manager's perspective: A grounded investigation and inductive model. *Academy of Management Journal*, *39*(6), 1479–1512.

Currall, S.C., Hammer, T.H., Baggett, L.C., & Doniger, G.M. (1999). Combining qualitative and quantitative methodologies to study group processes. *Organizational Research Methods*, *2*, 5–36.

Dougherty, D. & Hardy, C. (1996). Sustained product innovation in large, mature organizations: Overcoming innovation-to-organization problems. *Academy of Management Journal*, *39*(5), 1120–1153.

Locke, K. & Golden-Biddle, K. (1997). Constructing opportunities for contribution: Structuring intertextual coherence and 'problematizing' in organizational studies. *Academy of Management Journal*, *40*(5), 1023–1062.

Martin, J., Knopoff, K., & Beckman, C. (1998). An alternative to bureaucratic impersonality and emotional labor: Bounded emotionality at The Body Shop. *Administrative Science Quarterly*, *43*(2), 429–469.

Mats, A. (1998). Gender relations and identity at work: A case study of masculinities and femininities in an advertising agency. *Human Relations*, *51*(8), 969–1005.

Perlow, L.A. (1998). Boundary control: The social ordering of work and family time in a high-tech corporation. *Administrative Science Quarterly*, *43*, 328–358.

Pratt, M.G. (1997). Organizational dress as a symbol of multilayered social identities. *Academy of Management Journal*, *40*(4), 862–898.

Rafaeli, A., Dutton, J., Harquail, C.V., & Mackie-Lewis, S. (1997). Navigating by attire: The use of dress by female administrative employees. *Academy of Management Journal*, *40*(1), 9–45.

Sackmann, S. (1992). Culture and subcultures: An analysis of organizational knowledge. *Administrative Science Quarterly*, *37*, 140–161.

Warhurst, C. (1998). Recognizing the possible: The organization and control of a socialist labor process. *Administrative Science Quarterly*, *43*(2), 470–497.

14 Ethical issues and conduct in the practice of research

Objectives

At the end of this chapter you will be able to:

* *outline the main ethical issues in conducting research;*
* *explain the principle of informed consent and why it is important;*
* *apply principles of ethics in designing research studies, including gaining informed consent;*
* *describe how to conduct research to overcome ethical problems so that ethical issues are upheld; and*
* *identify the differences in following ethical principles when designing different types of studies (e.g., interview studies vs. survey studies).*

CONTENTS

Introduction	317
The main issues in conducting ethical research	317
Conclusion	325
References	326
Chapter review questions	327

Introduction

Prior to conducting a research project, the researcher needs to assess the design to determine if it follows ethical procedures. The researcher must also obtain formal permission to conduct the study from the ethics body from his or her institution. Good research design follows good principles for ethics, and some important issues are outlined here for researchers to consider.

The main issues in conducting ethical research

Presented below are issues that need to be considered by researchers in order to conduct research that is ethically sound.

- Prior to undertaking a research project, the researcher must consider the ethical issues involved and obtain ethical approval from the relevant institution.
- The research should be conducted according to the relevant professional body's code of conduct (e.g., Australian Human Resource Institute, Australian Psychological Society).
- The researcher should maintain his or her specialist knowledge and practice at an acceptable level of competence.
- Care should be exercised when advertising for/seeking research participants/respondents or using referrals by others (particularly with regard to the study's limitations or if it involves deception).
- The researcher should not exploit research participants (e.g., power, cost).
- The researcher should avoid conflicts of interest.
- The researcher should be particularly concerned when people are the research participants.
- The researcher must always respect the personality, rights, wishes, beliefs, consent, and freedom of individual research participants.

Setting up the research project

As a prerequisite, the project must have a purpose: aims, hypotheses, and potential significance. A research project should be scientifically valid and be able to yield reliable information according to accepted principles and research practice, concerning the hypotheses being tested or research aims being examined. The project should be worthy of being carried out, and the researcher should have a clear under-standing of the project (e.g., who will benefit from it).

Preserving confidentiality

Any information or data collected from respondents must be managed and handled carefully to safeguard confidentiality during and after completion of the research. Therefore, data must be stored in such a way that research participants' names are not available to others, unless they are staff who are responsible to the researcher. One method for preserving the confidentiality of research participants is to utilise unique identification numbers or codes. A private office should be used for interviews with research participants, and all information obtained from participants (e.g., interview transcripts or questionnaires) should be stored in a locked filing cabinet. Any disclosure of confidential infor-mation can only occur under strict conditions (e.g., written permission, documentation, court powers). It is the responsibility of the researcher to inform participants about any limitations on the preservation of their confidentiality (i.e., they should be informed of what may be disclosed and to whom this information may be disclosed). The analysis of data and reporting of the findings should be undertaken so that no indi-viduals are identifiable, unless they give their consent and this meets with the approval of the relevant ethics committee. Additionally, no information obtained from individual participants should be reported to the organisations that employ them. If an organisation requests data that the researcher has obtained from its employees who participated in a research project, this information should be made available only in aggregate form. Australian researchers must also comply with the *Privacy Act* of 1988 if personal information about individuals (e.g., records, file information, stored data where a person can be identi-fied) is taken from organisational records in a Commonwealth agency (i.e., the entire public sector) for use in the research. Finally, stored data should be destroyed after five years if it has no long-term value and the relevant information has been extracted. It is important that researchers ensure that the destruction of the data occurs in a confidential manner – for example, by shredding the transcripts or questionnaires before disposing of them.

Obtaining voluntary and informed consent

A research project must be explained to potential participants in some way prior to their involvement. The researcher must decide who will provide the explanation (this is usually carried out by the researcher him- or herself) and when this will occur (generally, at the beginning of the research project). In most cases, only a summary of the essential aspects of the project needs to be known before agreeing to participate. The only circumstance in which an explanation would not be provided is when ignorance of the purpose of the research is essential to its success.

Involvement in any research project must be undertaken on a completely voluntary basis. 'Voluntary' means that the participant freely, without threat or inducement, agrees to be involved in the research project (Sieber, 1992). This 'voluntariness' relates not only to their initial involvement, but also to their continued involvement, as research participants must be able to withdraw from the project at any time. Participants must provide informed consent, which means that they clearly understand the goals of the research (i.e., its aims and purpose). Informed consent also requires that participants are aware of the methods (i.e., the number of sessions, duration, cost, and effectiveness), alternative methods, any agreements or contracts, any potential negative side effects of the research, and the ultimate fate of the research (i.e., whether it is to be published or not) (Gregory, 2003). Clearly, it is important that research participants are capable of providing informed consent, and therefore the project should be explained using plain, non-technical language and permission should be obtained from a parent or guardian for participants aged under 18 years. Researchers also need to give consideration to any special relationship between the person explaining the project and the research participants; they should also question why one group of participants is asked to participate and not others (e.g., unfair imposition on particular groups of people). Dependent relationships between the researcher and the participant (e.g., the researcher is a teacher and the participant is a student; or the researcher is a senior manager and the participant is a junior employee) should be avoided. The power imbalance in these relationships can compromise the voluntary nature of participation. Research participants must not feel unduly pressured or coerced to provide data.

In order to obtain informed consent, researchers are required to provide participants with an explanatory statement, written in plain language, that outlines:

- the purpose of the study;
- the anticipated benefits;
- all methods or procedures;
- any demands on potential participants, including duration;
- the risks of harm;
- the limitation on the confidentiality of results;
- the participants' freedom to refuse to participate or to withdraw;
- information on results of the study; and
- the contact name and number for questions/concerns, and the address of the ethics committee to contact.

To assess how difficult terms or concepts used in the explanatory statement are to comprehend, researchers can ask pilot participants to read the statement and ask them to explain it using their own words. The explanatory statement should be modified until it is easily understood (Sieber, 1992). If the research project involves the voluntary return of questionnaires from participants, written consent is not required.

Researchers who wish to sample employees of an organisation should obtain permission from an appropriate representative of the organisation (often a senior person from human resources) prior to contacting employees about their potential participation.

How to collect the data to observe principles of ethics

In most cross-sectional studies the confidentiality of participants is preserved because their identity is not recorded (e.g., questionnaires are returned anonymously with no unique identifiers). However, researchers may wish to ensure that the people who have responded are those who were intended to respond and that their data are complete. In these situations the researcher may use temporarily identified responses. After comparing names with a list, or checking that the participants' responses have been completed, the temporary identifiers are destroyed. Researchers who need to identify respondents and non-respondents in a mail-out survey may use separately identified responses. In this case, the respondents are asked to return the survey anonymously; however, they are also provided with a reply-paid postcard and are asked to write their name on it and return it separately. This procedure allows researchers to determine those who have responded and provides them with an opportunity to send a reminder to those who have not responded. In longitudinal research, it is necessary to match individual responses collected at one time with responses collected at another. In these studies, researchers may ask respondents to record an easily recalled alias or code (e.g., a combination of their mother's maiden name and their date of birth). In order to ensure that this process is effective, it is important that the alias or code is sufficiently unique to avoid duplication and that it will be easily remembered (Sieber, 1992).

For internet-based surveys, the researcher should construct a website that provides an electronic version of the explanatory statement. Having read the statement, informed consent is indicated by participants clicking on a link taking them to the first page of the survey. The website should allow participants to respond anonymously (i.e., there is no record of their email or internet protocol address) and then save their data. The data should be electronically stored on a secure password-protected drive or website that is only accessible by the researcher. Participants can be invited to send a separate email to the researcher to indicate that they have completed the survey. This allows the researcher to track those who have not responded (if the population is known) and send a reminder (Johns, Hall, & Crowell, 2004).

In observational studies, people should not be observed without disclosure unless the behaviour is occurring in a public place (i.e., a place where it is not unusual to be observed by others). While observing people without disclosure reduces the potential of a demand characteristic bias, it is an invasion of privacy (Banyard & Flanagan, 2005).

If the research involves the collection of interview data, ethics committees usually require that participants provide signed consent, unless the potential interviewee is unlikely to participate if any identifying information is collected. The researcher should obtain permission from the participant to record the interview. All recordings should be stored in a secure place until transcription, and they should then be erased.

Researchers should consider any demands, inconvenience, psychological stress, or discomfort involved for the research participants. Researchers should make every effort to ensure that participants do not experience anxiety, stress, loss of self-esteem, or reduced self-confidence as a result of their involvement in the research (Warwick, 1982). If there is the potential for any of these outcomes to occur, the researcher (and the relevant ethics committee) should carefully consider how the potential harm will be handled and whether it is justified by the research benefits.

Handling deception

If deception is necessary for the purpose of research, it should be used minimally. In these circumstances, the researcher must debrief participants at the close of data collection about the true nature of the research. This also provides the researcher with the opportunity to evaluate the effects of the procedures and to have a system for dealing with problems (e.g., provide counselling to participants if required). Debriefing also affords the researcher the opportunity to obtain more information from participants in relation to the research (e.g., whether the participant suspected the real intent of the study). Once participants have been informed about the true nature of the study, they must have the option to elect to withhold their data from the research project (Banyard & Flanagan, 2005). The participants' right to withdraw their data is especially important if information on their private behaviour has been collected, or if they encounter discomfort resulting from disclosing information that they would have preferred not to disclose (Sieber, 1992). Researchers should never engage in deception regarding their own qualifications, education, experience, and training.

Use of measures and interventions to preserve ethical considerations

It is the responsibility of the researcher to ensure that the methods he or she has selected are able to test the research questions. As an example, the sample size should be sufficiently large to provide the requisite statistical power to yield significant results if they are there (i.e., detect the relevant effect size) and reduce measurement errors. However, the number of research participants should be minimised once this is taken into account. The researcher should also ensure that the limitations of the measures they use are made explicit, and that no attempt is made to conceal information relating to the reliability, validity, and norms associated with their measures. The selection of methods and measures should be based on the following criteria:

• effectiveness;
• empirical evidence;
• theoretical rationale;
• peer review;
• public acceptability;
• government regulations;
• side effects and after-effects; and
• systems for dealing with problems, etc.

Use of specialist research practices and by whom

Research should always be conducted by suitably qualified persons with appropriate competencies and facilities. It is important that researchers do not utilise techniques that they have not been trained to administer and interpret (e.g., use of psychological tests by non-psychologists). If it is essential to the research purpose that a specialist technique is applied, then the researcher should refer to professionals who are skilled in its use and who have received the necessary training. Researchers should also avoid attempting to interpret instruments from outside their area of expertise (e.g., the misuse of psychologists' work). If a study involves a training program intervention, participants should be provided with a description of the program, be informed of its design, and be given accurate and objective information regarding the outcomes of the training.

Benefits offered to participants

In social science research it is common practice for the researcher to offer some benefits to participants (e.g., summary of the overall results). Some researchers offer payment or a reward, which is usually quite small, for participation in their studies. In terms of the ethics of offering payment or a reward, the essential issue concerns the influence of the inducement upon the consent obtained from participants. Generally, ethics committees view offering reimbursements for participants' time or incurred costs, and offering of inducements to encourage participation, as appropriate. However, it is not acceptable to provide a payment or reward that could be considered coercive (i.e., a payment or reward that places the participant in a situation where he or she could not afford not to participate). Fry, Ritter, Baldwin, Bowen, Gardiner, Holt, Jenkinson, and Johnston (2005) examined research payment practices in Australian universities, research institutes, hospitals, and market research organisations. They found that there was considerable variability in terms of research reimbursement practices and that, when it occurs, it usually involves a small monetary payment for time or any expenses incurred by participants. The study also indicated that researchers who reimburse participants usually do so in the absence of any formal policy and procedures. The authors concluded that ethics committees should develop specific guidelines for research payment practices.

Writing to protect ethical standards

Researchers should never fabricate data or falsify results when reporting on the findings of their studies. They should also ensure that they report their results accurately in order to minimise the possibility that the findings are misleading. In circumstances when researchers discover a major error in their published findings, they should contact the editor or publisher and seek to correct the error (e.g., an erratum or correction). Plagiarism should be assiduously avoided. In published work, where ideas from others are used in any way, researchers must provide citations to acknowledge their sources. Additionally, direct quotes from other sources must be presented using quotation marks, and the author(s) and page number(s) must be cited.

Other relevant ethical issues for conducting research

Researchers should ensure that when they conduct their studies, they avoid engaging in discrimination. Discrimination occurs when certain individuals are treated less advantageously than others. In research, this may occur during the recruitment phase where participants are selected or excluded on some basis (e.g., age, sex) that is not relevant to the research. This is to ensure that the benefits and disadvantages of participation in research are fairly distributed within the relevant population. Discrimination may also occur in experimental and quasi-experimental studies when control groups are not provided with the treatment.

In terms of ownership, any data collected by a researcher is the legal property of the institution (i.e., university or research institution) that the researcher is employed by or is associated with.

If there is a disagreement between colleagues in the research process, researchers should avoid making any inferences about another colleague's professional competence. Any concerns regarding unethical research behaviour on the part of a colleague should be referred to the appropriate body, usually the relevant ethics committee.

Conclusion

Ethical issues need to be considered at every stage of the research process. It is important that researchers obtain informed consent from participants, and their involvement should be completely voluntary. Potential participants should be provided with an explanatory statement/letter of informed consent outlining the purpose of the research, as well as the benefits, risks, method, demands, limitations of confidentiality, their freedom to withdraw, and how to obtain information on the results. Prior to conducting a study, consideration should be given to any potential negative consequences for participants, and to how these may be avoided, minimised, or handled. If deception is essential to the research purpose, participants should be debriefed immediately upon completion. The research instrument and techniques should be valid, and the research should only be undertaken by those who are qualified and experienced in the particular technique. Participants should benefit from the research, and it is good practice to offer them an overall summary of the data. If payment or rewards are used, they should not be unduly coercive. Data obtained from participants should be handled and stored confidentially throughout the research project. In longitudinal studies where participants' time-lagged data need to be matched, participants should be asked to provide a unique and easily remembered alias. For web-based surveys, care should be taken to ensure that respondents remain anonymous and that their data are stored on a secure drive or website. Interviews require signed consent; however, in order to maintain anonymity, the return of a questionnaire constitutes informed consent in a mail-out survey. In terms of observational studies, people should not be observed without their consent, unless they are observed in a public space. When reporting their findings, researchers should not falsify data or plagiarise the work of others.

References

Banyard, P. & Flanagan, C. (2005). *Ethical issues and guidelines in psychology*. London: Routledge.

Fry, C.L., Ritter, A., Baldwin, S., Bowen, K.J., Gardiner, P., Holt, T., Jenkinson, R., & Johnston, J. (2005). Paying research participants: A study of current practices in Australia. *Journal of Medical Ethics, 31*, 542–547.

Gregory, I. (2003). *Ethics in research*. London: Continuum.

Johns, M.D., Hall, G.J., & Crowell, T.L. (2004). Surviving the IRB review: Institutional guidelines and research strategies. In M.D. Johns, S.-L.S. Chen, & J. Hall (eds.), *Online social research: Methods, issues, and ethics* (pp. 105–124). London: Peter Lang.

Sieber, J.E. (1992). *Planning ethically responsible research: A guide for students and internal review boards*. London: Sage Publications.

Warwick, D.P. (1982). Types of harm in social research. In T.L. Beauchamp, R.R. Faden, R.J. Wallace Jr, & L. Walters (eds.), *Ethical issues in social science research* (pp. 101–124). Baltimore, MD: Johns Hopkins.

Chapter review questions

1   What are the main issues in conducting ethical research?
2   How should the research project be set up?
3   How is confidentiality preserved?
4   How is voluntary and informed consent obtained?
5   How should the data be collected to observe principles of ethics?
6   How is deception handled, if at all?
7   How are measures and interventions used to preserve ethical considerations?
8   How are specialist research practices used and by whom?
9   How can benefits be offered to participants?
10   How do you write to protect ethical standards?
11   What are other relevant ethical issues for conducting research?

Index

95% confidence interval
  see confidence intervals

abstract
  in report writing, 281
acquiescence response set,
  172–173
action research, 18, 89–97
Adjusted Multiple R^2, 223
alpha coefficient
  see Cronbach's alpha coefficient
alpha criterion, 212
analysis of covariance, 233
analysis of variance, 211–212, 214,
  232–233
ANCOVA
  see analysis of covariance
anonymity, 320, 321
ANOVA
  see analysis of variance
appendix
  in report writing, 282
appreciative inquiry, 96–97
archival measures, 127
  see also documentation
association
  see correlation
assumptions, 200–203,
  224

benefits
  as related to, 324
beta coefficient, 223, 228

bivariate analysis, 192, 207–210
  see also correlation, correlation
    coefficient
bivariate correlation
  see correlation
Bonferroni adjustment, 213

case study, 18, 73–86
categorical variable, 194, 210,
  211
category, 254
  see also theme
causality, 15–16
  in case study design, 76
  in correlational field study,
    46
  in experimental design, 35, 42
  in quasi-experimental design,
    36
  in randomised pre-test–
    post-test experimental and
    control groups design, 38
centring, 227
centroid, 232
chi-square, 210–211, 231
chi-square test of independence
  see chi-square
citations
  in report writing, 281
closed-ended question, 113
codebook
  in quasi-statistical method, 258
  in template analysis, 255

coding
  in content analysis, 254, 264,
    266, 267
coercion, 320
Cohen's Kappa, 268
common method variance, 62–63
competency
  as related to, 323
complete observer
  see observation
complete participant
  see observation
component
  see factor
composite score, 161
conceptual framework
  see theory
concurrent validity, 157
confidence intervals, 212, 214
confidentiality, 318–319
confirmatory factor analysis, 168,
    169, 222, 237, 238
confounding, 9
confounding variable, 36
construct, 8, 150
  see also variable, latent variable
    or construct
construct validity, 155–156
content analysis, 251–269
  in documentation, 130
content validity, 157
  in scale development, 166
contingency table
  see cross-tabulation
continuous variable, 194, 223
contrived setting, 34
control, 9
  in experimental design, 35

in quasi-experimental design,
    36
control group, 20, 35, 36, 37, 39
control variable, 9, 198
  in correlational field study, 46,
    50, 51
controlling, 225
  see also partialling
convenience sampling, 55
convergent interview, 106
convergent validity, 156, 171, 306
  in content analysis, 269
Cook's distance, 203
correlation, 46
correlation coefficient, 151, 154,
    171, 192, 207, 210, 240
correlation matrix, 209
correlational field study, 17, 46–69
counterbalancing, 63
criterion variable, 222
  see also dependent variable
criterion-related validity, 156–157
Cronbach's alpha coefficient, 152
cross-sectional design, 19
cross-tabulation, 210–211
cyclical process
  see action research

data, 57–62
data analysis
  choosing a method of data
    analysis, 25–26
  initial analyses, 25
  multivariate analysis, 25
data collection
  choosing a method of data
    collection, 21–25
  developing a new scale, 25

in case study design, 80
observation and documentation, 23–24
questionnaires and interviews, 21–23
reliability and validity, 25
data triangulation, 81, 299, 305, 307
in documentation, 125, 129
deception, 322
definitions
in report writing, 285
dependent relationship, 319
dependent variable, 9
in correlational field study, 46
dichotomous variable, 194, 223
different source data, 59
discriminant analysis, 221, 231–232
discriminant function, 231–232
discriminant loading, 232
discriminant validity, 156
discrimination
as related to ethics, 325
discussion
in report writing, 296, 300, 303, 304
divergent validity, 171
see also discriminant validity
document analysis
see documentation
documentation, 23–24, 124–132
double pre-test, 40
double-barrelled questions, 165
double-negative questions, 165
d-test, 240
dummy variable, 223

editing analysis, 256
effect size, 57, 151, 212, 213, 214–216, 223, 224
eigenvalue, 235
empirical study, 10–11
future research, 11
eta-squared, 212
ethics, 317–326
ethnography, 135
evaluation techniques, 93
experimental condition or group, 35, 36, 37, 39
experimental design, 17, 33–42, 232
expert panels, 306
explanatory statement, 320
exploratory factor analysis, 168, 169, 222, 234–236
external validity, 82–83
in case study design, 82–83
in documentation, 127
in non-equivalent pre-test–post-test control group design, 40
in questionnaires and interviews, 108

face validity, 152
factor
see also independent variable
as used in analysis of variance, 211, 232
as used in factor analysis, 234–236
factor analysis, 169, 222, 233–237
factor loading, 168, 235
feedback loop, 306

FIML
  see full information maximum
    likelihood
focus group, 104, 106
F-test, 211
full information maximum
    likelihood, 206

General Linear Model, 238
generalisability, 82
  see also external validity
grounded theory, 259–260
group data, 60–62
group interview, 104–106

hard data
  see objective data
Harman's single-factor test,
    63
heteroscedasticity, 202
hierarchical regression,
    226
historical analysis, 132–133
historical data
  see historical analysis
history effect, 41
homogeneity of variance, 202, 224
  see also homoscedacity
homoscedacity, 202, 224
hypothesis, 11–15
  see also research question
  in report writing, 287

incremental effect, 226
independence, 224
independent variable, 8
  in correlational field study, 46,
    49, 51

indicator variable
  see observed variable
individual data, 60–62
inferential statistics, 212
inflated correlation, 63
informed consent, 319–320
initial item analysis, 167
interaction effect, 227, 233
interaction plot, 229
inter-coder reliability
  see inter-rater reliability
intercorrelation, 153, 235
internal consistency, 152–153, 173
internal validity, 16, 81
  see also causality
  in case study design, 81
  in documentation, 127
  in questionnaires and interviews,
    108
inter-rater reliability, 83, 140, 154
  in content analysis, 268
interrupted time-series design,
    40–41
interval scale, 193, 194
intervening variable
  see mediator variable
interview, 21–23, 102–121
interview schedule, 119

judgement sampling, 56

latent construct, 170
latent variable, 150, 165, 170
  as used in structural equation
    modelling, 238, 240
leading question, 116
least squares regression, 223
Levene's equality of variance test

see Levene's homogeneity of
variance test
Levene's homogeneity of variance
test, 202, 212
Likert scale, 166, 193
limitation, 9–10
methodological, 10
substantive/content-based
criticisms, 9
linearity, 202, 224
listwise deletion, 205
logarithm transformation, 202
logistic regression, 221, 223,
230–231
longitudinal data, 63
longitudinal design, 20

Mahalanobis distance, 203
main effect, 233
MANCOVA
see multivariate analysis of
covariance
MANOVA
see multivariate analysis of
variance
matching, 38
in case study design, 79
maturation effect, 41
maximum likelihood, 206
mean substitution, 205–206
measured variable
see observed variable
measurement error, 150, 323
in structural equation
modelling, 238
mediated regression, 229–230
mediator variable, 9, 229–230
in correlational field study, 52

meta-analysis, 222, 240–245
method effect, 63, 170
methodology
in report writing, 287, 288–292
missing data, 204
mixed-method design, 75
moderated regression, 226–229
moderator variable, 9, 226–229
in correlational field study,
52
multicollinearity, 203, 223, 225,
227
multidimensional construct, 161
multi-item measure, 161
multi-level modelling, 222
multinominal logistic regression,
231
multiple imputation, 206–207
Multiple R^2, 5–6, 223
multiple regression, 192, 203, 221,
230
multivariate analysis, 192
see quantitative data analysis
multivariate analysis of covariance,
221, 232–233
multivariate analysis of variance,
221, 232–233

negatively worded items, 166,
172–173
nested model, 239
nominal scale, 193
nomological network, 156
non-contrived setting, 34, 46
non-equivalent pre-test–post-test
control group design, 38–40
non-experimental design
see correlational field study

non-participant observervation, 134
non-probability sampling, 55
non-response bias, 67, 199, 200
non-zero chance, 54
normality, 200–201, 224
null hypothesis, 211, 212–214
null model, 169

objective data, 57–59, 63
oblim rotation, 235
oblique model, 169
oblique rotation, 235
observation, 23–24, 124, 134–143
observed variable, 150, 192
  as used in structural equation modelling, 237, 238
observer as participant
  see observation
observer error, 142
one-group pre-test–post-test design, 37
one-way between-groups analysis of variance, 211
  see also analysis of variance
open-ended question, 113
ordering bias, 54
ordinal scale, 193
organisational data, 62
orthogonal model, 169
orthogonal rotation, 234, 235
other-report data, 59–60
outlier, 203
ownership
  as related to ethics, 325

pair data, 60–62
pairwise deletion, 205, 225

parallel form, 155
paraphrased response, 120
partial correlation, 63
partialling, 224
  see also controlling
participant as observer
  see observation
participant observation, 134–140
participative action research, 93, 96–97
pattern matching, 261
pattern matrix, 235
PCA
  see principal components analysis
Pearson correlation coefficient
  see correlation coefficient
Pearson *r*
  see correlation coefficient
Pearson's product moment correlation coefficient
  see correlation coefficient
percentage agreement
  see inter-rater reliability
plagiarism
  in report writing, 280
positively worded items, 166
power, 57, 151, 170, 171, 202, 213, 214–216, 225
  see also sample size
power analysis, 216
  see also power
predictive power, 223
predictive validity, 156
predictor variable, 222
  see also independent variable

presentation
  in report writing, 278–280
primary data
  in documentation, 127
primary source, 78
  in documentation, 130
principal axis factor analysis,
  234
principal components analysis,
  168, 234
  see also factor analysis
probability (*p*) value, 212
probability sampling, 54
probing question, 118
product term, 227
projection, 81
promax rotation, 235

qualitative data, 16, 150, 276,
  296
  in action research, 92
  in documentation, 130
  in interviews, 102
qualitative data analysis, 26,
  251–269
qualitative report writing,
  296–308
quantitative data, 16, 150, 276
  in action research, 92
  in interviews, 102
  in questionnaires, 102
quantitative data analysis, 25
  multivariate analyses, 221–245
  preliminary analyses, 190–217
quantitative report writing,
  283–296
quasi-experimental design, 17,
  33–40, 42, 232

quasi-statistical method
  in content analysis, 258
questionnaire, 21–23, 46, 102–121
questions
  types of, 117
quota sampling, 55

random allocation, 35
  in experimental design, 35
  in non-equivalent
    pre-test–post-test control
    group design, 38, 39
  in quasi-experimental design,
    36
  in randomised pre-test–
    post-test experimental and
    control groups design, 38
random measurement error
  see measurement error
randomised pre-test–post-test
    experimental and control
    groups design, 37–38
ratio scale, 194
rationale
  in report writing, 277, 285, 287
reactive effect, 141
redundancy, 165
reference list
  in report writing, 282
reflection, 93
relationship
  see correlation
reliability, 25, 80–81, 150–155, 158
  in case study design, 80–81
  in content analysis, 267–268
  in documentation, 130–132
  in qualitative report writing,
    306–308

reliability (*cont.*)
    in quantitative data analysis, 204
    in questionnaires and interviews, 108
    in scale development, 170
replication, 82
research design, 16–21
research process, 4–27
    choosing method of data analysis, 25–26
    choosing method of data collection, 21–25
    choosing the research design, 16–21
    developing the research questions, 5–6
    finalising research questions or hypotheses, 16
    finding the underlying theory, 6–11
    reporting the findings, 26–27
research question, 5–6
response category, 120
response rate, 64–67, 107
results
    in report writing, 292–294, 304
return rate
    see response rate
rigour, 92, 151

same source data, 59
sample size, 56–57, 170, 213, 214, 216, 223, 323
    see also power
    in exploratory factor analysis, 236

in structural equation modelling, 239
sampling, 21, 53
    in correlational field study, 53
sampling error, 142, 213, 240
sampling frame, 54
sampling interval, 54
scale development, 161–174
scatterplot, 208
scree test, 235
secondary data
    in documentation, 127
secondary source, 78
    in documentation, 130
self-report data, 59–60
semantic differential, 166
semi-structured interview, 104
sequential regression
    see hierarchical regression
shared variance, 234
simple interrupted time-series design
    see interrupted time-series design
simple random sample, 54
single-item measure, 161
single-item reliability, 163
skew, 167
snowball sampling, 56
social desireability, 63, 172
soft systems, 93
Spearman's rank order correlation, 208
spiral process
    see action research
split-half reliability, 154
spurious, 10
    see also confounding
square root transformation, 202

squared canonical correlation, 231
stability
   see test–retest reliability
standard regression, 225
standardised effect size, 214
standardised interview
   see structured interview
standardised (*z*) score, 227,
   236
statistical power
   see power
statistical significance, 212–214
stepdown analysis, 233
stepwise regression, 225
story-telling question, 117
strata, 55
stratified sampling, 38, 55
stratum
   see strata
strength of association
   see effect size
structural coefficient
   see structural loading
structural equation modelling, 222,
   229, 237–240
structural loading, 232
structure matrix, 235
structured interview, 103
structured observation, 135,
   140–141
studentised deleted residual, 203
subjective data, 57–59, 63
subscale, 161
survey design
   see correlational field study
switching replication, 40
systematic observation
   see structured observation

systematic sampling, 54
systematic variance, 63
systematic variation, 227

tables
   in report writing, 282
TAP procedure, 111
template analysis, 255–256
terms, 7
test–retest reliability, 153–154
thematic analysis
   see content analysis
theme, 251–269
theory, 9, 259
   as related to research question,
     6
   in action research, 92
   in case study design, 75, 78
   in content analysis, 255,
     259–260
   in correlational field study,
     48–49
   in hierarchical regression, 226
   in report writing, 285
   in scale development, 164–166
   in structural equation
     modelling, 237, 238
time-series design, 79
tolerance, 203
treatment, 34
treatment group
   see experimental condition or
     group
true experimental design
   see experimental design
t-test, 202, 211–212
t-test for independent samples, 211
t-test for paired samples, 211

Type I error, 212
Type II error, 213, 214

unidimensional construct,
    161
unique variance, 225
unit of analysis, 18
    dyads, 18
    groups, 19
    in case study, 73
    individuals, 18
    industries, 19
    organisations, 19
univariate analysis, 192
univariate descriptive statistics,
    198
unobserved variable or construct
    see latent, construct latent
        variable
unstructured interview, 103–104
unstructured observation, 135

validity, 25, 150–152, 155–157

see also internal validity and
    external validity
    in content analysis, 269
    in documentation, 130–132
    in qualitative report writing,
        306–308
    in scale development, 170–171
validity coefficient, 157, 241
variable, 8–9
    as related to construct, 150
    in correlational field study,
        49–52
variance, 150
Variance Inflation Factors,
    203
varimax rotation, 235
verbatim response, 120
VIF
    see variance inflation factors
voluntary participation, 319–320

writing style
    in report writing, 280